REVISED AND UPDATED 2018 EDITION

EDEN
The Knowledge of Good and Evil

DR. JOYE JEFFRIES PUGH

"Eden: The Knowledge Of Good and Evil 666"
by DR. JOYE JEFFRIES PUGH

Copyright © 2006 by DR. JOYE JEFFRIES PUGH.
All rights reserved.

No part of this publication may be reproduced, stored in a retrieval system or transmitted in any way by any means, electronic, mechanical, photocopy, recording or otherwise without the prior permission of the author except as provided by USA copyright law.

This book is designed to provide accurate and authoritative information with regard to the subject matter covered. This book is designed to provide accurate and authoritative information with regard to the subject matter covered. Published by Sacred Word Publishing, LLC. for public consideration.

Edited, and formatted by Zen Garcia.
Cover Illustrative design by Gerard Hamdani
http://bookcloudcollective.com/
2nd Printing 2018
Sacred Word Publishing
www.sacredWordpublishing.com
SacredWordPublishing@yahoo.com
978-1-387-81478-7

Books and Music also by Dr. Joye Jeffries Pugh

POETRY
Colours of Joye (Limited Edition)

NON-FICTION
*(Available in Hard and Soft Back covers)

ANTICHRIST – The Cloned Image of Jesus Christ
*ANTICHRIST – The Cloned Image of Jesus Christ
Updated 2017 Edition

EDEN – The Knowledge of Good and Evil 666
*EDEN – The Knowledge of Good and Evil 666 Updated
2018 Edition

BEGUILED – Eden To Armageddon Volumes 1, 2 & 3
*BEGUILED – Eden To Armageddon Volumes 1, 2 & 3
Updated 2017 Editions

PARABLES OF JOYE – ON A GEORGIA FARM

E-BOOKS OF ALL TITLES AVAILABLE AT:
www.sacredwordpublishing.net

AUDIO

EDEN –The Knowledge of Good and Evil 666
(Abridged and Updated) 12 CD Disc Set

ALBUM---Music----
"BEFORE TIME STOPS"---"Dr. Joye"

Dedication

"To Those who have been called to walk alone,
To attain what God has called you to be—
March on—Christian Soldiers—March on."

In Memory of Mel, for believing in my quest for truth.
I miss you!

In Memory of my Mother, Stella,
thank you for teaching me to seek peace.

In Memory of Little One, my sweet kitty,
for the days and nights, you spent faithfully at my side
while I wrote this book.

To Zen and the staff of Sacred Word Publishing
thank you for allowing me to reach the world
and fulfill my destiny as one of your authors.

To Lillan and in memory of Garland,
thank you for your willingness to review a work
was totally on the water outside of the boat.

In memory of Mommie Elma, my beloved grandmother,
who took me to church the first week after I was born.
And Most Importantly,

To the 'One and Only' Lord and Savior Jesus Christ,
it is 'Pure Joye' to be offered the opportunity to "Publish
with the voice of thanksgiving, and tell of all thy wondrous
works." (Psalm 26:7).

Finally:
To all who read this work—
Always remember:
"In the Beginning,
the End was
in Satan's withered fruit
of deceitful knowledge."

"Dr. Joye"

Table Of Contents

Foreword ....…….....7
Author's Quest: To Expose........................….....…............9
The Garden of Eden....…..........................…..................18
Introduction: The Spiritual History of Mankind.............20

Part 5: Evil Unleashed - The New World Order

24. Roman Catholic Church and the Secrets of Fatima..….... 28
25. Tesla Technology...…...…..........….................. 82
26. Nanotechnology ….............….........…..........…98
27. Fallen Angels - The Alien Agenda …....…..........112
28. Animal Mutilations ...…….......…... …...........…150
29. Crop Circles ….............….......................…160

Part 6: Satan in the Flesh - The False Messiah

30. "666 - Is it Possible?" …...........…......…...… 196
31. ANTICHRIST - Prepare to Meet Satan.. …............264

Part 7: The Omega - Your Wake-Up Call

32. Good versus Evil - Your Choice …..................288
33. Psalm 26 and II Timothy 4:1-8 …...............308
Bibliography …............…......................... 310
Notes ….........….....................................322

Foreword

EDEN - The Knowledge of Good and Evil 666 is a comprehensive story of good and evil—brilliantly told, thought provoking, enlightening, and uniquely timely! Dr. Joye Jeffries Pugh has a tenacious grip on the history of the continuing journey of good and evil. This is a one-of-a-kind book paralleling the history of the Garden of Eden, with a Christian view, to the present time, with a credible exposé of the New Age Agenda for exactly what it is. This book is a must read for all people with inquiring minds, whether or not one agrees with all of the presented premises. Recognizing the evil forces that have brought us to this moment in history, the author presents a sense of awareness not seen in most publications today.

Many of us have been so absorbed in our mundane complex lives of extreme pressures; we have overlooked the evil seeds of secret ulterior agendas being planted in the Christian Church and other facets of our lives. To some Christians the information revealed may be frightening; to others it may be a wakeup call and spiritual reminder. To the general public it could be their first encounter with profound and basic truths that might be comforting as they discover answers to questions they have pondered and found troubling for a long time—answers that current mainstream books have not answered out of fear. Whatever unresolved conflicts or beliefs about good and evil you have experienced, after reading this book you will have gained a better understanding of the consequences of one's choice regarding them.

The author's diligence in her research is evidenced by her boundless intellectual curiosity in every area as she takes us through the 'never-beforetold' details of the Antichrist and detailed interpretations of the End Times with relevant accompanying Scriptures. This book contains recent scientific findings that will appeal to many researchers of different disciplines.

Dr. Pugh is a dedicated Christian and an insightful Biblical scholar, whose many years of devoted research in Biblical history and prophecy— including the paranormal and spiritual world—qualifies her for giving direction in making choices in one's life. Her compelling insights will linger in your mind as you begin to know the road you must use to travel through your life journey toward eternity. EDEN - The Knowledge of Good and Evil 666 is a book of distinction that should become an instant classic—it is much more than a book—it is a dynamic new vision!

Garland C. DuPree
Professor, Abraham Baldwin College (Ret.)
Published Author
(Now Deceased)

Author's Quest:
To Expose Satan

In an extensive review of history, one will soon discover that mankind has always been in search of higher knowledge. This quest seems to have immediately begun in the Garden of Eden with the Serpent tempting Eve with fruit from the Tree of Knowledge. Throughout the ages, different cultures have kept the quest alive. The Knights Templar's quest for the Ark of the Covenant and the Holy Grail during the Middle Ages has been written about in a variety of books. An interesting feature of their secret meetings and rituals involved blood oaths that were kept hidden from the public and not recorded in most books. In fact, not until recently have initiates of Secret Societies, whose very roots stem from the Templar, defected. These men explain how the blood oaths they took make them fear being killed by the elite Secret Brotherhood that governs all Secret Societies and their members. The higher level one achieves within the 'Craft,' the worse the penalty is for defecting. Men who have confessed about swearing to blood oaths, especially past the known thirty-third degree, have painted a horrific picture regarding the true agenda silently lurking in Secret Societies. Today a host of Secret Societies, like Freemasonry, exists in almost every country in our world and literally controls its members through fear.

Most members of local chapters of Secret Societies are not aware of the deceptive nature regarding these organizations. These men do not realize that they are victims of a bigger scheme of things where raising money for charity is really a funding project for an undercover agenda; in other words, they are using sheepskin to hide their motives. Attempting to locate just where their fund-raising money goes has revealed evidence of a well-kept secret. It is reminiscent of Black Budget Projects our Congress funds without details as to where the money goes. I am concerned about cover stories the public is being fed in order to manipulate them. It is clear that something with supernatural power has doctored our history and is secretly attempting to gain control of our future.

Does this mean that all members of Secret Societies who reach so called top degrees understand what is going on? No. In fact, most are not privy to that information. There are secret degrees above the publicized degrees, which few men are aware of. If a person is chosen to go higher into these levels, one must forsake all for the Brotherhood—the Illuminated Ones. Once in, you cannot ever leave. You belong to them forever. The only out is your death either by natural means or, if you decide to go public about what you know, it may well set one up for an untimely death, which in most cases is secretly carried out in such a way to resemble an unfortunate accident or suicide. Illuminated Degrees begin where the majority of degrees, like those found within Freemasonry, stop. For example, the 33rd degree of the Scottish Rite and the 10th degree of the York Rite are as far as most Masons believe they can go. Secretly, if one is of a certain genetic background, accepts Satan as their Lord of Enlightenment, and has the superior mentality, they can move to a higher rank within the Illuminated Orders such as the Round Table or the highest Order, known as the Illuminati. These carefully selected men oversee all Secret Society activities. At this level, they are well aware that all secret cults are really a branch of the same organization, which is, in turn, working toward a common goal. In order to control the game, they control all levels. This is how their hierarchy, placed at the apex of all Secret Societies, assures complete control.

The Illuminated Ones have at their disposal members of a group called the Bilderbergers composed of the most powerful and wealthy of the world. They also have established the agendas for the Trilateral Commission and The Council on Foreign Relations. It is said the Illuminati own the Monetary Trust Fund. In essence, they own the world. These Illuminated Ones pick the candidates that run for top offices in all countries and then they allow peons like you and me to vote in who we want in office. The process is to make us believe we have a choice in our government. Real democracy does not exist. We are, in reality, slaves to a higher power and fail to do anything about it. The web of control is now too big. Not one of those who have made it to the top will ever assist to help rectify this problem because they would be immediately eliminated based on their oaths. The Illuminated Ones have devised a brilliantly organized hierarchy that is ruled from the top down with a rod of iron that shows no mercy to anyone who does not do exactly as instructed.

Vital to the Illuminated Ones' agenda is the use of a form of secretly coded communication called 'Double Speak'—saying one thing but meaning another. It appears that those whom we are led to believe are overseeing the daily activities around the world may, in fact, be mere puppets on a stage. In other words, nothing is at it seems. Let us take a look at just one aspect of what is considered daily forms of 'Double Speak' being played out before our eyes. For instance, the United States Government reports to tax payers, who, by the way, pay the entire Nation's bills, that they do not fund a facility in the Nevada Desert called Area 51. Still, our tax dollars appear to be funding that secret testing facility. If the government does not own it, then exactly who, or what, does? Could it belong to the Illuminated Ones and house their secret technology, which, in turn, will be used against an unsuspecting public who funded it in the very first place? Oh, yes!

The plot of deception thickens when Unidentified Flying Object (UFO) documents are requested by the general public under the Freedom of Information Act for review. These documents are blacked out almost in their entirety and have very few tidbits of information that are decipherable because our government declares the censored portions are vital to National Security and therefore cannot be released. Yet at the same time, the government reports there is no threat from UFOs. That many pages blackened out in each Freedom of Information released document must mean there is a threat to something. Even information released on the atomic bomb is not censored as much as UFO documents are. So what makes UFOs of greater concern to National Security than the atomic bomb?

It quickly becomes evident, from carefully pieced together restricted documents, that there exists a secret organization handling the whole UFO affair. In return, they are releasing as little as possible on the phenomenon in order to maintain their covert agenda. Even elected officials holding Presidential and Senate offices have requested briefings and/or documents but have been left wanting. The Illuminated Ones, through various channels, deceitfully feed those seeking answers skewed evidence by claiming that there is no threat from such unidentified aerial phenomena. This Brotherhood of carefully selected men already knows the haunting truth about all paranormal activity, which is escalating at an alarming rate around the world. They know UFOs and USOs (Unidentified Submerged Objects) are merely identified flying objects (IFOs) posing no threat to their materialistic agenda because they are working with them to rule the world.

The powers-that-be around the globe, who are the real puppet masters, know that these entities piloting high-tech space ships have been on Earth with mankind from the very beginning. In fact, they are considered more terrestrial than extraterrestrial. They are the Fallen Angels and their father, Satan, whom God cast out of Heaven thousands of years ago. The success of the Brotherhood's Plan to conceal this fact has been very effective throughout history because the reality about what is really going on is so strange that most people will not believe the truth when someone like me attempts to expose it. This scenario, unfortunately, allows the Illuminated Ones, who have given their souls to Satan in return for His materialistic gifts, to continue their secret agenda uncontrolled and unchallenged by an unsuspecting public. It is the ideal situation in which to carry out a covert operation, and these wicked men have the power at their fingertips to discredit anyone who attempts to unravel their evil plans.

"And Yes, I do feel like 'little (King) David' with a slingshot and stone in my hand aimed at one huge all encompassing Giant of a Beast; but somebody's got to do it—The End is near!"

Time is running out, because the hidden plan instigated by Satan in the Garden of Eden to have mankind worship the created more than the Creator is nearing completion. 'Big Brother' is finally capable of monitoring every person on the face of this Earth. Surveillance technology is being expanded and set up daily under the unsuspecting banner of protection from terrorists. In reality, it involves nothing more than removing our individual human rights to personal confidentiality, freedom and democracy. If we fail to comply with this increase in surveillance, as part of their New World Order plot, then the Brotherhood has secretly developed technology to force mankind into doing exactly what they have termed as being 'politically correct.'

In the near future, the Illuminated Ones will take their control of mankind to a higher level by utilizing an advanced form of psycho-biological warfare with the sole intent of stealing our souls by taking away our capability of free will, which allows us to make choices. This technology will target control over our bodily functions through biological weaponry that will make it almost impossible to escape such evil and intrusive manipulation. Once they gain power over the human body through outside means, their intent is to make mankind servants to the Antichrist.

The human body's electrical system, known as the central nervous system, can be stimulated using electromagnetic beams from a distance. This technology allows these wicked men power to increase pulse rate, blood pressure, body heat, hallucinations, etc., using these beams. As a result, the mind does not have the capability to biologically fight against its own body or how it is reacting to that stimulus.

A perfect example of the loss of bodily function from an outside stimulus occurs in what has been termed as an

'Alien Abduction.' In these cases, humans report being controlled by an entity that has power over their human body's biological processes; such as making them completely paralyzed against their will. Also, these abductees report that their physical bodies are levitated and travel unharmed through closed doors and windows. This proves a higher level of physics and energy must exist. If these reports indeed are true, then we are already in the clutches of an evil genius who is exhibiting unprecedented control over the human body against its free will. There can be no doubt that this technology of the Fallen Ones has been harnessed and passed on through their teachings of Sacred Sciences to a chosen group of wicked men. It has been brought down through the ages by Satan's army to be unleashed full force upon this generation.

Their power to control of the Laws of Nature will become the major tool used by the coming Antichrist and his demonic followers to ensure mankind's full cooperation to his claim as the long-awaited Messiah. No wonder the Bible promises, as we get near the End of the Age, that time will be cut short. If God did not intervene, then not one human being could escape a power that has the ability to control the body against its own free will.

The Illuminated Ones have had access to the money needed over time to employ the best scientists to work on their behalf in bringing Satan into the flesh. This Brotherhood knows the true identity of their Prince who will deceive the world with miracles, money, manpower and control. These workers of iniquity have labored hard over the centuries, following mankind's expulsion from the Garden of Eden, to possess world dominion. Their Agenda is veiled from the public because the wicked do not want the masses to know what is going on until they are blind-sided by it. This demonic scheme derives itself directly from the ideology of Agnosticism, which is a pagan religious belief where mankind is led through rituals promising illumination and god-like immortality. The Illuminated Ones believe they have been chosen to lead humanity out of chaos by making us prisoners to their 'Propaganda.'

Whether we like it or not, we are the generation that is spoken of in the Bible that will see the Last Day because we are becoming completely controlled on a global scale. Most of humanity is too busy to notice what is really going on in the world and just who or what is actually dictating their lives. Daily pressures from debt and fear are tools used by the Brotherhood to keep mankind controlled. People are more aware of television shows, the latest movie, and the price of gas than what is going on within government or the true state of Planet Earth. Because of mankind's lack of interest in things other than what we are being spoon-fed, surveillance will soon be universally unopposed. Smart cards and implanted bio-chips, strategically placed under our skin, will identify and track us twenty-four hours a day. If you will but open your eyes, you will see the seeds of Satan working diligently to ensure mankind will be unable to escape their final 'Agenda.'

One of the aspects that I have tried hard to incorporate into this research regarding Satan's Plan is that of awareness. When you complete this book, like it or not, you will have acquired a world of knowledge that has been strategically hidden from public view. It is my hope that this information will assist you in avoiding Satan's trap and his followers' conspiracy in manipulating the world to ensure his age-old Plan comes to pass in our generation. From this day forward, you will never look at the paper, watch the news, or view politics and world events the same way ever again. Even the popular esoteric works like The Da Vinci Code will be decoded, and Harry Potter's Half Blood Prince will be revealed right before your very eyes. In fact, I am going to take you past those two New Age literary entrapments right up to Satan's doorstep and introduce him to you.

There is something playing a game of evil with our world. That something is here with us on Earth and does not want us to know the truth about their diabolical Plan. This evil gives us bits and pieces of what it wants us to know. The Agenda is designed to encourage wars, racial issues, two sided politics, money woes, and a host of other types of deception. These depressing issues are intended to keep the average person from having time to investigate the evil plots and plans that are being devised daily to control mankind. There is one thing for certain—this Evil Agenda that we are experiencing on Earth comes from behind the hidden curtain of an "Oz." In this book, you will soon discover that this "Oz" is a Wizard of a Lizard.

The Garden of Eden

The Garden of Eden is where it all began.
Mystifying as it may be, we fail to understand;
for it was with temptation
that we fell into Satan's Plan.
Wanting to step back in time,
to re-write the choice made by mankind;
I find our whole history distorted,
yet, we continue on blind.
It is with determination that I research,
it is with truth that I earnestly seek;
for my forefathers were misled,
by the evil seed of the serpent's head.
I trust with each day,
I will find the history that really was,
and expose the deceit in,
"Is there no help for the widow's son?"
Knowing the task may be long,
I travel up the mountain top alone.
Knowing at the top,
truth and innocence awaits
for, then, will I have reached Heaven's gate,
and not some misty mountain top experience.
I will have discovered
what Satan has hidden through the ages;
the secrets which have shaped our world
to deceive mankind.
In the end,
the seeds of Satan will not reign supreme;
but will be judged by those
they tortured through their Evil Plan.
It is with passion that I await
that Grand and Glorious Day!!!

"Come quickly,
Even so, Lord Jesus,
Come quickly"—
It is past time for Satan to pay . . .
"Dr. Joye"

Introduction:
The Spiritual History of Mankind

How did Satan manage to move through history undetected and maintain his hold on mankind? Why did those who knew of his deception in the Garden of Eden continue to uphold his desires to interfere in God's plan? These witnesses knew firsthand of the consequences and punishment God placed on anyone choosing to follow the agenda of Satan and the Fallen Angels. From living in a peaceful paradise, wanting for nothing, to toiling in the dirt just to survive. What makes worshipping Satan so appealing that generations have been willing to trade Heaven for Hell by choosing to follow him and his rebellion against the God who created all things?

What you are about to read is somewhat of a detective story that investigates ancient history and pieces together a wide variety of all the links that have brought the 'Agenda of Satan' through the ages to establish his final blow to mankind—the Antichrist. Many events have been hidden from those who do not understand Satan's crusaders. My objective is to expose their hidden agenda to the world so those who hear this message will not be deceived by these illuminated beings who originated from Satan's seed in the Garden of Eden. Many sons of Satan, who have been initiated into his Plan, serve today in positions of great power. They are the movers and shakers behind governments, financial institutions, religions, policies, research, medicine, education, technology, news media, etc.

Illuminated beings have been with us since the Garden of Eden, weaving their web of control, destruction, and deceit among the Children of God.

The hidden agenda, untold to the Children of God, is for Satan's purpose. He wants to take every soul he can acquire before his final battle with God at Armageddon. Satan must keep luring people to his side, because as they die they are no longer any help to him at this final conflict. Throughout this book, I will expose Satan's Plan. I will put to rest his ancient conspiracy, which has been designed to confuse those who want to follow the True God, our Creator and Lord—JEHOVAH—and His Son, Jesus Christ.

Our recorded history, from the very beginning, shows that civilizations have venerated the Serpent while others have abhorred it. In the earliest known civilizations of Mesopotamia, Sumer, and Egypt, the Serpent/Dragon was a sacred being. The Celtics of England used the Dragon as the symbol of their ultimate sovereignty. The Greeks believed Dragons were creatures that held the wisdom and knowledge of the true secrets to immortality. These Dragons were said to be spiritual and appeared in the form of Sea Serpents.

In direct opposition to these aforementioned beliefs, were the Christian and Hebrew concepts of Serpents. Christianity portrays the Serpent as the evil archangel who opposed God and brought about the fall of mankind. This is directly opposite of cult lore that says Lucifer was an enlightener and friend to mankind. It is in this opposition, between parallel histories and beliefs, that we will discover the real Truth. The Deceiver will be exposed!

The Earth and all that is, did not come from chaos. God's plan was perfect. Unfortunately, as God gathered His host of Heaven together, Lucifer became angry and jealous. He lashed out at God, because he wanted to be equal to God. Selfish sin overcame Lucifer and eternal division was forced into existence. God did not want this division, but Lucifer rebelled and chose his own agenda. Therefore, God removed Lucifer and his followers from Heaven by casting them out for all eternity. They can never return.

In the meantime, God's creation of Adam and Eve was His delight. He placed them within the Garden of Eden so they would always have everything they would ever need. God's presence was in the Garden and He carefully instructed them. Satan was furious when he saw the beauty of Adam and Eve, who, unlike him, were created in God's Own Image. The anger boiled inside Satan, and with his sin of jealousness he attacked earth.

God told Adam and Eve that they were created in His Image. He explained the need to stay away from the Tree of Knowledge, as it would bring them death. Satan watched, but he felt that Adam and Eve should be allowed to see both his and God's side of things. Therefore, Satan deceitfully used their innocence to entice them to do evil. He tempted Eve, and on that day, Christianity's foe, Gnosticism (evil), was born. At that moment, Adam and Eve's faith, their total trust in God Supreme, became infiltrated by Gnosticism, which was composed of secret knowledge, love of self and following Satan, who appeared to enlighten.

Life became a great chess game between the powers of good and evil. Gnosticism's promise of enlightenment gave mankind building strength; but in the end, it will bring sorrow. Knowledge gave mankind awareness of the ability to choose. Unfortunately, the penalty for not making the right choice results not only in physical death due to sin, as all mankind are sinners, but in eternal death to those that follow evil and do not choose to repent of their sin.

To those choosing to follow the will of God, the path of Christianity brings not an easier life, but the promise of resurrection and an eternity with our Creator. As Christians, we are all sinners, but it is through our faith in Jesus that we receive His grace and mercy, which washes us clean of our sin. Even though we are cleansed, we still have to die to inherit our reward into eternal life, unless we are caught up in the Rapture at the 'End of the Age' and are changed into our spiritual bodies in the blink of an eye.

The Gnostics believe through their power, control, and self-illumination that they will attain the keys to overcome earthly death and avoid eternal judgment. Throughout time, they have invested great energy in teaching their initiates that through the sacred mysteries they will become as god and reap immortality. Woe to the people of this deception, because it means an eternity without God. On the other hand, for Christians, ours is just a little sorrow of suffering on Earth, but with a wonderful promise of an eternity with God, our Father.

The wicked seeds of Satan, throughout history, have somewhat controlled humanity through various aspects of our daily life. Long ago, Gnostic sects conceived a plan to make themselves into an undercover organization. They made sure this mystery organization would not be subject to the ups and downs and uncertainties of political and social change that would occur throughout the ages. It is separate from all governments, but it indirectly controls them all. These wicked men have allowed an alternative history to be written that keeps mankind from the Creator. By secretly controlling history, they have manipulated how people view the past. This deceptive misinformation will be what they will use to massively influence how mankind accepts the future. It is a cleverly devised trap!

Many Christian Saints have been placed along the way to warn us about this deception. But their warnings have fallen on deaf ears. The problem has been mankind's inability to distinguish between Gnosticism and true Christianity. This is part of Satan's strategy. He wants to have his Agenda so close to Christianity that no one can be sure of what is truth. The more we look to the created for our answers and heed their words of wisdom, the less we search the Bible and pray to our Creator, Jehovah, for guidance. What a cleverly devised plan of deception! The Gnostics and their father, Satan, will soon present a man to the world who will appear to be the Messiah. This Beast will, seemingly, have the answer to all of mankind's greatest needs. The masses will embrace this so-called savior, without questioning whether he is God or Satan. This enormous acceptance of the future Antichrist will bring about the 'End of the Ages.' It will unleash the final battle between good and evil. The battle is known, prophetically, as that of Armageddon.

The history you are about to read will uncover Satan's plot to remove Jehovah as the good God and replace him with a false Messiah, the Antichrist. You will be led on a journey that proves, since Eden, that Satan has been in the background deceiving mankind. Satan's agnostic religion changes Jehovah from an honest God to a dishonest God. Gnosticism boldly teaches that Jehovah is responsible for keeping mankind in darkness through 'His Acts of Wrath.' It goes on to inform that Lucifer was true to man and had mankind's best interest at stake when he offered the forbidden fruit of knowledge to Eve in the Garden of Eden. Satan's enticement to eat the fruit opened Adam and Eve's innocent eyes from, what Agnostics term, 'ignorant darkness' and, in turn, gave them spiritual enlightenment. This form of false religion continues to deceitfully win the hearts of mankind, because it offers alternatives, tolerance, love of self, possible keys to obtaining earthly immortality, and the achievement of god-like wisdom without contemplating that there will be a 'Day of Judgment' for their souls.

Many have wondered, throughout the course of history, as to how Satan will manifest himself as the Messiah. His Plan is quite clever. Bible prophecy warns that he will deceive the whole earth and become mankind's false savior at the 'End of the Age.' The coming of the Antichrist is imminent. Of immediate concern is the fact that many, unknowingly, may be participating in Satan's agenda through their membership with various secret organizations. This book is a sound warning to unyoke yourself from these ritualistic and pagan practices now, before it is too late. From this day forward, no reader of this book will ever be able to stand before God and say, "No one told me that I was being deceived." You have been warned!

"And God spake all these words, saying "I am the Lord thy God, which have brought thee out of the land of Egypt, out of the house of bondage. THOU SHALT HAVE NO OTHER GODS BEFORE ME." (Exodus 20:1–3).

The First Commandment, "Thou shalt have no other gods before me," is the premises, 'the central theme and basis of argument,' for this very unique book. I believe God, over many years and through many trials, has prepared me to write it for this generation, because we are the terminal generation. It is my sincerest prayer that the reading of this research will offer each individual a better understanding of the fact that the 'End of the Age' is close at hand. It is important to me that all of God's People, who He created in His Own Image, realize the evil forces that have brought us to this prophesied moment in time.

"Beware of False Prophets, which come to you in sheep's clothing, but inwardly they are ravening wolves." (Matthew 7:15).

Our blessed hope of deliverance from the evil lineage of Cain and his father, Satan, will come soon. So:

"Watch ye therefore: for ye know not when the master of the house cometh (Jesus), at even, or at midnight, or at the cockcrowing, or in the morning: Lest coming suddenly he find you sleeping. And what I say unto you I say unto all, Watch." (Mark 13:35–37, Parenthetical comment mine).

Part 5
Evil Unleashed ~
The New World Order

Chapter Twenty-Four
Roman Catholic Church And The Secrets of Fatima

This generation is witness to the hierarchy of the Roman Catholic Church embracing and supporting some strange interpretations regarding the teachings of the Holy Bible. These leaders accept that the Jews are waiting for their Messiah to be born and condone that belief. What is the real reason behind their agreement with non-Christian Jews over this issue? Could the Roman Church leaders also secretly be waiting for the Messiah to be born?

The late Pope John Paul II, past Pope Benedict XVI and present Pope Francis I, all, very quickly became more and more tolerant of other religions based on a secret scheme not privy to the world at large once they took office. Were they made aware that the Antichrist has been born as a cloned replica of Jesus, who will soon emerge as the Messiah the Jews have been waiting for? Do they know that this time, instead of turning their backs on the Messiah, the Jews will embrace the Clone as their returned Prince of Peace who will promise to save them from their enemies?

According to a World News Report on Saturday-Sunday, August 20–21, 2005 edition of the Douglas Daily News, an Article entitled, "Pope Benedict XVI visits synagogue, warns of rising anti-Semitism," proves the Vatican was attempting to align themselves with Jewish leaders. The article of the Associated Press from Cologne, Germany, stated:

"The haunting tones of a ram's horn. Prayers before a Holocaust memorial. The Hand of Jewish friendship offered by a rabbi.

On Friday, Pope Benedict XVI became the second pope in history to visit a Jewish house of worship, and his time at Cologne's synagogue was filled with significance for the German-born pontiff—and for Jews worldwide.

"We need to show respect for one another and to love one another," Benedict said to applause, winning further praise for warning that anti-Semitism was on the rise.

The 78-year-old Benedict grew up in Nazi Germany. He called those times "the darkest period of German and European history" but did not mention his own trials, enrolled in Hitler Youth as a teenager and deserting from the German army near the end of the war."

The Jewish people hold the belief that Jesus was not the Messiah because He died on the cross. When His earthly body is brought back to life through the 'rebirth of His cells,' His image will "work great miracles," as well as "bring fire down from heaven." The majority of those living near the end of time, including the Jewish people, will joyfully accept this Cloned beast as their Messiah, thereby falling victim to Satan's deceptive plan.

The Cloned image of Jesus is not Jesus, but Satan desecrating the Holy Temple of God. All Christians should know that Jesus will return in the air and not be reborn. It appears the Roman Catholic hierarchy may be part of a global unification committee that is aiding Secret Societies in 'The Plan of The Prince of Darkness' to ensure the

Jewish people triumph in welcoming Satan as Messiah. This secret plan is revealed in the banned book, The Protocols of the Learned Elders of Zion, by Vic Marsden.

The leaders of the Roman Catholic Church, under Pope Francis I, have recently theorized that Heaven and Hell are not real tangible places. Yet the Bible explains that both were created by God and are very much in existence. Their new revelation declares and entices the average person not to have fear about spending eternal damnation in a place called Hell if they do not choose to follow Jesus. This esoteric teaching has the potential to lead many astray, right into the arms of those offering earthly immortality over spiritual immortality. Indications are that the famous esoteric Library of Alexandria, Egypt, was secretly passed to the Vatican and not destroyed. This could be where such blasphemous teachings have emerged. Supposedly, there are thousands of ancient esoteric books housed in secret vacuum-sealed vaults under the Vatican.

It is evident that something has infiltrated the beliefs and teachings of the Catholic Church in recent years. The late Pope, John Paul II, Pope Benedict XVI and Pope Francis I have met with religious leaders from a variety of false doctrines. Their promotion of religious tolerance is allowing religions to work together toward formation of a New World Religion. The main objective of this New Religion is acceptance of all beliefs as equal. Pope John Paul II first cited this unification of all religions would become the catalyst in achieving world peace. He, Pope Benedict XVI and Pope Francis I should know the very act of mixing Jehovah with the false religions of the wicked seeds of Satan was what brought about Solomon's downfall. Solomon, too, wanted peace and tolerance, but was destroyed for allowing worship of these same false religions within the Temple he had originally built for Jehovah.

Wickedness of Satan, his Fallen Angels, and their pagan teachings are why Jehovah brought the Great Flood in Noah's day. Mankind's acceptance to tolerate Satan and partake of his deception was the reason Jehovah drove Adam and Eve out of the Garden of Eden. How could anyone in the Catholic hierarchy have forgotten the most important First Commandment: "THOU SHALT HAVE NO OTHER GODS BEFORE ME?"

Embracing religious cults as equal to the religion of Jehovah, just because they believe in a god, is not biblically correct. The One True God is Jehovah - not Buddha, Allah, Mohammed, Krishna, Satan, or any other entity. If the Catholic Church hierarchy is, indeed, promoting unification of all religions as equal, then it appears they are trying to build a kingdom of man and not preaching the way to the Kingdom of God. John Paul II, Benedict XVI and, now, Francis I have done exactly what God forbade in Scripture, which was "not to yoke together with false believers" or "have any other gods before me."

There have been rumors the Roman Catholic Church's strategy is to pave the way toward a New World Religion so they will be in the superior position to have jurisdiction once the merger of all religions and cults are combined into one. The hidden plan in this merger is for the Catholic Church to gain world power and dominion. The late Malachi Martin recorded during the reign of John Paul II that the Pope commented he was waiting for the completion of something he called "fissioning" to take place, which would usher in the New Order of the World. He insinuated that the Vatican Observatory was presently looking to the heavens for signs that this fissioning had been completed.

The Vatican has spent millions of dollars over the years on their high-tech planetary observatory, which includes an enormous telescope that is constantly scanning the skies from Rome, Italy. They are secretly engaged in the application of the Hermetic Principle regarding astrology. This is the same wisdom, handed down through the ages, used to identify when planetary alignments are scheduled to take place in conjunction with their matching Earthly Megalithic Structures. The Vatican has also recently built a telescope in Arizona, named L.U.C.I.F.E.R., and the EPA (Environmental Protection Agency) did nothing to stop it from being built on an Indian reservation. Rumors are that the Vatican had to locate their telescope at this precise locale as they were tracking something of great significance they are secretly calling 'Wormwood.' Revelation 8:10–11 reveals,

"And the third angel sounded, and there fell a great star from heaven, burning as it were a lamp, and it fell upon the third part of the rivers, and upon the fountains of waters; And the name of the star is called Wormwood: and the third part of the waters became wormwood; and many men died of the waters, because they were made bitter."

To Hermetic practitioners, celestial alignments indicate a predestined event is about to happen. Elite Roman Catholic clergy appear to be schooled in sacred Hidden Mysteries and are eagerly awaiting these prophesied signs to transpire within this generation. Let us not forget the act of fission upon the cell of a human body will produce a replica of it, a Clone. Comments by the late Pope John Paul II regarding fission and his clergy looking to the skies seem to indicate the time is close at hand for appearance of the Prince who will usher in their New World Order.

Malachi Martin, who was a Catholic Jesuit Priest and bestselling author, before his death, wrote that a "Black Mass" was held in St. Peter's Cathedral. His comment from the historical section of his book, Windswept House, regarding this particular mass was that "The smoke of Satan has entered the sanctuary of God." It appears Malachi was aware of the fact Catholic Hierarchy had been mixing Jehovah and other gods together within the Vatican for some time. This act of abomination always brings about destruction, just as it did in times past. God will not tolerate mixing His Holiness with false doctrines of Satan.

Recent media exposure of satanic rituals and sexual perversion among priests, on-going acceptance of Masons into the Papal hierarchy, and uniting of all religions as equal are, all, part of a game plan being put into place to advance the kingdom of Satan. High ranking priests, like Cardinal Cooke, who spoke to several thousand Masons, are just one part of this continuing scheme. According to Newsweek Magazine, Cardinal Cooke spoke to several thousand Masons during their annual gathering and praised them for "loyalty to their rituals."

Here we have an important official of priesthood praising Masons openly for their commitment to pagan rituals, which are in direct violation to the Ten Commandments of Jehovah. These are, no doubt, strange comments coming from a priest, unless he, himself, is a member of the Order. One could not see fit to praise the rituals of Satan unless one agrees to the practice of his 'Craft.' The expressed approval of the Masonic Order by a high priest within Catholic hierarchy is additional proof Satan has entered the Vatican. When a priest endorses Masonic pagan mysticism, which originated with the 'Spirit of Cain,' instead of condemning it for its satanic occultism, the act sheds more light on the Catholic Church's newly approved 'doctrines and directions.'

Acceptance by Catholic priests of homosexuals and marriages between them is another area where Satan has infiltrated the church over the years. It has been kept quiet as to growing numbers of homosexual priests and nuns residing within the confines of the church. Even priests and nuns who have committed molestation upon innocent children are never prosecuted, but handled internally by the church in an effort to keep them hidden from the public and above the law. These criminals are many times moved to other parishes to keep the problem swept under the rug, thereby evading punishment from the law. Innocent victims' families receive enormous monetary restitution to keep quiet, but these children must live their lives as if it were their fault they were molested. Paying people off to keep them quiet and moving these criminals to other towns to commit the same crimes over and over again are an endorsement of Satan's practices.

The Bible specifically states homosexual behavior is of the Devil. Remember Jehovah destroyed Sodom and Gomorrah for these sins of the flesh. It is evident Satan is working his 'Craft' within the Catholic Church. With their tolerance of all things and acceptance of every religion under one canopy, Satan is putting in place his World Religion from which to wield his coming power. It appears ancient Rome has risen from the dead. It has again become a major city of cults and Devil worship in this century. Satanic practices and countries banning together, that were once part of the Old Roman Empire, which, later, became the British Empire, will soon spell success for the coming reign of the Antichrist. Our world is being prepared to welcome him with open arms.

One might wonder how Satan has managed to infiltrate the Roman Catholic Church. As you will recall, Satan's wisdom began with the lineage of Cain and was handed down by way of the Megalithic Builders to Sumerians and Babylonians. Catholic Popes often wear a mitre, a hat shaped like a fish, which bears a connection to Oannes, a figure who was half man and half fish. Oannes, according to Sumerian legend, was leader of a Brotherhood of Seven Sages, known to be semi-divine creatures that were half man and half fish/Serpent. They were sent by the gods to teach the arts of civilization to mankind before the Flood. Their wisdom included architectural building and engineering skills. They taught the antediluvian world the skills of writing, mathematics, agriculture, and the sciences. They were also the ones who made sure their 'Pillars of Knowledge' survived the Flood so mankind could be re-educated in ancient wisdom of the Hidden Mysteries.

Every Pope wears a Fisherman's ring some believe has connections to the ring of Serpents that came after the Flood. Others justify the ring symbolizes Jesus; not so. Christ being a 'fisher of men' is not the same as being part fish/Serpent and half man. Regalia of Popes are much more connected to a past with the Dragon Kings than to Jesus Christ. To prove this, walls of Pyramids in Egypt show Dragon Kings, known to Pharaohs as part gods, wearing the same mitre as the Pope. Oannes, the great Dragon Sage of

Babylon mentioned above, also is depicted in Assyrian architecture as wearing the same mitre on his head. These mitres all look like a big fish head with its mouth open on the top.

Amongst all pagan religions, rings were used by Dragon Kings to symbolize their power over men. Circles and rings were crafts originating from the science of Alchemy, which was performed by Megalithic Builders. Their geometric designs are very satanic in nature and represent Ouroboros, a Serpent swallowing its tail. Ouroboros was 'Fiery King of the Underworld,' and the circle represents his eternal reign. Furthermore, the papal crest, designed with the dome of St. Peter's Basilica and crossed keys of Peter underneath, deceptively form a skull and cross bones to 'those with eyes to see.' This emblem that originated with the 'Mark of Cain' equally serves as a symbol for the Order of Skull and Bones. Hitler's Nazi army also used the Skull and Bones on their uniform. This symbol connects all these organizations secretly to the wicked lineage of Cain.

On top of all of that, the Maltese Cross, which is so proudly worn by Popes, can also be found on the British Coronation Crown. This Cross is really a Knights Templar Cross. It was derived from an eight-rayed star believed to mark the equinox cross at the midpoint between two solstice events, the rarest symbolic translation of ancient astronomy. The Templar Cross can be traced back through their history to Cain's lineage where it originated as the 'Mark of Cain.'

The Catholic Church is definitely connected to a strange and mysterious past. All indications are the Roman Catholic Church's use of such pagan symbols can only mean one thing, and that is they were infiltrated by the Babylonian

Brotherhood. This all came to pass in 312 A.D. when Constantine bestowed the title of 'Pope' to Miltiades for his willingness to mix both pagan religion and Christianity together in order to give solidarity to Emperor Constantine's Roman Empire. Up until that time, these symbols had never been part of Christian teachings of the Church, which began with Jesus' Disciple, Peter. Yet the Catholic Church claims Peter was their first Pope. Yes, Peter was first in a succession of what had once been considered Bishops of His church, but in no way were the wicked seeds of Satan mixed in with his original doctrine!

Beliefs and wisdom of the Wise Serpent had spread to Egypt, Canaan, Palestine, and eventually covered all of Ireland, Scotland, Wales and England in the early days. Hidden Mysteries grew stronger through the Essenes, Templar, and Freemasons. In time, these pagan rituals crept into the Roman Catholic Church through nothing more than an agreement to mix with pagans in return for materialistic wealth. It was not long before paganisms of Freemasonry became accepted, even though they were once rejected by the Vatican due to their connection with the Templar Order that had been forced underground for heresy during the Inquisition. The Vatican knew Freemasonry was just a new name for the old Templar Order. Over time, the ban was lifted and the Vatican allowed their priests to be indoctrinated into Masonic rituals. This lifting of the ban allowed Satan total access to the Vatican. With this disastrous act of mixing the Canaanite religion with Jehovah, we are now witnessing deterioration of the Catholic Church as it once was. Jehovah left the Vatican a long time ago, if he was truly ever there in the first place. In the end, it will be destroyed for its promotion of mixing paganism with Christianity.

The Book of Romans warns that God rejects all those who worship anything other than the Creator by declaring:

"Who changed the truth of God into a lie, and worshipped and served the creature more than the Creator, who is blessed forever . . . Who knowing the judgment of God, that they which commit such things are worthy of death, not only do the same, but have pleasure in them that do them." (Romans 1:25, 32).

Even Jesus warned those following Him that His mother, the Virgin Mary, was not to be worshipped. According to Luke 11:27–28,

"And it came to pass, as he spake these things, a certain woman of the company lifted up her voice, and said unto him, Blessed is the womb that bare thee, and the paps which thou hast sucked. But he said, Yea rather, blessed are they that hear the word of God, and keep it."

Jehovah is not tolerant with His Commandments; that is why they are called Commandments. Whoever willingly turns his back upon the Lord and does not correct his error is forever cut off from the Lord and will perish.

In 1996, Pope John Paul II made an unsettling statement to those attending a conference of the Papal Academy of Sciences. He boldly claimed the Theory of Evolution was more than a hypothesis. Was he claiming someone may have had a hand in evolving mankind genetically so humanity could receive knowledge, or does he think we came from apes?

We know Charles Darwin's Theory of Evolution is bogus. Therefore, this Pope had to be insinuating a genetic evolution occurred where blind and imperfect man, created by God, was changed into a genetically illuminated man thanks to Satan and his Tree of Knowledge. Whatever Pope John Paul II meant the fact remains he believed an evolution of man had taken place and he was openly acknowledging it.

Within Illuminated Circles of the Elite, their Satanic Prophecies predicted preparation for the coming of a Prince would officially begin when a Pope took the name of Apostle Paul. Pope Paul VI reigned from 1963–1978 and was followed by John Paul I in 1978. This prophecy continued when the name John Paul II was chosen by the Slavic Pope, Karol Wojtyla after his predecessor John Paul I was found dead under unusual circumstances only after a month of becoming Pope.

There is no doubt that Wojtyla was part of a secret plan whose schemers had hand-picked to ascend to the papal throne; as he was only a junior cardinal. Wojtyla was virtually unheard of and had wanted to become an actor and not a priest. Not long after securing the office of Pope, photos of him sunning in the nude were all over the Italian tabloids. Other damaging and revealing information came to light he had worked for the Nazis in a chemical factory owned by I.G. Farben during World War II. I.G. Farben was responsible for tens of thousands of deaths at its chemical processing plant called Auschwitz. This death camp is where I believe only a certain lineage of Jews, which were really pure DNA Hebrews, were forced to work for a period (on average of three months) before being delivered into the gas chambers.

I.G. Farben is said to be a division of Standard Oil Company owned by the Rockefellers that was funded into existence according to David Icke's book, . . . and the truth shall set you free. John D. Rockefeller and Prescott Bush were supporting Hitler's rise to Chancellor through these channels while playing like they cared for the Jewish people. They cared only for Khazarian lineages not the Hebraic because the Hebraic, not Khazars, are inheritors of God's Promised Land according to Scripture. So just who were Hitler, Rockefeller, Bush, and the Khazarian Rothschild's slaughtering? God's 'Chosen People.'

The Rockefeller Foundation has always been secretly behind the United Nations' depopulation program. They helped Hitler organize the Hebraic mass murder program of Nazi Germany. These internationalists are connected to British Empire geopolitics and were not stopped after World War II. Their allegiance to Hitler's old Nazi regime poses a terrible danger to our world today. Rockefeller formed what he called a Foundation with his money and created the medical specialty called Psychiatric Genetics. For this new experimental field, the Foundation reorganized medical training in Germany. They actually created and oversaw the Kaiser Wilhelm Institute for Psychiatry and the Kaiser Wilhelm Institute for Anthropology, Eugenics and Human Heredity. Rockefeller's chief executive of these institutions was a fascist Swiss psychiatrist named Ernst Rudin. In 1932, when the British started their Eugenics' movement, they designated Rockefellers' protégé, Dr. Rudin, to become president of their worldwide Eugenics Federation. This movement called for killing and/or sterilization of races whose heredity made them a public burden. Then, these so-called "Racial Laws" were enforced in Germany. That is right, only a few months later, when

Hitler took over Germany, this Rockefeller and British backed program, with Rudin leading it, became part of the Nazi state. Hitler's regime appointed Rudin to oversee their Racial Hygiene Society. Then, Rudin, as part of the Task Force of Heredity Experts that was chaired by the evil SS chief, Heinrich Himmler, drew up Germany's sterilization law. What is most interesting is that during this time it was described as an American Model of Law. It was approved in July 1933 and then appeared in the September 1933, Eugenical News (USA), with Hitler's signature.

Then, Josef Mengele began writing medical/genetic reports to special courts which enforced this racial purity law against cohabitation of Aryans with non-Aryans (Pure Hebrews). This led to creating propaganda films that promoted right-to-die/mercy killing/euthanasia/ (DNR-do not resuscitate) to German citizens in order to brainwash them into believing this was okay. Then, under the Nazis regime, the German chemical company known as I.G. Farben and Rockefeller's Standard Oil Company became joint ventures in cartel arrangements. I.G. Farben, until 1937, was owned by the Warburg family. They were Rockefeller's partners in banking and establishing the Nazi German eugenics' programs.

Following Germany's invasion of Poland, in 1939, Rockefeller secretly promised his merger with I.G. Farben would continue even if the United States entered the war against Germany forces. This secret merger was totally exposed, during 1942, by Senator Harry Truman's investigating committee. Even, President Roosevelt took legal measures during the war to try and stop Standard/I.G. Farben from supplying our enemy, Nazi Germany's war machine. In 1940-41, I.G. Farben built a gigantic factory at

Auschwitz, Poland. There, they produced Standard Oil/I.G. Farben patents by forcing their concentration camp slave labor to make gasoline from coal. Get this, even Nazi SS guards were assigned to guard their Jewish and other inmates; as well as, select and kill anyone they deemed unfit to be I.G. Farben slave labor. Standard Oil's president, in Germany, Emil Helfferich, testified following the war that Standard Oil funds paid for SS guards at Auschwitz. If this was not bad enough, in 1940, a European Rockefeller Foundation official, Daniel O'Brian, wrote to the Foundation's chief medical officer, Alan Gregg, and said, "It would be unfortunate if they had to stop their research which had no relation to war issues." So, would you believe it, the Foundation continued full speed ahead financing the Nazi regime's psychiatric research projects during the war.

German inspired genetic research and their control over the real Hebrew lineages was paramount to them. Back in 1936, Rockefeller's own Dr. Franz Kallmann, a doctor of hereditary degeneracy, immigrated to America because he was half-Jewish. Kallmann went to New York and established the Medical Genetics Department at the New York State Psychiatric Institute. And guess what, the Scottish Rite of Freemasonry published Kallman's study of over 1,000 cases of schizophrenia, which tried to prove a hereditary/genetic basis. In his book, Dr. Kallmann actually thanked his long-time boss and mentor, Dr. Ernst Rudin. When Kallmann's book was published during 1938 in the United States and in Germany, it became the Nazi T4 unit's sole rationalization in 1939 to justify murdering all mental health patients and others they deemed defective, many of them children. The Nazi's used gas and lethal injections to kill around 250,000 people under this program. This prepared the Nazi forces for a broader murder program by being desensitized and trained to kill whoever without remorse.

In 1943, the evil geneticist, Josef Mengele, was made medical commander over Auschwitz. Rockefeller's Kaiser Wilhelm Institute for Anthropology, Eugenics and Human Heredity in Berlin, Germany financed Mengele's experiments at Auschwitz as part of the German Research Council. Then, with permission from Himmler, anthropological research was performed on various racial groups within the concentration camps and blood samples were sent to laboratories for investigation. Most important, was the fact, Mengele searched all railroad lines leading into Auschwitz, looking for twins; his favorite subject in psychiatric genetics. When found, once they arrived at Mengele's experimental station, all twins were forced to fill out a detailed questionnaire created by the Kaiser Wilhelm Institute. Genetic testing was intensive with daily drawings of blood looking for so-called "specific proteins". Needles were injected into their eyes for genetic research on eye color. There were experimental blood transfusions and infections given to people to research their reactions. Organs and limbs were removed, most times without anesthetics. Sex changes were attempted on men and women with females being sterilized and males castrated. Thousands upon thousands were murdered and their organs, eyeballs, heads, sexual organs and limbs sent to Rockefeller's Kaiser Wilhelm Institute.

In 1947, the Bureau of Human Heredity based in London was moved to Copenhagen. This new facility was built with Rockefeller money. The first International Congress in Human Genetics, following World War II, was held there in 1956. It was Rockefeller's Dr. Kallmann who, then, created the American Society of Human Genetics, which organized the 'Human Genome Project' which is, now, over a $3 billion multiculturalism effort. Dr. Kallmann became a director of the American Eugenics Society in 1952 and, then, again from 1954 to 1965. During the 1950s, the Rockefeller Foundation reorganized the United States eugenics research program by adding population-control measures and abortion groups. Then, the Eugenics Society changed its name to the Society for the Study of Social Biology in a vain effort to keep the public at large from knowing about their ongoing evil agenda since the days of Hitler. Rockefeller's Foundation had long financed the eugenics movement in England; thereby, repaying Britain's Royal serpents for the fact that British capital and an Englishman, partner, had started John D. Rockefeller out in his Standard Oil Trust. That is right; Rockefeller was funded to do all that he did. Royal serpent involvement is best noted in all of this when, in the 1960s, the Eugenics Society of England adopted what they called "Crypto-eugenics" by stating in their official reports that they would do eugenics through means and instruments not labeled as eugenics. So, with support from the Rockefellers, this Eugenics Society in England set up a sub-committee called the "International Planned Parenthood Federation", which for over twelve years had no other address other than the Eugenics Society. This private, international apparatus has, now, set our present world up for a coming global holocaust, under the auspices of the UN flag. Everything has been secretly put in place.

Even more shocking is the possibility that Hitler may have been a blood relative to the Rothschild family. According to The Mind of Hitler, a book written by Walter Langer, there is speculation Hitler's father, Alois Hitler, was the illegitimate son of Maria Anna Schicklgruber. She was living in Vienna at the time she conceived, while performing duties as a servant to Baron Rothschild, Salomon Mayer. He was a Freemason as well as the only Rothschild at home, and he was known to love young girls as his wife was sick and living in Frankfurt. When it was discovered Maria was pregnant, the Rothschild family sent her home.

Salomon was a very important man and had the Order of Vladimir conferred on him for his work with Russia. He was incredibly powerful in the world. To this day, Rothschild descendants still have control of the world's gold. They meet twice daily in London, where they now live, to dictate to the world what the price of gold will be each day. With their control over gold prices, they dictate what the 'Federal Reserve System' does in America. In other words, the Rothschild family owns monetary power over America. This only reiterates what Gordon Mohr wrote in his book, The Hidden Power Behind Freemasonry, concerning what old man Amsel Rothschild is reportedly to have said,

"Give me control of the economics of a country; and I care not who makes her laws."

The Rothschild dynasty has always known whoever has control of the money has control of everything.

In 1823, the Rothschild Empire took over financial operation of the Vatican's banking and papal treasures, forever linking Freemasonry, banking, the Vatican, and Rothschild family, together. They owe no allegiance to any religious belief. Rothschild money financed the Russian

Revolution and in the end, took the majority of Orthodox Christian Church's wealth. Once you understand who is pulling the strings of puppets around the world, you can better see that a centralized, powerful group is dictating their agenda with no regard to anything else. The average person means nothing to them.

Knowing all of this, now imagine the implications if Hitler indeed was a Rothschild. It gives great creditability to my theory that the whole Nazi attempt was to genetically identify and kill Hebraic Jews so there would be no linage left for direct claim to the Promised Land. The true Messianic lineage of the Hebrews would be extinct. Maybe that is why Hitler's swastika symbol, when placing an X (Mark of Cain) over it to connect the arms, becomes a perfect Maltese Cross of eight sharp sides. That same cross is proudly worn on regalia of the Roman Catholic Pope and British Royalty. In the past, Khazar Jews' ancestors, Knights Templar, wore it, further tying them all together as Lords of the Eight, those seeking materialistic immortality.

Science of genetics was first recorded by Theodor Heinrich Boveri of Munich University in Germany. In the 1880's, he listed the majority of information regarding cellular division and chromosome identification. This was an amazing scientific accomplishment, as he did all this without the invention of the electron microscope. Therefore, understanding of genetics did not recently surface. It has been around for more than a century. Hitler's plan was for his entourage of scientists to discover how to manipulate certain genetic markers in order to breed a perfect race—a New Man, the 'Second Adam.'

Hitler got his strange idea of recreating man from a book entitled The Secret Doctrine by Russian mystic and co-Mason, Helena P. Blavatsky. Blavatsky claimed she received knowledge to write this book from unknown masters. Hitler was so engrossed with this book that he read it many times and was said to have kept a copy always by his bedside. Hermann Rauschning, author of Voice of Destruction, said Hitler was always talking about a Cyclops Eye (a reptilian eye) located inside a person's head. According to Rauschning, Hitler stated,

"Some men can already activate their pineal glands to give a limited vision into the secrets of time."

Hitler also, according to Rauschning, told that a 'New Man' would be created using visions and scientific knowledge already being transmitted through these men's pineal glands. This so-called 'Superman,' which Hitler said was slated to arrive in the near future, would be large in stature, have a gorgeous physique, intuitive powers, have knowledge beyond his years, be gifted in a magical form of subliminal communication to mesmerize and brainwash humans, have complete power over Demons and nature, and control the world. Hitler believed nothing could prevail against such a man. He even called this 'Superman,' a 'Son of God.'

Hitler believed the secret behind creation of such a divine man would be from blood of the Holy Grail. According to Trevor Ravenscroft, in his book The Spear of Destiny, Hitler was in possession of the spear used to pierce the flesh of Jesus while he hung on the cross. The spear, if it had never been washed, could still have had blood stains on it, thereby offering a way to cultivate and identify Jesus' blood for evaluation and genetic testing. Hitler had the perfect setup in which to do this. His underground laboratory facilities were well away from eyes of a suspecting public and were being funded by the richest men on our planet, who were all members of the Secret Brotherhood.

Hitler and his Khazar buddies wanted to remove Pure Hebrews so they could recreate the New Messiah to their standards without anyone being suspicious. They forced captured Pure Hebraic lineages to undergo physical torture in many of their horrific so-called scientific experiments before killing them in the gas chambers. Their plan, although Hitler's regime was superficially disbanded, did not fail but as already noted resurfaced under a variety of names thanks to the Rockefeller Foundation which got its original funding from British Royal serpents.

This Plan still exists today where it always has—in the hands of the Secret Brotherhood. These elite men know if Christians and Hebrews remain in the world, then the Messiah they have recreated will have opposition. Therefore, their development of a New World Order is to have the true followers of Jesus out of the way—annihilated or locked up securely in detention centers (a new name for Concentration Camps being built all over America) to be brainwashed into submission. With no opposition, the world will then be their playground filled with pagan worshippers of a fake Jesus. But, it is the divine spark in Jesus' blood that had to be used to develop their Messiah because, according to Manly P. Hall, 33rd Degree Mason and author of The Phoenix, the recreated being had to be qualified enough to comprehend the mind of God. No human being, Fallen Angel, or Satan himself has that level of intelligence.

No wonder scientists of Nazi Germany seemed to be so much ahead of their time. That advancement is why these men were such sought after individuals following the war. On top of being offered huge salaries by the CIA and NASA, not one of them were ever prosecuted for their hand in carrying out what has only been described as evil experiments upon humans.

Efforts are still being carried out to try and identify various Jewish groups claiming Israelite descent. Dr. Ariella Oppenheim, a Jewish professor of genetics at Hebrew University in Israel, and five research colleagues reported in the American Journal of Human Genetics (November 2001) that Jews are closely related in DNA to Iraqis, Kurds, Turks, and Armenians. Meanwhile Sephardic (Middle East Jews) differ from European Jews, many of whom were found to be of Khazar (Turkic) stock.

Identification of all Jewish sects is the sole key to End Times prophecy. Satan wants very little competition when he ascends to his throne to rule mankind. The same extermination plan was used by Nazi's, as well as by Knights Templar, during the Crusades, to kill off Christians and true Hebraic lineages. This is also the future plan for getting all Jews to return to their homeland, Israel, without knowing they are being corralled for an attempted slaughter one more time. What is worse, Khazarian Jews are using their control over the media to beg sympathetic and unsuspecting Christians for money to help them achieve their diabolical plan.

Of course, there is no doubt Khazarian Jews put Wojtyla in office, especially since there is speculation he might have been married at one time. There is a suspicious period of time in his life where nothing is recorded; making one wonder what he had been up to that the powers-that-be did not want anyone to know about. Could it be Wojtyla was being schooled on his future papacy within Masonic Circles during this time period? Or, was he part of the Nazi regime? Karol Wojtyla was a student at Jagiellonian University studying theater, literature, philosophy, when the Nazis invaded Poland. The university was shut down and many were shipped off to Germany as forced labor. The future Pope avoided deportation by working at a limestone quarry that was directly associated with a Solvay chemical plant. In 1942, he started working at the plant itself, hauling chemicals so it makes you wonder about his Nazi involvement.

Interestingly enough, when Wojtyla was elected Pope, Cardinal Jean Villot (Masonic name "Jeanni," member Zurich Lodge #041/3 joined August 6, 1966, whom conspiracy theorists consider had a hand in killing the prior Pope John Paul I and making it look like a heart attack), put together a celebration party with the help of a group of Masonic Cardinals in Wojtyla's honor. Instead of singing hymns of victory and offering up prayers as was typical of papal celebrations, these men and the nuns they had invited had a champagne celebration. Wojtyla poured some of the glasses of the bubbly while singing a polish song called "The Mountaineer," according to Paul L. Williams in his book, The Vatican Exposed.

Wojtyla's association with such a large band of Masonic friends would have allowed him firsthand knowledge of the ancient prophecy concerning choosing the name Paul, because that is where prophecy of such nature is hidden. Why else would someone want to choose the same name as a Pope who was more than likely just murdered in office before them? Seems a little morbid when Wojtyla could have chosen any name he would have liked to have been known of as Pope. Why the name Paul, unless he knew full well he was fulfilling an ancient prophecy and he would have a role to play in preparing the way for the Antichrist?

Before Wojtyla became Pope, he was promoting geopolitics and had written and spoken openly about needing a New World Order. From this, one can be assured Wojtyla, under the name of John Paul II, was aware of his place in Vatican history. He allowed Satan's agenda to go forward, through his new directions and doctrines promoted by then-Cardinal Ratzinger; some of these directions and doctrines had never before been witnessed within Catholic hierarchy.

Today's generation will be witness to a Prince, whom the Bible calls the Antichrist. Malachi Martin, the late famous author and priest, wrote in the historical preface of his book, Windswept House, that

"The Enthronement of the Fallen Archangel Lucifer was effected within the Roman Citadel on June 29, 1963 . . . there could be no more perfect date for the Enthronement of the Prince than this feast day of the twin princes of the citadel—Saint Peter and Saint Paul."10

On June 29, 1963, Satan was enthroned and a timetable was set to bring the Prince of Power to life. Gradually, these priests began to secretly replace their worship of Jesus with their worship of Lucifer as the fruit of their plan. The complete transition was to be carried out under the noses of the church fathers. Good priests would be deceptively replaced with evil priests. Homosexuality would be promoted and used by the evil priests to violate the innocent and gain followers. Everything was planned right down to the last detail, and today, it is right on schedule.

The new generations of priests are dedicated to carrying out the Prince's scheme to rule the New World Religion from its highest pinnacle, the Vatican. Once in control, the Prince will move his headquarters to Jerusalem and the Pope will follow. There, he will reveal he is the newly built temple, a temple that is not made of stone but of flesh and blood. This Goat and his false prophet, the pope, will reveal that he is the Cloned image of the Lamb, who has returned to bring peace to the world.

Because the body of this Prince has been fissioned from the blood of Jesus, he will look identical to the image imprinted on the Holy Shroud of Turin. Everyone will be pleased that the Messiah has returned to Jerusalem to regain his rightful home and to rule as prophet, priest and king. Satan will have completed his task to be worshipped as the Savior of mankind. He will be sitting in Jerusalem and residing in the rebuilt (Cloned) temple of Jesus. The Bible refers to the human body as a temple where it states,

"Know ye not that ye are the temple of God, and that the spirit of God dwelleth in you? If any man defile the temple of God, him shall God destroy; for the temple of God is holy, which temple ye are." (1 Corinthians 3: 16–17).

Each moment that passes by, Satan's tentacles are gaining more and more hold on the world. Tolerance is being preached toward acceptance of abortions, death, Cloning, homosexuality, global unity, religious differences, cults, and a host of other issues. A laissez-faire attitude now predominates in our society to an extent that almost any occurrence can happen without the first eyebrow being raised. Love of self, power, wealth, scientific advancement, sexual pleasure and materialism all breed secularization. Man looks at what he has created for himself and never looks to God. Secularization is the foundation for Satanism of the world. Those assisting Satan behind his sinister plot are willing to give their own blood to push our world into the hands of Lucifer and his false prophet, the Pope.

In preparation of this, Pope John Paul II, first, allowed Masons into the top positions of his clergy. He did not stop nontraditional teachings such as homosexuality and New Age rituals from becoming rampant within the church. The Vatican refused to punish those in the clergy who were guilty of molestation with immediate removal. Punishment for doing wrong appeared to be of little concern. The late Pope was too caught up in fulfilling his destiny of preparing the way for the coming Prince. He traveled around the world to shrines, temples, cathedrals, and cultic places of worship attempting to unify them into one religious group. He went so far as to participate in occult ceremonies, witchdoctor antics, and met and blessed those who participated in such rituals.

Pope John Paul II even invited another one of the world's religions to participate in a sacred ceremony with him at St. Peter's Basilica. On June 29, 1995, Pope John Paul II of the Roman Catholic Church and the visiting head of the Orthodox Church (Christian Church originating in the eastern Roman Empire) gave an unprecedented ceremony to onlookers who stood below the balcony of St. Peter's to watch. The official journal of the Holy Trinity Monastery of the Orthodox Church called the Orthodox Life (Vol. 45, 1995) covered the monumental event as follows:

"John Paul II, head of the Roman Catholic Church, and Patriarch Bartholomew, symbolic head of Orthodox Christians, together, on Thursday, June 29, from the balcony of the basilica of St. Peter, blessed their faithful all over the world. They addressed a common appeal for the reunification of the Christian churches, separated for 1,000 years. The two religious leaders came to participate at a mass in the Vatican, where they undertook to redouble their ecumenical efforts.

The Patriarch underlined, "today . . . we have arrived at maturity." The Pope, in turn, suggested that papal authority would have to be supreme in a unified Church because Christ had given Saint Peter, the first pope, free power to rule the flock on earth."

Following the John Paul II's comments, Patriarch Bartholomew asked for prayer, and at that exact moment, a lightning bolt struck the basilica. This was just a sign that things within the Catholic Church have been going awry for some time.

It was on October 28, 312 A.D., that Miltiades, a 62 year-old man serving as the 32nd Bishop of Rome, whom his followers called "papa," became the first so-called Pope. He lived in a world of poverty, persecution, and self-denial, wearing an old robe and working as a commoner in the marketplace like all the bishops who had come before him, including Peter. Each one of them had equally followed the path of Jesus as a suffering servant who took no pleasure in materialistic gain. Unlike those Bishops before him,

Miltiades broke this tradition forever when he agreed to become the first Pope and accept the title of 'Pontifex Maximus,' which was given to him by the Roman Emperor, Constantine.

Constantine believed that a cross he had seen in the sky before a battle had led to its decisive victory in his favor. Since his kingdom was divided and made up of Christians and pagans, he decided to combine their holidays in honor of his victory. In reality, he was being selfish and made the decision to approach the Catholics in order to hold his huge kingdom together. He gave his first Pope, Miltiades, material wealth so that he would agree to this mixing of the religious and pagan practices in the Roman Empire.

In order prove his allegiance to Miltiades, Constantine went the so-called 'extra mile' to get the Pope's full cooperation by building a basilica on the spot where Peter's bones had been buried. It is worth noting here that this basilica, known as St. Peter's Basilica, was not a church, but a huge pagan structure built where the Emperors of Rome, carved into huge white statues, could be worshipped as gods. Because Miltiades agreed to such nonsense, Constantine also built him the Pope's Palace on Lateran Hill, where every Pope since Miltiades has resided since that time.

As the Catholic religion grew, workers had to be hired to assist the new Pope and were called Cardinals (Supporters). Overnight, the church of the poor became the wealthiest in the history of the world. All that had been required was that they had willingly agreed to mix with other pagan religions in return for materialistic wealth. The church sold its soul for a little silver and a little gold, just like Judas had done.

This was the same temptation that Satan had offered to Jesus in the wilderness, and He turned it down.

"And the devil, taking him up into an high mountain, shewed unto him all the kingdoms of the world in a moment of time. And the devil said unto him, All this power will I give thee, and the glory of them: for that is delivered unto me; and to whomsoever I will I give it. If thou therefore wilt worship me, all shall be thine. And Jesus answered and said, Get thee behind me, Satan: for it is written, Thou shalt worship the Lord thy God, and him only shalt thou serve." (Luke 4:5–8).

If the Catholic Church is the true vine of Jesus, they did not follow protocol. Roman Catholicism became something entirely different. It is not from the same roots as those found in the Biblical Christianity of the early church or its martyrs. Instead, it became the old paganism of Rome resurfacing under the veil of Christianity by using similar terminology and ritual. When Rome fell, the Pope and Roman Catholicism continued to exist and that is why, to this very day, the Pope exerts so much power. These same doctrines, toward greater unification of Christianity with pagan religions and their rituals, continue to survive today within the Vatican. No wonder a bolt of lightning hit the Basilica on June 29, 1995.

Unfortunately, the lightning bolt did little to deter John Paul II's quest for harmony between religious doctrines. In January 2000, Pope John Paul II bowed and kissed the Koran, the holy book of the Muslims as Patriarch Raphael I of Iraq and his delegation looked on during their visit to the Vatican. The Koran instructs Moslems to kill the infidels—infidels meaning Christians and Jews. Why would John

Paul feel it necessary to kiss such a book unless maybe he agrees that all Christians and 'Hebraic' Jews need to be dead? This is a possibility, since these two groups are the only ones standing in the way of a Universal religion as the true inheritors to the 'Promised Land.'

On June 27, 2000, Mikhail Gorbachev was invited as a guest of honor at a Vatican press conference to celebrate the Church's new orientation called Ostpolitik. This new process was a policy of "dialogue" and accommodation with Communistic regimes (Russia, China, etc.) that persecuted the church. Interestingly enough, the reporters at this press conference were prohibited from asking questions. In other words, it was a broadcast that allowed 'those with eyes to see' that the New World Order was coming along as planned.

Then, on November 4, 2000, Gorbachev was again invited to the Vatican to address the Pope and high ranking clergymen at the "Jubilee of Politicians." This event included a ceremonial dinner of 5,000 rulers from the world's secular republics. The fact that the ceremony was heralded as a Jubilee is an abomination because a Jubilee was known in Old Testament times as a spiritual event. Now here the Pope is, holding such an event with discussion of secular matters and attempting to merge it with the church toward tolerance of a modern civilization.

If that was not enough, Pope John Paul II met a second time in Assisi, Italy, on January 24, 2002, for the World Day of Prayer for Peace. Religious leaders representing the Buddhists, Catholics, Protestants, Jews, Hindus, Moslems, an African witchdoctor, Jains, Confucians, Asian Shaman, and Zoroastrians were transported from the Vatican to

Assisi in what L'Osservatore Romano called "a peace train," in an effort to promote unification of the world's religions toward peace. These major representatives of their various religions, including the witch doctor, gave speeches from a wooden pulpit in the lower plaza of the Basilica of Saint Francis.

As part of this unification/mixing ceremony, the pagan religions were each given a room inside the Basilica to perform their pagan rituals and offer prayers for peace to their gods. Then they all lit oil lamps to signify to the world their total commitment to inter-religious brotherhood and world peace. What is worse is that the Pope commented that they all had commonality in that they worshipped the one true God. Anyone who knows anything about all these religions is quite aware that pagans worship hundreds, if not thousands, of gods. How could Pope John Paul II even consider that there was any connection between these pagan gods and Christianity, when God's First Commandment to all Christians is "to have no other gods before me?"

Just as King Solomon did in the Temple, John Paul II followed suit, as he also opened up the Vatican to the worship of other gods. When the Basilica was hit by lightning, Jehovah may have been sending a sign from Heaven that He would never cohabitate in such a place with Satan. Maybe that explains why the commemorative coin issued by the Vatican with Pope John Paul II's photo includes three pagan stars having six points—in other words adding up to the diabolical number of 666. Even when this Pope took over the papacy in 1978, the Vatican issued a set of stamps with a Pyramid and an 'All Seeing Eye' on them—symbols used by Secret Societies since ancient times.

Over time, Pope John Paul II's position on Jehovah's Son, Jesus, began to wane. In January 2002, the Vatican issued a revised doctrine that stated that, "The Jewish wait for the Messiah is not in vain." So if the Jews are waiting for the Messiah to be born, then something is amuck in the hierarchy of the Roman Catholic Church; unless, of course, you already know that he has been cloned, reborn, and now lives again in the flesh. The change in John Paul's prayers and daily devotionals were noticeable because he rarely mentioned the name of Jesus Christ in his latter days. But then again, if he believed that Jesus was living amongst us, then who would he be praying to? He even removed the crucifix when his non-Catholic and pagan visitors complained that it bothered them when they came to visit him.

Pope John Paul II did not call himself a Roman Catholic or refer to the church as the Roman Catholic Church. As Pope, he already knew that a New World Religion was in major progress. He had been chosen, from the beginning, to fulfill this diabolical Plan of the Illuminati in order to solidify all religions banning themselves together under one big umbrella.

According to Malachi Martin's book, The Keys Of This Blood, hatred for the Roman papacy's control over religion had to be secured if the Masonic Order's agenda was to become a reality. Therefore, the Permanent Instruction was drawn up between the years of 1819–20 by the Grand Masters of the Lodges in France, Austria, Italy, and Germany, which read:

" . . . we must turn our attention to an ideal that has always been of concern to men aspiring to the regeneration of all mankind . . . the liberation of the entire world and the establishment of the republic of brotherhood and world peace . . . Among the many remedies, there is one which we must never forget . . . the total annihilation of Catholicism and even of Christianity . . . What we must wait for is a pope suitable for our purposes . . . because, with such a pope, we could effectively crush the Rock on which God built his Church . . . Seek a pope fitting our description . . . induce the clergy to march under your banner in the belief that they are marching under the papal banner . . . make their younger, secular clergy, and even the religious, receptive to our doctrines. Within as few years, this same younger clergy will, of necessity, occupy responsible positions . . . Some will be called upon to elect a future pope. This pope, like most of his contemporaries, will be influenced by those . . . humanitarian principles which we are now circulating . . . the medieval alchemists lost both time and money to realize the dream of the "Philosopher's Stone" . . . The dream of the secret societies (to have a pope as their ally) will be made real for the very simple reason that it is founded on human passions . . ."

The above statements reek of the Communist Karl Marx, a Khazar Jew, whose roots were in Masonic Ideals. Communism and Masonic ideology go hand in hand. They both want mankind's happiness to be fulfilled in this world without intervention from a divine God coming from the spiritual realm offering eternal life as a goal for all humans—in other words; forego the wants of materialism in this life for the promise of eternal life. Pope John Paul II became the geopolitical leader that Secret Societies had been waiting for.

Pope John Paul II was born on May 18, 1920—the same day as a solar eclipse. He fulfilled an ancient prophecy of Saint Malachy that the 264th pope would be born under the sign of labor solis (the classical expression for a solar eclipse). Amazingly, his funeral, which forced Prince Charles and Camilla's wedding date to be delayed, was held on April 8, 2005—the only day that year for a total solar eclipse. From the moment Karol Jozef Wojtyla became Pope, 'those with eyes to see' knew that he was the pope they had been waiting for.

At 8:17pm, on October 16, 1978, the very day Wojtyla had been elected to the papacy, he stepped out on the balcony overlooking St. Peters Basilica in the heart of Rome and gave a hand gesture to the world that identified him to all Secret Societies as one of their own, for whom they had been waiting. His hand positions were a code. All popes who had come before him had displayed to the awaiting public the exact same hand positions—that of both hands at breastbone level with palms to palms, fingers on fingers, and thumbs crossed. This hand position is the normal Roman Catholic gesture of prayer and divine worship used by popes immortal. But Wojtyla's hands were quite unique, as they were tightly fisted and crossed over his chest, with the right forearm over the left and each fist touching the right and left shoulder. That is right; the newly elected pope was giving the secret hand position of the Order of Skull and Bones before the world. The Permanent Instruction was finally coming to fruition just as planned.

The Black Madonna is considered the true Queen of Poland, the now deceased Pope's birth place. She has been the icon of Poland for over 6 centuries. His fascination with Mary Magdalene, the 'Black Madonna,' was not only in his blood from his upbringing in Poland, but was also truly Masonic in every sense of the word. Pope John Paul II, from the beginning of his appointment, was actively involved in the Order's Plan to assist the Prince of Darkness in gaining future power over all the nations on earth. The 1963 Enthronement of Lucifer at the Vatican apparently brought about the present condition of the Roman Catholic Church.

Pope John Paul II was aware of his place in history, due to the Prophecies of the 'Three Secrets of Fatima.' On May 13, 1917, three young children believed they were visited by the Virgin Mary. The Virgin is said to have appeared to Lucia, Jacinta, and Francisco a total of six times in Fatima, Portugal. During the apparition, she revealed three prophecies that would come to pass before the return of Christ.

The First and Second Secret Prophecies came true just as the Virgin had predicted. The First was the end of World War I. The Second was that Russia would become a superpower promoting atheism and communism following a World War II. The Third and final Secret has not been revealed. It has been carefully concealed and kept from the public because of the terrible nature of the prediction.

Internal leaks within the Vatican say that the Third Secret is about the Antichrist. Sources close to the hierarchy report that Satan will come to control the Vatican and become the head of the Roman Catholic Church. Strangely enough, the late John Paul II announced it was his mission to fulfill the Fatima Prophecy. Cardinal Ratzinger (Pope Benedict XVI) even wrote bogus reports trying to link the secret to an earlier assassination attempt on John Paul's life. He and Pope John Paul II, both, worshipped the Black Madonna.

When Pope Benedict XVI traveled to America he was recorded live on a newscast bowing before and kissing a small statue of a Black Madonna and child. The filming crew quickly tried to move their live feed to just him kneeling so the general public would not see the statue.

On October 13, 1917, over 50,000 people came to the site of the Virgin apparitions. During prayers, the sun appeared to tremble, rotate, and change colors. Everyone present was able to look directly at the sun without it hurting their eyes. The sun began a dance that made it appear to be moving toward the earth. The sun's colors changed from red to yellow to purple. Those present could feel great heat as it got closer. The sun moved to the height of the clouds and rotated extremely fast for about eight minutes. There was a blue column of smoke that appeared above the three children's heads. It was a clear beam of light, which rose up and disappeared into the sky. The dance of the sun was observed within a 25 mile radius of Fatima.

Because of the reported dance of the sun, many pilgrims traveled to Fatima by the thousands. What is really strange concerns the reported reaction of the Freemasons in that area towards these pilgrims and the event itself. On October 23, members of the local Masonic Lodge vandalized the Holy Site. They cut down the tree where the 3 children had seen the Virgin on October 13. Besides taking the tree, they took an altar, a wooden arch, lanterns, and crosses that had been placed there in the Virgin's honor. They set these items up in a house and charged people admission to view them. These same Masons even carried the stolen items through town in a paradelike fashion, mocking them to those that watched.

The Masonic Order also organized demonstrations at Fatima to keep those traveling to the site from praying. The demonstrations included bringing a herd of donkeys to the site and agitating them so they would bray so loud that the visitors could not pray together. The Masonic leaders actively ridiculed religion through speeches and the handing out of negative literature to the visitors. Their actions failed to stop the pilgrims from traveling to visit Fatima.

Over the course of a couple of years, money was collected and a statue was erected to Mary. It was carved based on the description of the three children. A chapel was then built to house the statue. These events enraged the local Masons. On March 6, 1921, the Masonic Lodge placed five explosives inside the chapel. Four of the bombs took out parts of the chapel and completely destroyed the roof. The fifth bomb had been placed on the oak stump, which was left from the tree they had cut down earlier, where the Virgin appeared. Amazingly, that explosive did not go off. One can only wonder what it was about the Fatima prophecies and signs of the Virgin Mary that shook the core of the Masonic organization. Clearly, it was the Black Madonna and not the Virgin Mary that these men had been worshipping all the time.

In 1139 A.D., the Archbishop of Ireland, Saint Malachy, said God showed him that there would be a total of 112 Popes before the 'End of Time.' Pope John Paul II was #110 and Pope Benedict XVI was #111. Benedict relinquished his title; something unheard of in modern times. Interestingly enough, a lightning bolt hit the Vatican not once but twice the same day Benedict told the world he was resigning as Pope. The 112th Pope, Malachy recorded, would defect from the Catholic Church and, like the Third

Secret of Fatima predicts, turn from Jehovah to worship Satan (Antichrist). Saint Malachy named this final Pope Peter Romano II, the Defector. So far, all of Malachy's prophecies have come to pass as he predicted they would.

Therefore, it is fitting, that the #112 Pope is Francis I and he is fulfilling the prophecy as the final pope. His parents were of Italian descent. He chose his name as Pope from an Italian, St. Francis of Assisi, who was a friar and a preacher that spent most of his time in Rome. St. Francis's real name was Pietro---Peter. The fisherman ring Pope Francis received at his installation mass in St. Peter's Basilica on March 19, 2013 had the image of St. Peter holding a fishnet and keys. Several rings had been shown him but he chose this one. The design was originally drawn up for Pope Paul VI but he wore a commissioned ring due to the Second Vatican Council. Pope Francis's ring is gold plated silver. He is a Jesuit, the first to ever become a Pope. Francis I wears black shoes instead of the traditional red ones. His signet ring also serves as his mark or signature. Since the days of the Apostle Peter, Pope Francis I is the official 266th Pope.

As mentioned earlier, the late Pope John Paul II stated his mission was to fulfill the remaining prophecy of the Third Secret of Fatima. He appointed 135 Cardinals, the most a Pope has ever appointed, and from which the present Pope was chosen. Peter Romano II, the Defector, was among those in line waiting. It was John Paul II who made, now, Pope Francis I a Cardinal on February 21, 2001.

Even Cardinal Ratzinger, before he was Pope Benedict XVI, released a version of the Third Secret of Fatima that many called a fake to take the heat off having to reveal the real secret. This release of disinformation by him proves the Vatican is hiding the truth sandwiched between lies. The five Popes before John Paul II would not release the secret because it was claimed by them to be too horrible. Yet the information released by, then Cardinal Ratzinger was not gruesome at all. He clearly did not reveal the whole truth concerning the Third Fatima Secret.

Older leaks regarding the Third Secret agree with Saint Malachy that the Antichrist will gain power over the Vatican through a Pope who will serve as his False Prophet. The Bible prophesies that the Antichrist will rise from a United Empire of Nations: Daniel 2:42–44; 7:7, 24; Revelation 12:3; 13:1; 17:12, 16) to unite the world under a World Religion (false church: Revelation 17:1–6; Revelation 13:3–8, 11–15), as revealed in these passages below:

United Empire: "And as the toes of the feet were part of iron, and part of clay, so the kingdom shall be partly strong, and partly broken. And whereas thou sawest iron mixed with miry clay, they shall mingle themselves with the seed of men: but they shall not cleave one to another, even as iron is not mixed with clay. And in the days of these kings shall the God of heaven set up a kingdom, which shall never be destroyed: and the kingdom shall not be left to other people, but it shall break in pieces and consume all these kingdoms, and it shall stand forever . . . And this what I saw in the night visions, and behold a fourth beast, dreadful and terrible and strong, exceedingly; and it had great iron teeth; it devoured and brake in pieces, and stamped the residue with the feet of it: and it was diverse from all the beasts that were before it; and it had ten horns . . . And the ten horns out of this kingdom are ten kings that shall arise: and another shall rise after them; and he shall be diverse from the first, and he shall subdue three kings . . . And there appeared another wonder in heaven; and behold a great red dragon, having seven heads and ten horns, and seven crowns upon his heads. And I stood upon the sand of the sea, and I saw a beast rise up out of the sea, having seven heads and ten horns, and upon his horns ten crowns, and upon his heads the name of blasphemy . . . And the ten horns which thou sawest are ten kings, which have received no kingdom as yet; but receive power as kings one hour with the beast . . . And the ten horns which thou sawest upon the beast, these shall hate the whore, and shall make her desolate and naked, and shall eat her flesh, and burn her with fire."

World Religion: "And there came one of the seven angels which had the seven vials, and talked with me, saying unto me, Come hither: I will shew unto thee the judgment of the great whore that sitteth upon many waters; With whom the kings of the earth have committed fornication, and the inhabitants of the earth have been made drunk with the wine of her fornication. So he carried me away in the spirit into the wilderness: and I saw a woman sit upon a scarlet coloured beast, full of names of blasphemy, having seven heads and ten horns. And the woman was arrayed in purple and scarlet colour, and decked with gold and precious stones and pearls, having a golden cup in her hand full of abominations and filthiness of her fornication: And upon her forehead was a name written, MYSTERY BABYLONTHE GREAT, THE MOTHER OF HARLOTS AND ABOMINATIONS OF THE EARTH. And I swathe woman drunken with the blood of the saints, and with the blood of the martyrs of Jesus: and when I saw her, I wondered with great admiration . . . And I saw one of his hands as it were wounded to death; and his deadly wound was healed: and all the world wondered after the beast, and they worshipped the dragon which gave power unto the beast: and they worshipped the beast, saying, Who is like unto the beast? Who is able to make war with him? And there was given unto him a mouth speaking great things and blasphemies; and power was given unto him to continue forty and two months. And he opened his mouth in blasphemy against God, to blaspheme his name, and his tabernacle, and them that dwell in heaven. And it was given unto him to make war with the saints, and to overcome them: and power was given him over all kindreds, and tongues, and nations. And all that dwell upon the earth shall worship him, whose names are not written in the book of life of the Lamb slain from the foundation of the world . . . And I beheld another beast coming up out of the earth; and he had two horns like a lamb, and he spake as a dragon. And he exerciseth all the power of the first beast before him, and causeth the earth and them which dwell therein to worship the first beast, whose deadly wound was healed. And he doeth great wonders, so that he maketh fire come down from heaven on the earth in the sight of men, And deceiveth them that dwell on the earth by the means of those miracles which he had power to do in the sight of the beast; saying to them that dwell on the earth, that they should make an image to the beast, which had the wound by a sword, and did live. And he had power to give life unto the image of the beast, that the image of the beast should both speak, and cause that as many as would not worship the image of the beast should be killed."

Pope John Paul II was the first to coordinate efforts toward uniting nations and religions to prepare the world for a coming New Order. The groundwork was carefully laid toward this agenda with his appointment of some very liberal and progressive Cardinals to the Vatican, who were located in pagan capitals of the world. Because of these appointments, over the course of the last several years, the world has witnessed some amazing changes in the teachings of the Catholic Church involving the tolerance of what once were condemned as very sinful actions. This change in Catholic doctrine that first appeared in the Permanent Instructions, written by Masons, appears to be laying the groundwork for the Antichrist, who is destined to rule the world with the approval of the Pope as his False Prophet.

Nothing could be more eye-opening to this clandestine agenda than the cover of the late John Paul's final book, which was released right before his death, entitled, Rise, Let Us Be On Our Way. The work is very Masonic in nature and more than likely is giving a coded message 'to those with eyes to see.' The photo on the cover reveals the Pope with only one open eye showing. It is depicting, no doubt, homage to pagan worship of the 'All-Seeing-Eye' (Great Architect of the Universe), venerated since time immortal by secret orders. His one eye showing could also be a double reference to what Hitler referred to as the 'Cyclops Eye,' the reptilian eye located in man's pineal gland that can receive transmissions from the master of deception, Satan, who is the Masonic 'Great Architect of the Universe' if the gland is stimulated.

On the cover, John Paul II is also holding his sepulcher of a broken cross with his left hand in a manner depicting the Hiram Abiff "lion's paw" hand grip. This grip is known to Masons as the 'raised from the dead' grip and is given to their fallen Master during Masonic rituals. Please note the word 'fallen' before Master—as in Fallen Angel. The arms of the crucified image of Jesus on the Pope's sepulcher form a perfect triangle pointing down, while his legs form a triangle pointing up. This is known as the Hermetic Principle: 'As Above, So Below.'

A few of the hidden words retrieved from the title of his book include 'lion,' 'paw,' 'eye,' 'so below,' etc. Even in his death, Pope John Paul is speaking through this book cover from his grave to initiates around the world. Through intelligently coded messages, he is telling them to rise up because the time is come to make the world conform to their way. This same evil agenda was continued and escalated to greater magnification under John Paul II's right hand man, Cardinal Ratzinger—who became Pope Benedict XVI.

Cardinal Joseph Ratzinger served as 'Perfect of the Congregation' for the Doctrine of the Faith under Pope John Paul II. This Roman Catholic Church's leading doctrinal hard-liner was quickly voted in to succeed John Paul. Ratzinger was born in Nazi, Germany, to his parents, oddly named Mary and Joseph. He was the first German to serve as a Pope since Victor II's reign from 1055–57. Of greater interest is the fact that Ratzinger served as a Nazi soldier and was captured. He spent seven years in an American Prison Camp. "Nazi Ratzi" declares he was forced into joining Hitler's army.

Ratzinger, who chose the name of Pope Benedict XVI, stood on the balcony of St. Peter's Basilica and blessed the crowd as their new Pope on April 20, 2005. In a photo of this event, made available to the Associated Press by the L'Osservatore Romano Vatican newspaper, Ratzinger displays more of an evil grin than a smile on his face. His hands are not in the correct Roman Catholic gesture of blessing; instead, he has his thumbs and forefingers positioned such that they form an up and down triangle—the Hermetic Principle: 'As Above, So Below.' Equally fitting to his hand display of the hidden principle of the ancient Egyptians is that this photo captures, to Ratzinger's right, a real Egyptian obelisk, located in the center of Vatican square. It is standing stately in the background as if he is paying homage to it. This was no quick photo but a cleverly planned one, distributed so that 'those with eyes to see' know he is another servant to the Brotherhood.

During Ratzinger's address to all those who came for this first blessing from the balcony of St. Peter's Basilica, he called himself "a simple, humble worker in the vineyard of the Lord." This seems quite strange that a man with such a fierce and forward style would use these words to describe himself. It almost appeared like he was trying to deceptively hide his true persona behind such innocent words—like a wolf in sheep's clothing. Then it all falls into place when you look 'with eyes to see' and discover the true meaning that I had sensed from the beginning. The word simple equals (6) letters, as does humble (6) and worker (6). In other words, to the people watching his address or reading the Associated Press Release, Pope Benedict XVI was declaring to the world that he is 'A' (6)(6)(6). Notice he says he is 'A' simple, humble, worker and does not use the word 'The' before the three words of six letters; meaning he is not 'The Antichrist' (The 666). In other words, Ratzinger is a promoter of the coming Antichrist.

The words 'A SIMPLE, HUMBLE WORKER' appeared boldly over the Press Photo of the Pope's introduction to the world. That is right; there he was with his hands forming the esoteric symbol of 'As Above, So Below' and an Egyptian obelisk over his right shoulder, with the words above his photo clearly implying that he is 'a' 666. Just how blind can the public really be? From his past aggressiveness as Cardinal to drafting and changing Council documents during Vatican II, where he proclaimed that a non-Catholic need not convert to the true Church either for salvation or for unity, 'A' '666' (Antichrist ideology) fits him a whole lot better than just "a simple humble worker in the vineyard of the Lord."

On the cover of Newsweek, May 2, 2005, which proclaims "Benedict XVI What He Means for American Catholics," Benedict XVI is shown raising his arms and hands to the sky with thumbs open and his other fingers together forming a perfect 'V' shape (Virgin). This V-shaped hand signal to the world is the Masonic and Rosicrucian sign of Admiration and Astonishment. Texe Marrs, a leading researcher unmasking 'Double Speak' and the symbolic language of Secret Societies, writes in his book, Codex Magica, pg. 181, that

"The sign of Admiration, or Astonishment, is practiced in the sixth degree of Royal Arch Masonry—the Most Excellent Master ritual. During this same ritual, the participants bow their heads low toward the floor exactly six times, balance six times, and then balance six more times. Thus, 6+6+6, or 666. And this happens in the ritual for the 6th degree (Duncan's Masonic Ritual and Monitor, p. 212–213). It is taught that the sign of Astonishment or Admiration is given in remembrance of the emotion felt by Masons in the days of King Solomon at the moment they viewed the inner sanctuary of the newly completed Temple of God in Jerusalem."

Remember that the masons in Solomon's Temple were pagans, as the Israelites were used as mere slave laborers because they were not skilled in masonry. Therefore, if Benedict is comparing himself to these masons with his hand gestures, then he is a brother to all Masonic Orders around the world. What a powerful message in simple hand gestures that Pope Benedict XVI (with the cooperation of Newsweek) was delivering 'to those with eyes to see' worldwide. We have already noted that he claims to be a Simple (6) Humble (6) Worker (6) in the Lord's vineyard, just like the pagans skilled in masonry were in the inner sanctuary of Solomon's Temple before it was eventually destroyed.

With all this said and done so openly, it was very interesting to watch how Ratzinger fulfilled his role as Pope. There is no doubt he was put in place to prepare the way for the final Pope (Peter the Roman/ Pope Francis I); as well as, the enthronement of 'The Antichrist' as Messiah. His quick election as the newest Pontiff was due in part to his unusual interpretations of Catholic doctrines, events such as miracles and apparitions. For example, Ratzinger openly discredited Sister Lucia, one of the three children who witnessed the Fatima Secrets, as being nothing more than a seer. He reasoned that her vision incorporated images that she might have seen in her devotional books. In other words, he beguiled the world by claiming all three of the prophecies at Fatima had been fulfilled; therefore, no need for further discussion.

Ratzinger fraudulently misrepresented the Fatima messages and also concealed them deceitfully in a vain attempt to destroy them from the Church's traditionally held beliefs. His acts as Cardinal at the time were so blatant that following a press conference in regard to the subject held on June 26, 2000, the Los Angeles Times sub-headlined the following in an effort to buffer his attack:

"The Vatican's Top Theologian Gently Debunks a Nun's Account of Her 1917 Vision that Fueled Decades of Speculation."

Sister Lucia, who passed away in 2005, died with the Third Secret of Fatima still not revealed. She had been promised by the Vatican's officials that the final secret would be released years ago, but to no avail. Upon her death, her room was locked and her writings, as well as her diary, were confiscated. Friends of Lucia speculated that she may have still been having visitations and was recording what she was being told. Vatican insiders would never have allowed the wrong people to get their hands on something of that nature if, indeed, she was still receiving information from someone she thought was the Virgin Mary.

Imagine attacking a nun's creditability after so many years. But Sister Lucia was not the only person to ever be viciously attacked by Cardinal Ratzinger. Father Nicholas Gruner probably is the most abused. He openly resisted the new orientation of Ratzinger, which sought to de-emphasize the Fatima Message. Gruner's failure to follow this new protocol resulted in the Vatican sending excommunication papers to him in an effort to silence him.

According to The Pope Versus The Professor by Kenneth Westhues, Professor Herbert Richardson and Father John Kelly encountered the wrath of Ratzinger, too. In the 'Introduction' to Westhues book, Richardson states that it was Ratzinger who initiated his dismissal from the

University of St. Michael's College after being a professor there for 16 years. On top of that, Ratzinger also fired College President Father John Kelly, who Richardson reports died suddenly only a few weeks later. Richardson claims that his own dismissal involved being harassed and mobbed for not submitting to the authority of the Roman Catholic Church because he was a Protestant theologian. Due to his unprofessional treatment, Richardson expressed great concern over Ratzinger becoming Pope. These are the haunting words he wrote on April 19, 2005:

" . . . if you begin to wonder how 115 Cardinals could have been guided by the Spirit to elect a man widely known to be an "Eliminator" as the Infallible Vicar of Jesus Christ on earth, then you will be asking yourself one of the most disturbing theological questions that could ever be posed."
Vatican controllers want their agenda to remain hidden and will do all that is necessary to ensure their diabolical plan goes off without a hitch. These men are in submission to a well-prepared timetable with a date demanding that the World undergo the necessary diabolical paradigm shift in order to bring the Antichrist to power. They are carefully eliminating any opposition.

This means they know time is drawing near by watching for signs in the Heavens that will herald the 'End of the Age.' According to Biblical Scripture these signs will be seen in the sun, moon, and stars.

" . . . and the sun became black as sackcloth of hair, and the moon became as blood; And the stars of heaven fell unto the earth as a fig tree casteth her untimely figs . . ." (Revelation 6:12–13).

"And the third angel sounded, and there fell a great star from heaven, burning as it were a lamp, and it fell upon the third part of the rivers, and upon the fountains of waters; And the name of the star is called Wormwood." (Revelation 8:10–11).

It should not surprise readers to learn here that the Vatican has one of the largest Space Observatories in the world on its premise; one can only speculate their enormous activity in watching the skies. We already know they have a sacred and hermetic interest in anything that appears abnormal or unique regarding the alignments of planets with Oracle sites on earth. A papyrus stored at the Vatican even tells about a UFO that was witnessed in Egypt around 1500, B.C., when Tuthmosis III was pharaoh. The Vatican hierarchy, interestingly enough, stays very up to date on all UFO activities occurring around the world.

Peter Levenda, Nazi researcher and author, in an interview held live on the air October 13, 2005, by George Noory, host of Coast to Coast AM Radio, which is heard around the globe, stated that the Vatican had recently built another observatory. Their new one, according to the report, is located near the University of Arizona, near Tempe, here in the United States. Levenda explained that Vatican officials had to have it built to a very specific location and broke all EPA Regulations in doing so. No one stopped them, and all the EPA (Environmental Protection Agency) issues were brushed aside. He went on to state that his sources had indicated that the Vatican was watching something very closely in the heavens and had to have their observatory where the object could be tracked daily. The informant went on to say that these Vatican officials had given a name to the object they were so intently tracking, called

Wormwood. The Observatory on Mt. Graham is manned by Jesuit Astronomers. In 2010, next to the Observatory, a new infrared telescope attachment to the large binocular telescope, already there, was named 'L.U.C.I.F.E.R.' and was designed by Germans to supposedly see how stars are born.

The Vatican in Rome is built on a sacred Megalithic site that was marked in ancient times by a Standing Dragon Stone. The dome at the Vatican is situated over an ancient Oracle site of the Sun. Under the dome is the proclaimed tomb of St. Peter. The tomb lies beneath the Basilica at the Vatican. The position of this tomb is identical to the tomb and crypt that lies under the Capitol Building in Washington, D.C. Next to the dome of the Vatican, in St. Peter's Square, is an Egyptian obelisk called Cleopatra's Needle. Obelisks, according to legend, are said to affect the energy fields of the earth by harnessing solar energy. At the Vatican, these esoteric monuments are surrounded by a circle like that of a sun dial, reminiscent of Stonehenge.

St. Peter's Square makes up the very heart of the Vatican. The square is a sacred geometrical design revered by Freemasonry, which originated from the Hidden Mysteries. 'Being on the Square' means total commitment to this evil ideology. The term Vatican comes from the Latin Word 'vates,' which means Prophet. For those in the Vatican willing to open their pineal glands to Satan, their location, which sits on top of an Oracle site, is secretly positioned on the earth to allow an easy connection. This sacred site has the potential to alter consciousness and allow all those who want hidden knowledge an antenna (a 'Third Eye') in their pineal gland to receive Satan's transmission.

The late Malachi Martin, whose work was quoted earlier, was also a Jesuit priest, exorcist, and a close associate of Pope John XXIII. He verified that contact had been made with Satan at the Vatican in his historical account regarding the Roman Catholic Church. His specific comments were that,

"The Enthronement of the fallen angel Lucifer was effected within the Roman Catholic Citadel on June 29, 1963."

To verify that Satan had gained a strong hold in the Vatican, Pope Paul VI, in his Papal address of June 30, 1972, commented on this very same occurrence when he, also, said that,

"Through some crack the smoke of Satan has entered into the Church of God."

With transmission lines having already been open to Satan for a while now, all that remains for the Vatican to do, in the near future, is become the False Prophet of the New World Religion and welcome their Chimera Prince as Messiah.

The last and final Pope, Peter Romano II (Petrus Romanus), Pope Francis I, is secretly awaiting his destiny as the Defector. Satan and his wicked seed are preparing him daily on how he will announce to the world that mankind's long-awaited Savior has finally arrived. Ratzinger, who became Pope Benedict XVI, at 78 years of age, was a prime candidate to replace John Paul. Insiders knew the time was short before the coming of the Antichrist, or they would have elected a younger man for the papacy. This strategic move in pope selection is exactly what Vatican officials thought as the following was recorded in the Vatican City Associated Press release of 4/20/05 entitled, New pope selected:

" . . . Ratzinger turned 78 on Saturday. His age clearly was a factor among cardinals who favored a "transitional" pope who could skillfully lead the church as it absorbs John Paul II's legacy, rather than a younger cardinal who could wind up with another long pontificate . . ."

The decision to elect an older Pope on the premises that he would die was a very strange attribute to consider. Since he did not die, as planned, he resigned his role as Pope in order to place Peter the Roman, Pope Francis I, in power to fulfill the role as False Prophet at the predestinated time. So, the election process of the Vatican's Cardinals and their total out-of-character decision in making such an unusual move, concerning their appointment of Pope Benedict which was, then, followed by his resignation only a few years later, does give great creditability to St. Malachy's Prophecy of the Popes. These prophecies can be downloaded at www.catholic-pages.com, with a complete printout of each Pope and how they have all come to pass just as he predicted. His vision concerning the Final Pope of the Roman Catholic Church is haunting about him being a Defector and False Prophet along with what the 3rd Secret of Fatima is said to have predicted,

"In extreme persecution, the seat of the Holy Roman Church will be occupied by Peter the Roman, who will feed the sheep through many tribulations, at the term of which the city of seven hills will be destroyed, and the formidable Judge will judge his people. The End."

No Pope has ever taken the Title of Peter due to holy reverence of the Apostle Peter. So, it is interesting that on Wednesday March 13, 2013 at 16:43 EDT that Jorge Mario Bergoglio, age 76, took office as Pope Francis I. He was born in Buenos Aires, Argentina to Italian parents and worked as a chemical technologist and night club bouncer before attending seminary. As Pope, he acts concerned about the poor but he is much more focused and totally committed to liberal interfaith relations and unification of the masses into a one world order. This makes sense as to why Bergoglio chose the title of Pope Francis I because it came from St. Francis of Assisi whose real name was Pietro (Peter). Pope Francis also chose to receive his papal fisherman signet ring embossed with the Apostle Peter holding a net and keys. So, his signet ring is signing and sealing all his papers with his hidden signature really as 'Peter'.

On the Feast of the Holy Rosary, the Vatican was hit by lightning and it was hit by lightning again on October 7, 2016. In 2017, Pope Francis continued to replace conservative Cardinals with liberal Jesuit Cardinals. On July 3, 2017 he replaced Muller as 'Perfect of the Congregation for the Doctrine of the Faith' (CDF) with a Spanish Jesuit, Luis Ladaria Ferrer. Francis I, also, declared the Shroud of Turin to be authentic and he released new evidence supporting his claim that dated the Shroud at the time of Christ. This announcement came on Easter in 2013 immediately following his election as Pope on March 13, 2013.

Then, if that was not enough, Pope Francis displayed Saint Peter's bones for the very first time in history during Mass at St. Peter's Square on Sunday, November 24, 2013. The 9 pieces of bone were housed in a jeweled box inside a bronze display case at the side of the altar while Pope Francis I gave Mass. These bones had never been seen publically. Francis prayed before the fragments at the start and then held the box in his arms a long time after his homily. This first time event displaying St. Peter's bones was very interesting, because a book written, in 2012, by Bruno Bartoloni, a Vatican correspondent, entitled The Ears of the Vatican had previously stated:

"No pope was ever permitted an exhaustive study of these bones to prove they belonged to the Apostle Peter because a 1000 year old curse, attested by secret and apocalyptic documents, threatened anyone who disturbed the peace of St. Peter's tomb with the worst possible misfortune."

It is so obvious that Pope Francis I is secretly 'Peter the Roman' and that he is fulfilling St. Malachy's prophecy right before our very eyes as the final pope and False Prophet.

Chapter Twenty-Five
Tesla Technology

Nikola Tesla was a genius who, through his engineering capabilities, invented alternating current as a power source that harnessed electricity for the world. He invented the system between the years 1886 and 1888. Tesla was somewhat of an alchemist who dabbled in the occult. He was aware, like the Megalithic Builders, that the Earth possessed currents that had the ability to stimulate the human brain. Tesla felt that this neo-physical impact upon the brain could be harnessed and used upon the unsuspecting masses as a control tactic.

Earth currents are where ancient Oracle sites and, later, Gothic Cathedrals were built so that their energy could stimulate the pineal gland into submission by an unseen power who offered answers to anyone seeking advice. The chief feature of an ancient Oracle site was that the replies to questions of an inquirer were delivered by a man or woman who had been put in a trance over the Oracle site and who was receiving information from their subconscious mind. This person posing as the medium would speak answers to the inquirer's questions with a changed voice and different personality than what was typical of their natural self. Their body became some type of paranormal speaker that was able to transmit and receive data. The ancient Greeks believed it was Apollo, messenger of the Gods, also known as Hermes, who was speaking through these mediums.

Instead of a messenger, it was Satan who was speaking through the willing person being used as his transmitter. When the medium returned to normal consciousness, they did not recollect what had been said. Therefore, independent stimulation of the pineal gland can be achieved by anyone meditating over an ancient Oracle site. These ancient sites are well-hidden under Gothic Cathedrals. It is through the energy of the earth currents running below these Oracle sites that a willing subject can invoke paranormal contact and receive satanic transmissions.

Throughout his life, Tesla conducted many experiments and made new discoveries. He proved that radio waves bounce off the Earth's ionosphere.

This transmission of waves could light up the entire night sky. In 1940, Tesla invented what he called the 'death ray.' He was essentially harnessing free energy and was capable of sending it wherever he aimed it. This invention laid the foundation to today's particle beam theories. It also gave rise to many German inventions under the auspices of Hitler.

There has been speculation that Hitler's greatest minds were building rockets and space ships using Tesla's technology. Following World War II, the United States and their ally, the Russians, split the German Scientists up and gave them refuge in exchange for their technology. These Germans went on to build NASA's Space Program and the Russian Cosmonaut Program. The technology that these German Scientists undoubtedly possessed was much more advanced in the science of electromagnetic energy than anything the United States and Russia had ever known. Without German intervention, the United States and Russian Space Programs would have emerged much later, or not at all, if Germany had won the war.

The United States and Russian interest in Germany's scientists was secretly protected from the public at large. Not one of these scientists was ever punished for their crimes against what I believe were certain Hebraic lineages only, in which they performed all types of horrendous experiments. They were working diligently with Hitler to genetically produce the perfect race using blood samples taken from selected Israelite lineages.

Today, that same agenda is being carried out in laboratories all over the world in search of immortality. Secretly hidden under the cloak of human bioengineering, they are re-designing humans into perfection through acts of cellular fission called Cloning. Hitler had envisioned the genetic processes needed to produce an indestructible warrior. Bio-tech laboratories are working toward improving on Hitler's idea of a human without a death gene.

Tesla was not secretive about his advancements in science and would often give demonstrations of his innovations to the elite Brotherhood. He produced wireless power that he called 'Balls of Lightning.' These 'Balls of Lightening' tend to occur naturally as part of nature all over the world. They are also associated with the UFO controversy. This free form of natural energy, discovered by Tesla, was immediately blackballed by the powers-that-be. They forced his discovery underground, because no one could make money off of energy that occurred freely in nature. These elite men were all members of the Masonic Order. They wanted to get rich off of new inventions and not give anything to the public that was free. Because of their selfishness, they were instrumental in breaking Tesla, both publicly and financially. He died a poor man.

What Tesla was undoubtedly unaware of was that these same elite men took his technology underground and began using it for their clandestine projects. With free energy sources in the palm of their hands, these men, whose plan was to control the world, could go about their secret business without governmental or public awareness. The elite Brotherhood knew Tesla's technology possessed the capability their Order needed to exercise power over the masses. Tesla had already proven to them the energy's capacity to be used as a mind control tactic. He had shown these men that the powers of electricity directly affected the electromagnetic fields and, in turn, produced altered states of consciousness within humans.

Tesla pointed out to the Brotherhood that the earth resonates. It has the same musical pitch as that found within the Pyramids and the Gothic Cathedrals. Tesla had in his possession the knowledge of sacred geometry, which he used to expand the capabilities of his own inventions. Resonance, he proved, could be used to cause interference in the weather patterns, changes in the health of humans, and induce unsuspected altered states of consciousness. Tesla's knowledge was so powerful that the world's 'Puppet Masters' had to do whatever it took to secure it for their sole use. They publicly destroyed Tesla so that no one would take his work seriously.

Today, we are witnessing of the resurgence of Tesla technology in what is being called non-lethal weaponry. Radio frequency beams can be aimed at an unsuspecting public without their knowledge. These Extremely Low

Frequency waves (ELF) vibrate the neurons in the brain. They produce an effect on an unsuspecting person, who does not realize their biological reactions such as fear, panic, heart racing, sweating, etc., came from a source outside their body. This technology has the capability to take over the brain's ability to instruct the body to perform biological functions against the person's will. Humanity cannot fight back, as the body does exactly what the brain tells it to do. If one is beamed information into their brain that it is cold, then the body will shiver even though it is 100 degrees outside. Humans have no way to block these biological hackers from tapping into their main computer, the brain. It is the perfect weapon in the arsenal of psychological warfare, where the enemy never has to fire a shot to totally secure or annihilate their victim.

Tesla's invention of the 'death ray' harnessed similar technology to that which is now found in X-rays, lasers, and particle beam technology. Through transmitters strategically placed around the world, Tesla's energy will be used in the near future to manipulate and control mankind. The Top Secret Star Wars Project is proof that Tesla's inventions are being mainstreamed into daily life. In fact, the public has never been fully briefed as to where this Star Wars technology originated.

The money hungry Brotherhood would never want the people of the world to know their secrets. They definitely wanted to keep Tesla's discovery of free energy hidden. If they had not, then every home would be maintained without any cost of electricity. It would have widely gained public approval, as Tesla's energy did not pollute the atmosphere, thereby giving people a better world to live in. Unfortunately, those that believe they are so illuminated want his technology for their purposes. It will be a while before they divulge all of Tesla's discoveries, as that would mess up their financial status and stronghold on an unsuspecting public. These powerful men will instead gradually release bits and pieces into the mainstream such that no one will question where the process originated.

Tesla technology is presently being utilized to control the weather through a military-funded project called HAARP (High-frequency Active Auroral Research Project). This project possesses the power to change weather patterns anywhere in the world. It can also halt all communications around the globe. HAARP has the potential to be used as a massive tool toward psychological warfare, as it can affect the brain of all living things from a great distance. It holds the power of particle beam technology and can essentially 'death ray' anything it targets. This force of energy, derived from Tesla's technology, is unlimited and cannot be matched by anything else on the planet. It is but one of the secret weapons that will be used in the near future to control the world.

Tesla discovered that energy waves can be charged to produce gravity waves. These waves have the potential to be harnessed and used to power aircraft. This may very well be the answer to the question as to what kind of energy is being used in the propulsion systems of UFOs. Being able to produce gravity and anti-gravity actively involves manipulating and controlling the Laws of Mother Nature. This Sacred Science of harnessing the key to nature's forces is the premise behind the 'Unified Field Theory' proposed by Albert Einstein. Possession of it would mean god-like power.

Black budgets are used to fund a variety of secret projects. The purposes of these clandestine game plans are well-hidden, far from the public's view. Funding strategies are so secretive that very few members of Congress even know where or how the money they have allocated from the taxpayers' dollars is actually being spent. What this so-called democratic process amounts to is that a secret group is using your taxes in a planned and coordinated effort to eventually control you.

Everything from the CIA, to private laboratories, and intelligence organizations around the world are owned by this wealthy Illuminati Brotherhood. Employees working within these black budget organizations are operating in what is called a "Black World." They have certain classifications and cannot discuss their work even with their co-workers unless they are working within the same classification. Not adhering to these strict employment guidelines results in immediate termination, or depending on one's level of clearance, death. The Illuminati mean business when it comes to maintaining secrecy.

Tesla technology has further been used in developing high tech surveillance systems. Eavesdropping can now easily be accomplished with great accuracy on all technology including telephones, cellular phones, computers, and Internet, radio, and fax machines. Increased surveillance became part of the Homeland Security Act following 9–11, as a program to control not only terrorists, but the American public. It will soon be used as a secret bullet in a bloodless war involving a form of surveillance to monitor your every move. 'Big Brother' will be watching you.

The power to control and manipulate Tesla's powerful microwaves will allow the Order to disable, confuse, and even kill a person. The hidden use of these waves of energy makes it appear that the person died of natural causes. Microwaves are a cost effective weapon, and one of the most dangerous ever developed due to their profound effect upon the brain. The human brain functions in 4 wave frequencies: beta, alpha, theta, and delta. Beta waves (13–35 Hertz) occur in normal outward thinking and are where agitated states can originate. Alpha waves (8–12 Hertz) indicate the body is in a relaxed state. Theta waves (4–7 Hertz) are involved in controlling internal functions within the body. Delta waves (3–5 Hertz) occur during deep sleep. If any of these brain waves are manipulated by a wave from an outside source, the person will experience sleepiness in low wave states and agitation if hit with higher frequency waves. Microwaves produce a host of chemical releases within the brain. These chemical releases generate feelings of fear, anxiety, depression, and weakness.

Extremely Low Frequency (ELF) waves, between 1–10 Hertz, cause loss of consciousness. These electromagnetic fields have a direct affect on heart rhythm, blood pressure, and the body's metabolism. They can also produce visual hallucinations, hearing problems, seizures, and the formation of tumors. A constant low frequency wave of 3–5 Hertz can kill a human. Enhancement of what appears to be ominous phenomena can be increased to make something unreal seem real to the person who is being subjected to these waves. When a person's right to think and choose is violated and controlled from an outside source, it is the most evil thing that can be done to that person.

Free will is what God gave humans but it allowed Adam and Eve to eat from Satan's Tree of Knowledge because they were not robots, they had a choice. God warned them not to eat but they still had free will to make their own decisions. We, all, have an ability to choose between good and evil. Removing free will and the ability to have control over our bodies through psychological warfare is a tool the Antichrist is planning on using in order to make all people politically correct and accept him when he comes to power. Mankind, without internal control of one's biological processes, will become nothing but programmed robots. This future event is a major reason one should desire to become a Christian, so they can be caught up in the air as part of the Rapture and not left behind to endure such torment.

Wireless transmission of electrical power was a grand accomplishment of Tesla. This type of free energy, as we have already discovered, would financially ruin companies that today charge mega dollars for electricity. Tesla's technology, no doubt, has given a powerful free source of energy to the Illuminati to fulfill Satan's Plan. These elite men are making good use of this hidden energy by devising ways never imagined to control mankind in the near future. The Antichrist will also garner its seemingly miraculous powers over the Laws of Nature to mesmerize humanity into total submission.

Within circular formations known as the phenomena of Crop Circles, there is a proposed theory that a type of Tesla's technology may be what is being used to form the circles. According to Dr. Paul LaViolette, president of the Starburst Foundation Research Institute, this technology could be the process by which Crop Circles are made. He states,

"We might theorize that in producing its propulsion beam, a UFO spacecraft is projecting downward an intense column of Tesla-type microwave radiation; that is, shock-type microwave emissions that have the ability to exert forces on the material they intercept. As Tesla observed, shock emissions tend to collimate themselves into a beam."11

It appears that this micro-beam technology, which Tesla discovered back in the 1800's, may well be the energy that is used by UFOs to propel themselves upward, as well as create Crop Circles. These micro-beams have different frequencies, which produce harmonics in a sonic and ultra sonic range. In other words, the beams are actually singing to us through a sacred form of musical geometry. This is the same form of Sacred Harmonic Geometry that was used by the Megalithic Builders in ancient times. Micro-beams using laser technology are capable, today, of producing holographic images, as well as broadcasting Extremely Low Frequency (ELF) waves that can directly affect the human brain. This advanced technology will eventually be used to make the masses believe God is speaking to them, as they will see an image and hear a voice. Biologically, the unexplained phenomena will terrify them into becoming submissive to the Antichrist. It will destroy free will.

Dr. Steven M. Greer led a project to allow the military and others to testify to the evidence of UFOs. He claims that many people know that present technological discoveries involving the generation of energy and propulsion have resulted from the study of UFOs through an investigative process called backward engineering. Greer also believes there is a connection between this new energy source and the innovations of Tesla.

The similarity that exists between the two involve the fact that the new energy uses a secret form of physics that does not require the burning of fossil fuels or ionizing of radiation to generate power. In Greer's opinion, he believes if the men possessing this secret knowledge would come clean by allowing the declassifying of this new energy source, they would have the power to create a civilization of mankind who would not have a want. Poverty would be a thing of the past and, most importantly, there would be no environmental damage from its usage. The high cost of electricity and gas, as well as the wars fought around the world to control those items, would be history. This new energy source has the potential to bring about world peace, but it would break the oil and electrical companies in the process. What a pity.

The world's financial leaders and Puppet Masters prefer to make millions of dollars off the unsuspecting and ignorant public. They believe their plan for society keeps us in line as we need them for our livelihoods. These elite men fully enjoy their global power. We, the working class, are forced to buy their products, thereby supplying them the financial means to play games against their enemies. We are their puppets.

Think of how many people are forced into war, while those belonging to the elite orders of Secret Societies somehow bypass this threat of death. If the world were to have nuclear war, those same elite men, who control the power to push the button, have their ready-made bunkers for survival already built, while the rest of us would perish. Yet it is the common man's high taxes and every penny made that are spent on payments for gas, oil, electricity, etc., that have paid for these bunkers to be set up for only a select few to escape such a disaster. What is even sadder is that this clandestine group, with a secure place to hide, is the real cause of most disasters in the first place.

Take a moment to just imagine free electricity and free travel without gas pumps. Imagine clean air without pollution, which is responsible for causing so many diseases. Today, there are millions of cases of cancer that are annually caused by air pollution. And just think, the Illuminated Ones do not even blink an eye that their neighbors are suffering. Very simply put, these elite men serve mammon (money and self) and not God. It makes no difference to them if common man lives or dies. Their goal for humanity is just to control us, work us to death, take our hard-earned money, deceive us, and make us so unhappy that we will give up our souls in all the agony.

The secret Order of the Illuminati wants to keep mankind so busy that we will not have the time to see what they are up to or have the money and/or power to do anything about it. Because of Satan's Plan, this elite Brotherhood will continue using secret technology to increase their control over mankind instead of using it to help us, all the while deceiving mankind into believing that what they are doing is in the world's best interest.

For example, Skull and Bones member Laurance Rockefeller funded a study on Crop Circles. The study concluded that Crop Circles are the effects of a newly, yet to be discovered, energy source from a type of laser technology that is being beamed down. This energy source may be new to the so-called ignorant, but not to the Puppet Masters. So what was Laurance up to by funding this project? The Rockefeller Empire has been around for a long time. I am sure Laurance knew that John David Rockefeller and J.P. Morgan were big buddies. He had to have been aware that it was J.P. Morgan, the world's financial power source, who personally broke Nikola Tesla and supposedly destroyed Tesla's technologies.

In 1907, J.P. Morgan, the huge banking mogul, caused a panic by spreading rumors about a competitor's bank failing. This false panic caused Congress to convene and establish the National Monetary Commission. In 1910, J.P. Morgan's hunting club on Jekyll Island, Georgia, became the location where J.P. Morgan and John D. Rockefeller's interest were formulated for America's Central Bank—The Federal Reserve. It appears that Morgan and Rockefeller were great at the satanic 'Craft' of deception. Their money was used to contribute to Thomas Edison's light bulb technology, where an enormous amount of money could be made off the general public by them selling electricity instead of giving it away freely through Tesla's technology.

It is interesting that an heir of the Rockefeller Empire now wants to identify the energy that may be producing Crop Circles. Maybe Laurance has been given the responsibility, by the elite, of letting the ignorant public in on the sudden discovery of a new energy source; one they want us to think has just been discovered. This is just a small sample of how their evil scheme works. Tell the public as little as you have to. Keep them satisfied so they will not ask too many questions. Make them think the powers-that-be are also just now learning of the discovery of this new form of energy. This is a simple tactic used by the Illuminati. When mankind starts to ask too many questions about technology, feed them deception with a little truth to pacify them.

Questions remain as to how Tesla's technologies have been and are presently being used. There can be no doubt that the Star Wars Project is a direct result of his technology. Along with this project, we have already discovered that his inventions have the ability to control the world's population from space through world radar, the ability to cause earthquakes, manipulate brain waves, produce laser beam energy/weapons, create ELF microwaves, and change weather patterns.

There is some speculation that Tesla's technology is being propagated to produce and control the paths of devastating hurricanes; the first being Katrina (August 2005), which totally destroyed New Orleans, Louisiana, and Gulf Port and Biloxi, Mississippi. The manipulation of this same energy source has the power to destroy all communication networks of any city from space.

J.P. Morgan's cover-up and takeover of Tesla's technological feats were to the advantage of him and his Puppet Master buddies. If they had not intervened, Tesla would have dominated the world instead of them. Tesla was a direct threat to their control agenda and he had to be stopped.

Reviewing the Crop Circle study funded by Laurance Rockefeller, it apparently has come time for the Brotherhood to release their new energy source through tidbits of information. They can afford to do this now, because the wicked seeds of Satan have completed the building of their arsenal using this technology to completely control mankind. If they were not in the driver's seat, nothing would have been forthcoming about the discovery of these new energy systems. For the rest of mankind riding in the back of the truck that these elite men are driving, start praying and hold on. A tribulation beyond measure is about to begin because the gas is about to run out.

Chapter Twenty-Six
Nanotechnology

Nanotechnology is the revolutionary new wave of the future. Nanorobotics is a vital part of this new science. It involves miniaturized robots, which are smaller than bacteria and are powered by nanotransistors to go where no other technology has ever gone before. These robots can be inserted into your body through an injection or simply by swallowing them. They are controlled by computers.

The robots can also receive signals through transmitters and antennas, some of which are being secretly set up around the world. Unfortunately, in the wrong hands, these tiny robots are capable of being programmed to attack you internally if you are perceived, by the enemy, as a threat or just plain politically incorrect. Nanorobots have the capacity to be secretly injected into a person during a mandated vaccination program. These robots could be issued easily to people around the world if an outbreak of small pox or some other life-threatening disease were to occur. The unsuspecting public, rushing to receive immunization from the dreaded disease, would never know they have been internally invaded.

Nanotechnology, which can place robotic chips inside the body, works exactly like the Global Positioning Satellite (GPS) that is used to track cars, ships, and airplanes through built-in transmitters. Small implants are now available to humans for medical, military, and safety purposes. The Global Positioning Satellite is able to locate a person, with an implanted biochip, within one foot of their exact location. Nanotechnologies are presently being promoted for personal, as well as national, security. In early 2006, the United States Department of Agriculture (U.S.D.A.) announced a mandatory law stating that by 2009, all horses had to be chipped. These officials claimed the mandated chipping was for identification of animal to human diseases like Encephalitis and West Nile Virus so they could be contained quicker. In the future, nanorobotics will to be used for some very similar and sinister justifications against humanity.

Implants and nanorobots have the potential to control the world. Their unique capability eerily reminds one of the 'Mark of the Beast,' which is described in the Book of Revelation. Scripture there states,

"And he causeth all, both small and great, rich and poor, free and bond, to receive a mark in their right hand, or in their foreheads: And that no man might buy or sell, save he had the Mark, or the name of the beast, or the number of his name." (Revelation 13:16–17).

A person might willingly choose to get the implanted Identification Chip for medical purposes without the knowledge that, along with their chip, nanorobots were secretly injected as well. Security agencies plan to promote the ID implant for the safety of all newborn children to help assist them if the child is ever kidnapped or lost. There is already a governmental mandatory vaccination program in place for all children who attend school. If these vaccinations were secretly laced with nanorobots, the future of that entire generation could be successfully monitored.

As in all cases of new scientific discoveries, Nanotechnology will be promoted for all its good purposes and intentions. Promoters of nanorobotic technology claim it has the programming capability to target and search out cancer cells and eradicate them without destroying good cells within the body. Major government funding was set aside for immediate release to support Nanotechnology in January 2000 by then-President Bill Clinton. At that time, Nanotechnology was heralded as a new science that promised to revolutionize our present world.

Nanotransistors are being developed today, which are smaller than a single molecule. These tiny transmitters have the potential to be linked to antennas like the HAARP (High Frequency Active Auroral Research Project), located in Alaska. HAARP's production of Electromagnetic Low Frequency (ELF) waves could then be broadcast to these transmitters and used as psychological warfare against anyone injected with a nanorobot. We have already discovered in an earlier chapter that ELF waves can produce hysteria, hallucinations, agitation, increased pulse rates, tumors, and even drive a person insane. Masses of people could be targeted much more easily if they are also recipients of this technology. They would not only have their pineal glands receiving the ELF effects, but would also have robotic transmitters helping in this reception.

Holograms, which are 3-Dimensional pictures or illusions, can be generated in the sky using HAARP technology. Through the implant, a person's brain can be made to believe they are in danger when it is only an illusion. Nanotechnology offers many possible surveillance options that are readily accessible to the Brotherhood. The use of this new science has the potential to brainwash all those who will not open up their pineal glands to Satan. It is an advanced step in the wicked seeds' effort to rule the world.

The desire to control the world has been the ongoing goal of the elite within Secret Societies. One of their own, Dr. Jose Delgado, Professor at Yale University, where the famous Skull and Bones Order is located, said,

"We need a program of psychosurgery for political control of our society. The purpose is physical control of the mind. Everyone who deviates from the given norm can be surgically mutilated. The individual may think that the most important reality is his own existence, but this is only his personal point of view . . . Man does not have the right to develop his own mind . . . We must electronically control the brain. Someday armies and generals will be controlled by electronic stimulation of the brain."[12]

Dr. Delgado's scientific work began in the 1950's, when his mind control tactics were funded by the Naval Intelligence and the Air Force. He proved through his vast research that individuals are defenseless against direct electrical manipulation of the brain because it deprives the person of the most intimate mechanisms of biological reactivity. By using electrical stimuli, the subject is unable to stop the biological response in his body. A person cannot override what the brain fires for the body to respond to. The individual is therefore rendered completely helpless. This discovery led to the 1960's investigation into the strategy of directing microwave beams at targeted human beings from a distance. These studies found that microwave (ELF) beams created enormous anxiety and hyperactivity in those targeted, so much so, that it led to their complete physical exhaustion.

The plan to take over the mind of humans has been developed in stages. It has been going on for quite some time, and uniquely, it incorporates much of Tesla's technology. The intent of Satan's Plan is to take away a person's capability of recognizing the difference between good and evil, thereby hindering their biological ability to exhibit freedom of choice. It is an evil system designed to allow the politically correct and so-called illuminated men to make all decisions for you and your family with their free will, while robbing you of yours. This has been Satan's ancient agenda; to create a collective consciousness that will ensure evil progresses without defiance by Christians.

With the science of Nanotechnology in the wrong hands, dissenters will be faced with two choices after they have been implanted. That is, to either be surgically slaughtered internally by nanorobots for failing to follow the Antichrist, or simply just following the Antichrist out of fear of being internally slaughtered. Either way, one must follow the New World Order or their death will be immediately programmed and the robots will take action toward that end. Those around the person will think the individual died due to natural causes and will never suspect what is really going on. As nanorobots are perfected, they will have the capacity to attack the brain and damage areas where human emotions exist. This will produce an instant solution to the control of any rebel not willing to go along with the New World Order.

The positive aspects of what nanorobotics can offer humanity will continually be promoted without referencing the potential horrors of the technology. For example, the positive attributes include treating all kinds of medical conditions that now require invasive procedures.

Nanotechnology will offer a host of non-invasive options to the patient, such as swallowing pills that can photograph and send back real time images as it moves through the digestive tract of the body. Nanorobots will have the ability to surgically cut and take biopsies internally, while immediately evaluating the tissue. These procedures will be done with the person fully awake, with no need for anesthetics. Within moments to a few hours, many of the human body's complete internal systems will be able to be viewed and evaluated medically.

Vaccines are being developed that will incorporate the use of nanotechnology. These vaccinations, as we have already discussed, will be heralded as advantageous for mankind without ever mentioning their sinister possibilities. With bio-weapons being manufactured by terrorists that target certain races, the nanotech vaccine can be a successful, as well as sinister, antidote. In this case, the vaccine seeks out a genetic marker to rid those that carry certain genes that are being targeted by terrorists, thereby killing the person who has those genes. These bio-weapons are set up to target certain individuals and therefore will not set up a contagious disease process to spread uncontrollably to others. This form of nanodeath could be targeted at any genetic marker, such as those with certain diseases, particular races, blood types, etc. No one would be safe if they carried the targeted marker that was chosen to be eradicated.

In 1995, health workers started questioning why the tetanus vaccine was causing young women in the Philippines to abort and become sterile.

Someone who developed the tetanus shots had included a chemical called Human Chorionic Gonadotrophin (HCG). They did not warn all those poor unsuspecting women that they were really being targeted for creating an immune response to pregnancy rather than mere protection from tetanus. This situation could very easily happen today with all the panic surrounding the threat of biological terrorism and the rush to vaccinate large numbers of people in a short time. There have been speculations as to whether AIDS was intentionally developed to target underdeveloped countries and it got out of hand. A possible link to this scenario involves a polio vaccination program that occurred in Africa prior to the first AIDS outbreak being diagnosed.

With a Congressional subcommittee hearing in Washington, D.C., on September 28, 1994, which revealed that up to 500,000 Americans were endangered by secret defense-related tests between 1940 and 1974, our government's secret involvement in such atrocities is appalling. Their willing hand in exposing the mentally retarded to radioactive material hidden in their oatmeal, watching black men die in the Tuskegee Syphilis Experiment of venereal diseases, and other covert experiments involving mustard gas, LSD, and biological agents is truly reprehensive. The fact that each of these experiments were administered to unsuspecting persons by those so-called following orders 'to the glory of science' can only make one believe that similar covert operations are still continuing but exercising a lot more caution to avoid being caught. Their hope of not being discovered until much later means very little can be done about it.

Another example of government knowledge that was kept secret involves the use of Agent Orange during the Vietnam

War, which caused military men to produce impaired children and/or become sterile. Today, there is much speculation that the Gulf War syndrome resulted from a mixture of vaccinations hurriedly given to troops to avoid biological warfare. Apparently, all the different vaccinations these troops were given could not be assimilated in the body and actually attacked the immune system predisposing soldiers to a host of unresolved complications.

The CIA (Central Intelligence Agency) Project code named 'Operation Paperclip' involved the hiring of Nazi psychiatrists to the USA to further enhance their psychochemical brainwashing techniques. Psychedelic drugs such as LSD were developed to be utilized in mind control operations. A vital member of this Nazi group was Dr. Hubertus Strughold, who was known as the 'father of space medicine' and had direct connections with NASA.

Nazi scientific knowledge continues to show up in the strangest places. For example, the new drug sweetener Splenda, sweeping the country as a replacement for sugar, is touted not only as the Diabetic's best friend but is marketed also to those just wanting to lose weight. Unbeknownst to the public is that production of this sweetener involves a chlorine-type process where a molecular change can cause it to become unstable and poison the body. This same chlorination process used in the manufacture of Splenda was identical to the one used by Hitler to chemically kill captured Jews in his death camps. When unstable molecules are released, their chemical processes deteriorate, causing the kidney and liver to enlarge. This chemical mixture will even abort pregnancy in rabbits.

Splenda is manufactured by the makers of Tylenol as being safe. Yet Tylenol is not as safe as it seems because in larger doses, it also attacks the liver's ability to filtrate. Without adequate filtration from the liver, the body's toxins back up. This sewage backup has the potential to lead to immediate death and/or cancer. Keeping known carcinogens in the body for extended periods of time will ultimately break down the cell's defense DNA and cause cancer. It does not take a rocket scientist to figure that out, but no government agency is running to take these types of products off the shelves. Instead, they go after products with too much sugar to force the public to eat altered substances that the body cannot assimilate.

Bioengineering food substances for human consumption are a cause for alarm. Look at the labels on your foods, and you will soon discover the enormous amount of chemicals being used in them. Beware, modified food means a chemical change has been made to what you are about to consume. These foods have proteins from other organisms spliced into them, and who knows what else? Where is the Food and Drug Administration, one might ask? Going along with the Plan; that is right, they appear to just be blindly going along with the plan.

The World Health Organization (WHO), under the control of the United Nations, has been actively involved in vaccination programs around the world for a very long time. Bill Gates, of Microsoft fame, has given a lot of money recently to the Global Alliance for Vaccines and Immunizations. The renewed interest in vaccines by Bill Gates and others could only mean there will be a need for advanced computer software to successfully produce and tract the vaccinations of the future.

New strains of Avian Flu (H5N1) are cause for concern, due to it possibly producing a Bird Flu pandemic, so money is being poured into the hasty development of vaccines for the entire world's population. Scare the public to death, and they will submit to anything. The H5N1 virus is touted as being much more lethal than the Spanish Flu epidemic of 1918, which now is also believed to have been a bird flu that mutated to humans. Scientists worked for over 10 years reconstructing the Spanish Flu virus from lung tissue of two soldiers and an Alaskan woman who died in 1918 from that strain of bird flu. According to an article in The New York Times:

"The findings, published in the journals Nature and Science, show a small number of genetic changes that may explain why this virus was so lethal. It is significantly different from flu viruses that caused the pandemics of 1957 and 1968. Those viruses were not bird flu viruses but were human flu viruses that picked up a few genetic elements of bird flu."

Could the Illuminated Masters already have known that genetic crossovers were the cause of such diseases? Are they planning to develop high-tech vaccines that are purported to be in defense against such epidemics, when in fact these vaccinations are for the secret purpose of depopulation in order to further exercise power over the world? Remember, in the past it has been their protocol to plan a crisis, with their evil tactics already in place to seemingly handle the crisis so that they monetarily and powerfully gain benefit from their planned outcome.

For an example of how such an evil plan works: Genetically alter a virus, scare the public with some deaths, make them hand over large sums of money for vaccination development (even though you secretly already have the antidote), give the vaccinations to all people, either with an implanted nanotechnology tracking device or a tainted mixture to make them sick later, and you never had to fire a shot to indirectly take over humanity. In other words, at a given time, people get sick or you control their body from an outside source through their implants, which they did not know they had. The time of Great Tribulation is quickly drawing nigh.

"And when he had opened the fourth seal, I heard the voice of the fourth beast say, Come and see. And I looked, and behold a pale horse: and his name that sat on him was Death, and Hell followed with him. And power was given unto them over the fourth part of the earth, to kill with sword, and with hunger, and with death, and with the beasts of the earth." (Revelation 6:7–8).

The sinister plan for nanorobotic technology will be to police and control the human body. Swimming within the blood, a nanorobot can lodge itself in various organs. In the brain, these little robots can produce a variety of sensations. One of these sensations is secretly said to render a person unable to perceive what is real and what is falsely being conjured up in the brain. This modification in perception can be used to make soldiers fearless and march for a common cause. At this point, the human body becomes a computer-programmed shell that takes orders from a nanorobot in the brain. As we have already discussed, the human body does not have the biological capacity to fight back at itself. The body is the slave to the mind; therefore, he who controls the mind controls the body.

The intent of those behind the sinister side of nanotechnology is to eventually link all men together through their minds. In the 1981 book written by Brad and Francis Steiger entitled Gods of Aquarius, they propose connecting all of mankind to a super brain. They write,

"The only viable solution is to link the brains of all men into one giant super brain. It is the entire species which has been developing, and it is the entire species which now must be linked into one super being".13

What better way than to use nanotechnology to yoke all mankind together toward a unified purpose. Everyone would then be politically correct all of the time. With their pineal glands tuned into Satan's transmissions, everyone would become enlightened beings. The Masonic timetable to create, 'order out of chaos' would be successfully accomplished. The entire world at that point will fulfill Biblical prophecy as 'they will all marvel at the Beast.'

"And they worshipped the dragon which gave power unto the beast: and they worshipped the beast, saying, Who is like unto the beast? who is able to make war with him?" (Revelation 13:4).

The human brain has always been envisioned by the Secret Brotherhood as a machine that can be manipulated through outside intervention. These elite men know the power that can be used to completely control a person's every action. They understand there is no biological resistance to this form of psychological warfare. The unsuspecting public continues to believe they have free will when they are not aware outside sources are producing their thoughts and behaviors. This deceptive bliss of secret control over the masses is exactly what the Satanic Brotherhood has worked so diligently to attain. Back in 1953, Bertrand Russell, a member of the Illuminati, wrote The Impact of Science on Society, which purported the advantages of mind control. He said,

"It is to be expected that advances in psychology will give governments much more control over individual mentality than they now have . . . Education should aim at destroying free will, so that, after pupils have left school they shall be incapable, throughout the rest of their lives, of thinking or acting otherwise than as their school master would have wished."14

Global citizenship has always been the quest of Secret Societies. This quest involves unifying mankind to rebuild the Tower of Babel against our Creator. These societies promote this because of their hidden knowledge that predicts mankind can be perfected to become like God. With the implementation of the science of Nanotechnology, it appears that the long-awaited goal of the Brotherhood is nearing completion.

There is evidence that our bodies are presently undergoing a change without our knowledge. Dr. Brenda Fox, a holistic practitioner and former consultant to Fox TV Network, came across some interesting findings in her research regarding immunology. Fox found that the blood samples she had been collecting since 1980 showed humans are developing what she believed to be a third strand of DNA. She attributed her patients' complaints regarding aches and pains of unknown origins, hormone fluctuations, inability to concentrate leading to confusion, dizziness, feelings of light-headiness, and euphoria as being directly connected to this DNA change, occurring silently at the molecular level.

Just who and what could be affecting our bodies on a molecular level? Apparently, someone is aware of this and does not want it revealed. Remember Marilyn Monroe's own fate when she, too, made comments about disclosing hidden secrets? When Dr. Fox chose to go public with her findings and unmask the Brotherhood's secret agenda, her office was raided by the U.S. Food and Drug Administration. It is believed by those who knew her best that she immediately went into hiding to avoid being unjustly persecuted.

How do we fight against something we cannot see happening to us? Will new advances in nanotechnology and vaccination plans further push our bodies into a completely controlled state? Can we escape the clutches of Satan? Yes, but only if one is a Christian. Jesus Christ prophesied about these distressing times when He said,

"And except those days should be shortened, there should no flesh be saved: but for the elect's sake those days shall be shortened." (Matthew 24:22).

Chapter Twenty-Seven
Fallen Angels-The Alien Agenda

Albert Pike, who served as Grand Commander of the Ancient and Accepted Scottish Rite in Washington, D.C., wrote Morals and Dogma, which is given to all Masons. It is a book filled with hermetic and occult sciences. Pike acknowledged in his lifetime that he believed in the existence of Angels, whom he called Amshaspends. He wrote that these Angels were placed among mankind to promote free will and freedom of choice. Pike felt if one interacted with these Angels, they would offer them eternal life. In other words, it required a person to open up their pineal gland to receive this communication and sacred enlightenment.

Another famous writer of the occult, who we have already discussed in an earlier chapter, was philosopher Helena P. Blavatsky, author of The Secret Doctrine. She called the Amshaspends the builders and creators of humanity. Blavatsky believed Hermes had been very much in contact with these Fallen Angels and through their direct intervention with him, brought additional knowledge to mankind. Her writings are highly regarded and worshipped by elite members of Secret Societies in their quest to create 'Heaven on Earth.'

The Masonic ritual of laying a cornerstone through the use of a foundation chart is to precisely bring celestial beings to participate in the earthly ceremony. This, as we already know, is the Hermetic Principle that connects the celestial bodies to Earth—'As Above, So Below.' The 'Heaven on Earth' ritual of laying cornerstones in a sacred fashion exists around the world. This mystical act acknowledges the belief in seeking angelic intervention in human endeavors.

There is no other explanation for continuing such a planned and secretly demonic ritual. There are millions of buildings around the world that have had these astrological ceremonies performed at their inception. Every one of these structures has been built on the shifting sands of the worship of strange gods. Their very foundations have been laid for Satan and not Jehovah. What is even more shocking is the number of churches whose cornerstones have been laid using these principles. Even the very flag of Israel has an up and a down triangle forming a six pointed star, secretly professing the demonic principle, 'As Above, So Below.'

Within the teaching of Gnosticism lies the belief that the world is ruled by Archons. These spiritual beings are said to be invisible. Their powers are rumored to be designed to keep humans in turmoil through commandments, laws, and bondages. They are not able to kill, but to torment. Gnostics believe these Archons are from the realms of Jehovah. They envision Jehovah as the wicked god who drove Adam and Eve from their rightful place in the Garden of Eden. Gnostics, in turn, worship Lucifer as the good god and the bringer of enlightenment to mankind. They claim Lucifer's Fallen Angels are here to help mankind progress through stages of development, which will lead them to god-like illumination and wisdom of all things.

Many belonging to the royal hierarchy throughout the generations have believed that spiritual beings were at work in the lives of mankind. James I, the King of England, was an avid believer in Demons and their demonic powers. He wrote the book, Demonologie. This work established the fact that James was a true believer in the reality of active demonic beings walking among mankind. He felt these demonic beings were Satan and his Fallen Angels who had been cast to earth, just as the Bible stated. James wrote that this spiritual realm was very active with and against humans. He conceived Jehovah's good Angels were in constant battle with Satan and his bad Angels for the souls of mankind.

Author and UFO researcher Whitley Strieber established a direct link between the similarities of Fallen Angels and what we, today, term as 'Alien Abductions.' In his book, Transformation, the Breakthrough, Strieber states,

"I have learned a number of important things from my experience.

1. The visitors are physically real. They also function on a nonphysical level, and this may be their primary reality.

2. They have either been here a long time or they are trying to create this impression . . .

3. They have the ability to enter the mind and affect thought, and can accomplish amazing feats with this skill.

4. They have taught me by demonstration that I have a soul separate from my body. My own observations while detached from my body suggest that the soul is some form of conscious energy, possibly electromagnetic in nature.

5. They can affect the soul; even draw it out of the body, with technology that may possibly involve the use of high-intensity magnetic fields.

6. They used few words to communicate with me. Their primary method was a sort of theatrical demonstrations, richly endowed with symbolic meaning.

7. When I challenged my own fear of them they responded by taking me on a journey deep into my unconscious terrors . . .

I suspect that the visitors may have been here for a long time. It has even crossed my mind, given their apparent interest in human genetics that they may have had something to do with our evolution."15

It appears from various studies being generated by UFO researchers that Aliens cannot precede with their genetic breeding programs unless they have the involvement of human subjects. The Fallen Angels and Satan are continuing in their lusts upon humanity, just as they did following the fall of mankind from the Garden of Eden. These evil Angels and their leader, Satan, have corrupted mankind from the beginning and will continue in their relentless pursuit until the End of Time. The Alien Agenda is identical in philosophy to that of Satan's agenda. They are, merely, one and the same.

In the practice of modern day sorcery, a Demon by the name of 'Rehctaw' is called upon. This name is really 'Watcher' spelled backwards. Those involved with the witchcraft movement have been calling upon the 'Watchers' for decades, because they know the ability these

Fallen Angels possess. Their mystical powers have always been worshipped by those involved in the 'Craft.' This sacred 'Craft' originated in the beginning with the ancient Megalithic Builders and continues through today with the Illuminati Brotherhood. The world is surrounded with those that worship Satan as their god. They are leading others blindly to the altar of Satan by making them think they are worshipping a universal god who accepts all faiths as equal.

Satan and his Fallen Angels have power over the elements. Just take a look at the Book of Job where Satan caused calamities, increased the wind, brought fire down from heaven, and displayed power over the air. He and his army of Angels are capable of producing signs and wonders to capture mankind's attention. Our sky is presently being filled with more and more strange phenomena.

Shen Shituan, a well-known rocket scientist who is President of Beijing Aerospace University and serves as an honorary director of China's UFO Research Association, believes something strange is going on in the skies. Shituan stated,

"All this UFO phenomena is worth researching. The Chinese have always watched the skies for signs."

The year of 2002 was the year of the Dragon. Years that fall on the Dragon are recorded in Chinese history as a time of major crisis and change. It is an interesting fact that UFO sightings in China have gradually increased to an all-time high, just as have UFO sightings around the world.

Hartwig Hausdorf, a German researcher and author of The White Pyramid and Satellites of the Gods, claims that a

Chinese Roswell-type UFO crashed 12,000 years ago in China. He reports that there are graves containing the skeletal remains of Alien looking beings that stood four feet tall with unusually large heads. According to Chinese legend, they are referenced as the 'sons of heaven' who came to Earth in fiery metallic Dragons. These 'sons' are credited with building over 100 Pyramids throughout China, including the Great White Pyramid in the valley of Qin Lin. It stands 1000 feet high, compared to the Great Pyramid in Egypt, which is only 481 feet. The China Pyramids resemble the Mayan Step-Pyramids with flat areas or temples on top, and like the Pyramids of Mexico they, too, are frequently visited by UFOs.

Unidentified Flying Objects are real, even though tabloids make jest of them. These tabloids are a tool being used as a conditioning process to allow a gradual change in our thinking without shocking mankind and causing mass panic. Essentially, the powers-that-be want to make humanity aware of the possibility of strange phenomena, laugh at it, and then hit them with a little truth, gradually, until the possibility is accepted as fact. It is somewhat easier to tell the people of the world that they are being watched by Aliens than to admit that they are being watched by Fallen Angels. The UFO phenomena is not a 20th Century anomaly, but has been documented from the earliest recordings of man's history. Credible UFO cases stretch from ancient Babylon through today. Many of these cases prove that UFOs were witnessed before the invention of aviation. Throughout history, UFOs have left landing traces, were able to be tracked on radar, and accelerated at speeds that far exceed the capability of manmade aircraft.

Thousands of very intelligent and credible people from all corners of the globe are aware of and have even witnessed UFO activities. Victor Marchetti, the former Special Assistant to the Executive Director of the Central Intelligence Agency (CIA) and the first CIA employee to go public, stated in his article entitled, "How the CIA views the UFO Phenomenon," in Second Look, Vol. 1, No 7, May 1979, that:

"We have indeed, been contacted perhaps even visited by extraterrestrial beings, and the US government, in collusion with the other national powers of the Earth, is determined to keep this information from the general public."

A serious researcher of the phenomena includes Dr. Barry Downing, a Presbyterian Minister. Dr. Downing believes UFOs are from the spiritual dimension. In the October 1988 issue of The MUFON Journal (pp. 10–13), Downing's explanation regarding UFOs is based on what he terms the "God Hypothesis." His theory states that UFOs come from another dimension, which exists within the midst of us. He believes the entities piloting these space ships have somehow been involved with humanity since the time of our creation. Downing further speculates that these beings are from a spiritual world where humans go at death.

The Holy Bible records that the Fallen Angels and Satan are immortal beings residing within the spiritual realm. Satan wants mankind to be able to change mortal flesh into immortal flesh so as to avoid the spiritual realm where he and God exist. Satan wants to keep mankind continually alive on Earth through Cloning and other forms of life extension technology, since he has power over the flesh. He knows that when a person dies, they are no longer any help to him in his rebellion against God. Satan is very aware that sinners have no hope for eternal salvation, but will burn eternally in Hell with him and his Fallen Angels at the 'Day of Judgment.' Satan's only kingdom is here on Earth. He is tempting mankind into believing that if death is eradicated, humanity will never need to worship Jehovah out of fear again.

Satan's promise of immortality of the flesh deceitfully offers an alternative for a person to live out their earthly lives, any way they want to, by removing the fear of death and judgment hanging over their heads. When death is abolished, man will 'worship self' and 'praise the created instead of the Creator.' Right now, if most people knew they could live indefinitely on earth, how many would continue to go to church, pray to Jehovah, and look forward to a paradise they cannot see unless they die? Satan is right on track with his game plan, which promotes the sin of selfishness among mankind.

The majority of people will do whatever is necessary to stay alive, including giving their soul to the Devil for the knowledge and technology that has the potential to bring immortality to their physical body so they will never die. By giving man seemingly eternal mortal flesh through various scientific discoveries, and at the same time confusing humanity as to what is right and wrong, Satan's power over the world is growing by leaps and bounds.

The ambition to physiologically control the Laws of Nature is part of the New Age strategy that is being highly promoted by Aliens during human abductions. Under hypnosis, humans taken aboard UFOs claim their captor's mandate that they follow a religion involving nature worship. The entities tell about how it is the responsibility of humans to protect and love 'Mother Earth.' This encouragement to love nature is identical to 'loving the created more than the Creator.' It is the age-old worship of nature, known as Theosophy, which has always been promoted by the Fallen Angels and their father, Satan.

The Bible records the increase in the pagan worship of nature, as well as the powers of Demons and strange occurrences in the skies near the 'End of the Age.' Scripture also says that the increase of evil during these last days will be 'like unto the days of Noah.' Remember, the Great Flood was brought about by Jehovah to rid the Earth of the evil half-breed race called the Giants, who were born through the wicked lineage of Cain and the Fallen Angels. Jehovah wanted the Spirit of Cain, which is the 'Spirit of Selfishness,' to be removed from the earth. Because we are witnessing the Alien's promotion of nature worship with abductees, there can be no doubt that we are living in the last days spoken of in the Bible. As prophesied, it will take the 'Second Coming of Jesus' to rid the evil hold Satan and his Fallen Angels have on the world.

Just as the Fallen Angels and Satan possess great power between the physical and spiritual worlds, so seemly can reported Aliens move in and out of our physical dimension. The Aliens, like the Angels, do not come from another planet. They come from another dimension that can manifest itself in and out of our world. When humans are exposed to Alien Abductions, they report experiencing strange physiological phenomena. These events include air blowing, becoming partially paralyzed, blinded, going through walls, traveling in a beam of light, receiving painful probing with strange looking apparatus, medical procedures, healings, sickness, and strange symbols placed on their skin. With the increasing reports of UFOs and Alien Abductions, researchers are having to not only rely on a form of scientific investigation, but are also having to allow for the spiritual dimension to be addressed to better understand these unwanted visitations. The problem is not going away. It is increasing. Hundreds of sightings occur monthly, on a world-wide basis. The UFO phenomenon is in desperate need of academic study.

If a person ever experiences a UFO sighting, or even worse, an Alien presence, they will never laugh about such events again. 'Seeing is believing' and from that point it becomes a life-altering inwardness that is never forgotten. Pretending that Fallen Angels/Aliens do not exist will not make them go away. They present serious consequences that the powers-that-be know they cannot protect mankind from. That is why no government will forthrightly admit the reality of UFOs. They already know they cannot protect an individual from the spiritual world. If people really read the Bible and understood the existence and daily threats of these demonic Alien assaults, it would either cause mass panic, or people would be in much more prayer. There is but one line of protection and it requires individuals to claim Jesus as their Savior. No one can protect humans from the attack of the spiritual world except Jesus. That fact is something Satan and his minions do not want you to truly understand, know about, or rely heavily upon, or their so-called gig would already be up.

Sitting here reading this book, does it bother you to know that something is really watching you—something that no one can protect you from except Jesus Christ? I want to assure you that you are being watched and that the Bible warns mankind of this when it tells us to,

"Put on the whole armour of God that ye may be able to stand against the wiles of the devil. For we wrestle not against flesh and blood but against principalities, against powers, against the rulers of the darkness of this world, against spiritual wickedness in high places." (Ephesians 6:11–12).

There are a few UFO researchers who have come to the conclusion that there is, indeed, some sort of religious connection between Aliens and demonic beings. Jacques Vallee, in his work entitled, The Invisible College (1975), called UFOs a "New Form of Religion." John Mack, MD, the late author of Passport to the Cosmos: Human Transformation and Alien Encounters (1999), stated that research findings from his abduction case studies indicated that Aliens were trying to take mankind back to something he called the "Source." As was previously discussed, Dr. Barry Downing, UFO Researcher and Pastor of 34 years, terms the UFO phenomena a type of "God Hypothesis." Even though these three famous UFO Researchers describe the Alien Agenda using different terms, they are all, in essence, describing it as having religious connotations. Dr. Downing goes a tad further when he explains that the UFO phenomenon does not consist of:

"a bunch of little green guys from Mars." 16

Downing also clearly expresses that the Aliens are not God—just playing like it. He further states,

"ET's are not God, but they are so powerful they can trick us into thinking they are God, which causes the religious response of Betty Andreasson, Whitley Strieber, and many of the "experiencers" reported by John Mack, MD."17

From on-going UFO research, it appears that Aliens are promoting religious revelations like that of demonic beings. The spiritual world does exist and has many levels. It is where Jehovah lives, along with all of His Angels. Unfortunately, the spiritual realm also contains a lower dimension where Satan and his Fallen Angels exist. Jehovah resides in the highest level of the spiritual realm called Heaven. When Satan and his Angels were forced out of Heaven for rebelling against God, they were condemned to reside in the lowest spiritual dimension within and under the Earth.

Throughout the Bible, the spiritual world has been documented as being able to manifest itself in our physical dimension of reality. Aliens are reportedly exhibiting these same manifestations between dimensions in cases reported around the world. When we eventually understand the UFO and Alien Agenda, it will lead us back to the satanic sacred mysteries and the realization that a spiritual world of demonic beings has existed all around us since the beginning of time. The forces of good and evil have been at play every second of our existence after mankind was removed from the Garden of Eden.

It seems very logical that the ancient gods, goddesses, Giants, Fairies, etc., are what we now term as Aliens. We know that these strange entities and their offspring are not human. According to ancient history, highly intellectual beings were said to be actively involved in the affairs of mankind. Satan and his Fallen Angels had a direct hand in producing the lineage of Cain, which advanced mankind in the knowledge of physics, music, metallurgy, architecture, geometry, astronomy, numerology, the sciences, and astrology, as well as seeking 'the god within' to promote selfishness.

Across the many generations of mankind's history, there have been sightings of strange beings who exhibited miraculous and magical capabilities. The Celtic/Druid era of human history produced an enormous amount of documentation concerning 'Fairy Sightings.' These Fairies were always reported to have been seen near the ancient Megalithic Structures. The concept that Fairies and Aliens could be one in the same was recently proposed by Chris Aubeck in his book, Return to Magonia. Aubeck states,

"Folklore and ufology overlapped in the first half of the twentieth century and this overlap is stranger than what many writers have shown so far."[18]

Aubeck reveals in his work that there are physical similarities between Fairies and Aliens. He sites in his research that they are both documented to be grey in skin color, not quite four feet tall, and wearing seamless clothing like a frog suit. His research also contends that Fairy Folk were reported to have abducted humans in a manner similar to Alien Abductions, which are being investigated today. Aubeck goes on to establish a strong correlation between hybrid babies of women who claim to have been Alien abducted and Fairy babies, which folklore literature called changelings.

As you will recall, in ancient times, the 'Watchers' (Fallen Angels) and human women produced hybrids that the Bible recorded as Giants. Alien hybrids, Fairy changelings, and the Giants have always been alluded to as existing. They are mentioned in the Bible, as well as in literary works of mythology and folklore as being offspring from the sexual relations between Demons, gods, and humans. These relationships, occurring between the physical and spiritually demonic world, should not be taken lightly. We can no longer pretend that this phenomenon does not exist.

According to Peter Meyer in his Psychedelic Monographs and Essays #5 entitled, Apparent Communication with Discarnate Entities Induced by Dimethyltryptamine (DMT), upon one's use of the drug, there are documented cases of contact with Aliens, elves, and spiritual beings. The hallucinogen DMT allows users to visit into another dimension with beings that seem to be highly intelligent. This psychedelic drug not only alters human consciousness, but enlightens the user, which is similar to what the brain neurotransmitter serotonin does. Serotonin stimulation is why so many drugs causing the brain to uptake more of the substance are now on the market for depression such as Paxil and Zoloft. It, along with melatonin, is produced by the notorious pineal gland—interestingly enough, the gland I fully believe is involved in higher dimensional transmissions.

DMT is a white powder and, when ingested, will cause one first to feel as if some form of illuminated energy is descending upon them. This experience is quickly followed by geometrical patterns, then a tunnel, and eventually contact with non-human beings that look like little elves with big, piercing eyes. So just how is something like this possible? The fact is that humans only use about 10% of brain capacity. DMT molecules target the very neurons of the brain, causing it to function differently, just like switching channels on a television—same television but entirely different channels; a radio picking up different stations would also represent the same concept. The areas of the brain that are stimulated take over, even if those areas might not have been used before. In other words, precise manipulation of our central nervous system allows brainwave transmissions to take place, just like they do over ancient Oracle sites or during intense meditation practices.

Evans-Wentz, in his work, The Fairy Faith in Celtic Countries, states that Fairies existed in France and Britain and were believed to exist by anyone willing to enter a meditative trance. Leaving this 3 dimensional world in a meditative state invoked the exact same beings as those seen in people using psychedelic substances like DMT. This process of contact is no different than what is known to occur in Asia with those practicing Shamanism or the meditative Jewish practice of Kabbalah. If indeed these beings from another dimension exist, then they can be contacted and are waiting for a willing human vessel to invoke them. There is too much evidence to their existence not to understand that they are indeed watching us from another dimension, just as is recorded in the Book of Daniel:

"I saw in the visions of my head upon my bed, and, behold, a watcher and an holy one came down from heaven . . . This matter is by the decree of the watchers, and the demand by the word of the holy ones: to the intent that the living may know that the most High ruleth in the kingdom of men, and giveth it to whomsoever he will, and setteth up over it the basest of men." (Daniel 4:13, 17).

Notice in the above Scripture that it first mentions a holy one, which can only be one of God's Angels. The 'Watcher,' mentioned above as the second being, is not referenced as holy; therefore, it has to be a Fallen Angel. So in other words, the 'Watchers' decree' means an official order, while the holy ones 'demand' is an act of asking especially with authority. The word 'basest,' used to describe man, means inferior. Therefore, man is under the authority of the Most High, according to the holy one, but falls below the order of the 'Watcher.' Scripture proves that God made man a little lower than the angels:

"What is man, that thou art mindful of him? And the son of man, that thou visitest him? For thou hast made him a little lower than the angels, and hast crowned him with glory and honour." (Psalms 8:4–5).

It would behoove us to remember that these angelic visitations happened to Nebuchadnezzar in a vision or dream; either way, it was during an altered state of consciousness. The troubling vision was not dismissed by the Prophet Daniel as nonsense but was interpreted by him, further proving that there is indeed something out there capable of making contact with humans through transmissions during altered states of consciousness. The book of Colossians tells us that God made a lot of things that we as humans cannot see:

"For by him were all things created, that are in heaven, and that are in earth, visible and invisible, whether they be thrones, or dominions, or principalities, or powers: all things were created by him, and for him. And he is before all things, and by him all things consist." (Colossians 1:16–17).

Could it be that the Ark of the Covenant was some form of transmittal device for the voice of God to speak through? Did God have Moses to build the Ark so that individual people would not open themselves up using pagan incantations to a spiritual realm filled with other beings, not understood by man due to his inferiority? The average human being would not have been able to discern which beings were instructing them—the holy ones or the 'Watchers'—unless they had been mighty prophets of God like Daniel and Ezekiel. Correct instruction from only Jehovah was crucial in the early days while traveling through the wilderness because the Israelites had just left the pagan practices of the Egyptians. In Egypt, the Fallen Angels were having a field day mixing with mankind by stimulating their pineal glands.

If the Hebrew Children had tried to go into a meditative state like Egyptians taught by sitting in a cobra position in order to seek Jehovah's will, they more than likely would not have been able to distinguish the difference between good or evil spiritual beings. The reason for this confusion is that Satan also comes in illuminated light, deceptively imitating the pure and true light of God. This is the very reason that mankind does not need to open up to mediation and chanting.

Discernment is a gift of the spirit, and unless the Holy Spirit is upon you, then your inferiority to the spiritual realm puts your soul at great risk. This means most people today, who are promoting that they are so-called 'crossing over and talking to the dead,' more than likely are really talking to Satan. Jehovah warned against necromancy (conjuring up spirits) and other forms of witchcraft because of Satan's powers in those realms.

"There shall not be found among you any one that maketh his son or his daughter to pass through the fire, or that useth divination, or an observer of times, or an enchanter, or a witch, or a charmer, or a consulter with familiar spirits, or a wizard, or a necromancer. For all that do these things are an abomination unto the Lord: and because of these abominations the Lord thy God doth drive them out from before thee." (Deuteronomy 18:10–12).

"For we wrestle not against flesh and blood, but against principalities, against powers, against the rulers of the darkness of this world, against spiritual wickedness in high places." (Ephesians 6:12).

It is important that we understand our limitations and heed the warnings of Jehovah to avoid using the tools of witchcraft. To better understand the dimension in which we live and how to stop Satan from having such control over our lives is what really matters. Surprisingly, there are many highly educated researchers who are willing to risk their professions to get to the truth about what is really going on in the heavens. One such person is Edgar Mitchell, Sc. D., a former Apollo Astronaut. Dr. Mitchell appeared before Congress calling for governmental disclosure of the UFO cover-up. He believes the government's silence regarding UFO's has gotten out of hand and is posing a danger to the democracy of the United States.

The late U.S. Congressman Steven Schiff, a Jewish Republican from New Mexico, requested before his untimely death that the Government Accounting Office (GAO) search for documents concerning the famous July 1947 UFO Crash in Roswell, New Mexico. In 1995, the GAO responded to his request by stating that the Roswell Air Force Base's Administrative records from March 1945 to December 1949 had been destroyed along with ongoing messages from October 1946 through December 1949. These documents, Congressman Schiff was told, were destroyed without any record of authorization to destroy them.

This all seems very suspicious, as government regulations were not followed in the destroying of governmental property. It is interesting that the only destroyed records are from a time period that has been so thoroughly investigated regarding a UFO crash and the retrieval of Alien bodies. With the addition of Schiff's premature death to a volatile form of skin cancer, when he was never one to be out in the sun, makes one wonder if those attempting to reveal the secrets of UFOs will continue to have their aggressiveness to expose a cover-up cost them their lives.

According to Power of Prophecy, May 2003, (Vol. 2003-05), Texe Marrs wrote that mysterious deaths and casualties are a common occurrence in those struggling against the evil men of the Illuminati. He sites, for example, the mysterious shooting of William Cooper, the author of Behold a Pale Horse. Marrs goes on to mention that author Jim Keith, who wrote Black Helicopters over America and Saucers of the Illuminati, also suffered an untimely death. Even more unnerving, according to Marrs, was the fact that Keith's publisher, Ron Bonds of Illuminet Press, died after ingesting a mysterious and fast-acting poison at a restaurant in Atlanta, Georgia. In addition to these men, there are the deaths of Marilyn Monroe, the Kennedy Brothers, and even Princess Diana, in which all of them made comments hinting that they knew about some secret that would rock the world before their tragic deaths.

In an effort to keep the UFO agenda secret, governmental and commercial airline pilots are told to refrain from speaking to the press or going public with their hundreds of sightings. The National Security Agency (NSA) does not want the truth to be known publicly. Deceit is being used as part of this ongoing cover-up campaign. The fact is that the elite within these agencies already know that the true identity of the Aliens is none other than Satan and his Fallen Angels. They also know the Plan is to allow evil to produce miraculous manifestations in the final days before the Apocalypse.

Apparently, the elite Brotherhood within the NSA has a working relationship with their so-called benevolent space brothers. That is why the NSA states that there are no such things as unidentified objects or beings and secretly records such phenomena as Identified Flying Objects (IFOs). It is quite possible these IFOs are piloted by demonic Angels/mixed hybrids that cannot live totally in the spiritual realm. Because these entities are mixed, their flesh can die. This might explain why so-called strange, alien-looking dead bodies were recovered from the 1947 UFO crash at Roswell, New Mexico.

These hybrids died, just like their mixed descendants the Giants, who perished in the Flood. The fathers of both the hybrids and Giants are the same. They are the 'Watchers'

(Fallen Angels) who are totally spiritual beings and who, according to Sumerian Clay Tablets, escaped the Flood in their heavenly boats. Apparently, they have taught their hybrids how to fly those heavenly boats in order to escape any future disasters.

The formation of the Jewish state of Israel, in 1948, and the removal of the Gentiles from its governance, in 1967 during the Six Day War, has pushed mankind closer to the countdown of the Battle of Armageddon and the return of Jesus Christ. The increase in UFO activity being documented on a daily basis all around the world indicates that time is running out for Satan and his wicked seed. They appear to be in high gear, with the goal of attempting to deceive as many souls as possible so they can successfully pull off Satan's enthronement as Messiah.

Their puppets, the Elite Brotherhood, are strategically employed in prominent positions to assist Satan in his diabolical plan and keep it on schedule. They are doing all that is necessarily possible to ensure his plan is never exposed. Therefore, all UFO related information is retained in the hands of an extra-constitutional group, functioning outside the normal channels of governments, which are located around the world. Maintaining this level of secrecy could only be accomplished by an Elite Illuminated International Brotherhood—a clandestine group that owes no allegiance to the public or any political leadership. These men want Satan to be totally in charge without mankind knowing the truth, and they will do everything in their power to keep it a secret.

Satan and his followers cannot afford exposure or bad press involving their game plan. Mankind must be forced into accepting that Satan, as the God of Light, and his Angels are really here to assist humanity in creating a paradise on earth. The human race is being kept from knowing that it is Satan and his Demons who are daily tempting us, manipulating us, using us to his service in his rebellion against God, putting stumbling blocks in our way, making us feel failure, filling our bodies with sickness and pain, and taking our souls if we choose to follow an evil lifestyle. As long as Satan stays somewhat hidden or veiled, he can entice more souls into his kingdom through his deceitful 'Craft of Enlightenment.' Satan knows he will need a big army on his side when he and his Fallen Angels finally come face to face with Jesus at the Battle of Armageddon.

Take a moment and think about the UFO phenomenon. It has an element that is totally covert and largely full of deception. The techniques used by the Aliens against mankind are manipulative and deceiving. The Aliens promise not to hurt those they abduct, but in most all reported cases a degree of pain is involved. The Aliens say one thing and do the opposite. After an Alien Abduction, some form of psychological trauma occurs in a vast majority of abductees. The abduction experience itself appears to resemble a type of spiritual encounter. Abducted humans tend to return with information about a new religion. This religion is identical to an ancient philosophy that promotes 'nature worship' called Theosophy.

Theosophy involves a transmutation of thought in which its intent is to perfect man and nature by worshipping 'Mother Earth' as a Goddess. In the later part of the 19th Century, around 1870, a small portion of the secrets and teachings of Theosophy were released to the world through the

Theosophical Society. The Society was co-founded by Madam Helena P. Blavatsky at Adyar, India.

Theosophy was the religion of the Ancients, who were said to be an inner cadre of enlightened sages. Their teachings were hidden in subterranean vaults and temples, which were guarded in utmost secrecy. The secret teachings required one to go through stages of initiation to open up their 'Third Eye' of illumination, which they called 'The Awakening'. This was considered a spiritual process, which would lead the person to seeing an invisible universe that exists in the voids of space. The teachings claim that between the visible planets all space is filled with sentient beings. When 'the god within' is tapped by opening up the initiate's reptilian 'Third Eye' (pineal gland), those beings can then have a relationship with that particular human. This inner awakening promotes the love of self and nature over the worship of the Creator.

Many abductees reveal that the Aliens are promoting the saving of planet earth. The Aliens tell their abductees that in the near future, they are going to be living here among them. When this comes to pass, the Aliens report that mankind will live eternally in peace, and everyone will have their rightful places on this wonderful and perfected earth. This ideology sounds like 'Heaven on Earth,' and it is the basis of those promoting the New World Order. The Alien Abduction program is apparently an integration program for those who will be ruled by the Antichrist under the New World Order. This program of indoctrination into the religion of Theosophy is occurring at an accelerated rate because the time is short.

Dr. Barry Downing, an author and minister mentioned earlier, says the Vatican has gotten into the act of accepting the reality surrounding the UFO phenomena. Dr. Downing states,

"Monsignor Corrado Balducci of the Vatican has gone on record saying he believes UFOs are real, but he believes they come from the natural order, not the supernatural order. The Balducci statements put Roman Catholics in a reasonable position just in case governments start releasing UFO information".19

Downing has theorized that it is very possible the Aliens and the Biblical Fallen Angels are one and the same. He believes this explains why UFOs have not landed on the White House Lawn or tried to take over our world. They have been here all the time with mankind, from the very beginning. Only their names have changed. Satan and his Fallen Angels have been dubbed Watchers, Pagan Gods, Fairy Folk, Demons, Incubus, Succubus, Devils, and are now being called Aliens. This explains why those reporting Alien Abductions say that if they begin saying the Lord's Prayer or the name of Jesus, their abduction immediately terminates.

Research into known abductees orally reciting the Lord's Prayer and the name of Jesus to stop an Alien Abduction is presently on-going. No other known course of action has surfaced as an antidote to stop an abduction that is in process until now. Apparently, when an abductee openly chooses Jesus, the Aliens have no choice but to leave them alone. In cases where the abductee had been involved in multiple abductions, once that person chose to call out to Jesus it accounted for the complete termination of that and any future Alien encounters. This is additional evidence in support of the fact that Aliens are actually Satan and his Fallen Angels who are attacking mankind.

Choosing to follow Jesus would truly release the spiritual power necessary to over come all evil beings. Our Creator promised mankind that if we call upon the name of the Lord we shall be saved. This is the very reason these Aliens/Demons cannot continue their attack to hurt us. If the person experiencing the abduction continues to appeal to God, the Aliens quit showing up. When a person calls upon Jesus, it signals to these spiritual beings that they have no power against that person's choice. The Aliens are immediately forced to depart and the abductee regains a full wakened state of consciousness. This would prove that Jehovah God possesses superior power over all demonic manifestations and that these Aliens do not have the ability to defeat Him—now or ever.

Ann Druffel, in her book, How to Defend Yourself against Alien Abduction, has also reportedly uncovered the unique connection between Alien Abductions being terminated by the calling on God for protection. She is no newcomer to the field of Ufology, as she has been studying the phenomenon for over 44 years. There can be no denying that there is a major element of religion involved in all reported cases of the abduction phenomena.

UFO research is increasingly pointing toward Aliens being Angels who fell from grace along with their rebellious leader, Lucifer (Satan). God created all spiritual beings and has authoritative power over them. When He cast Satan and his followers out of Heaven, they had no ability to stop their Creator's decision. They were forced out of eternal bliss and will never be allowed to return. In retaliation to God's punishment, their rebellion has continued. It has caused many souls to be lost. Mankind must not be afraid to address the truth behind the Alien Agenda if we are to survive their attacks.

The Bible clearly states that spirits of Devils will be seen in the coming days before the 'End of the Ages.' John the Revelator wrote,

"And I saw three unclean spirits like frogs come out of the mouth of the dragon, and out of the mouth of the Beast, and out of the mouth of the false prophet. For they are the spirits of devils, working miracles, which go forth unto the kings of the earth and to the whole world, to gather them to the battle of the great day of God Almighty." (Revelation 16:13–14).

The Apostle John described demonic spirits as being frog-like. Many reports and descriptions of Aliens and Fairy Folk mention the entities as having skin akin to that of a frog. Their skin is said to be without seams and similar to the tightness and slickness of a wetsuit. This is yet another correlation between Aliens and Fallen Angels, which should not be dispelled as mere coincidence.

In 1486, two Dominican Friars, Jacob Sprenger and Heinrich Kramer, wrote Malleus Maleficarum, which still serves today as the most authoritative subject on witchcraft. Sprenger was then serving as Dean of Theology Faculty at the University of Cologne. He and Kramer were concerned that humans and Demons could procreate and have children. They investigated the possibility that humans could be physically taken and transported by demonic beings. These issues are the same concerns involving Alien Abduction research, which investigators must come to terms with today. Screen memories, scars, marks, lost pregnancies, sperm collection, and hybrid babies were also discovered to be occurring in Sprenger and Kramer's 1486 Study of Demons. An identical scenario of their published research on Demons is now being witnessed in the field of Ufology regarding Alien Abduction.

Demonic encounters and Alien Abductions seem, according to researchers, to be occurring within an altered state of consciousness, which propels one into another dimension. Demonic creatures were determined by Sprenger and Kramer's research to be composed of mostly air, and like the Aliens, could take on various forms through shape-shifting capabilities. Aliens and demonic beings appear most of the time to never be wounded by weapons. They tend to divide and rejoin if attacked, due to their mixture of being half flesh and half spiritual being. Although most have the supernatural ability to avoid being injured by manipulating control over the elements, some have died. Like we discussed earlier, according to various reports concerning the 1947 UFO Crash in Roswell, New Mexico, the Alien beings found at that site were all said to have been found dead, except for one who was believed by some earlier researchers to have been captured.

Cases where communication has been reported as taking place between humans, Demons, Fairies, and Aliens are described by contactees as being telepathic. Alien abductees recount that they are able to hear words inside their heads, but the Aliens' lips never move. There is speculation based on witness accounts that Aliens and Demons do not breathe. These entities appear to move through the air without regard to gravity and seem to float. They are masters of deception and illusion. Their magical 'Craft' is designed to make humans see, think, and feel a variety of sensations that are not real. From Sprenger and Kramer's research on Devils and Demons, they provide evidence that manifestations are an ongoing assault against mankind. Their agenda has remained the same, but is just packaged within the framework of different names to continue to lure mankind into following Satan's rebellious Plan.

George P. Hansen, a parapsychologist/PSI researcher, wrote in his book, The Trickster and the Paranormal, that UFOs have been with mankind for thousands of years. He calls the Aliens "Tricksters." According to Hansen, Tricksters travel between the heavens and the earth without limitations to time boundaries. They are, he records, involved in a secret plan of deception aimed at all mankind. These Tricksters, while elusive, are participating in an ongoing interbreeding program with select human beings, Hanson conceives. This involves the same process of procreation as recorded in the Book of Genesis, where the 'Watchers' bred with earthlings and produced the race of Giants. Hansen goes on to state that Hermes/Mercury was chosen as the Tricksters' 'Bringer of Knowledge' to mankind following the Flood. This sacred knowledge was again used to fuel the course of the Tricksters and continue their deceptive manipulation of humanity.

Hansen gives quote to a 1997 article written by Gerald Haines, a historian at the National Reconnaissance Office, which says that the USA studies psychic phenomena associated with UFO's. The reason for the USA's increased interest is that, according to Haines, almost all of the government's psychic spies have encountered

UFO's/Aliens in their Remote Viewing excursions. That is not surprising. What these psychic warriors, who are trained by the government, do not understand is that they are opening up their pineal glands when they are engaged in the 'Craft' of Remote Viewing.

Opening up the pineal gland always invokes the presence of an enlightened being. It allows the reviewer to become a receiver for all of Satan's transmission. That is the sole reason for their encounters. Anyone who willingly opens themselves up to an altered state of consciousness risks having their body, mind, and soul taken over or possessed by Demons, Fallen Angels, and/or Satan himself.

The late Malachi Martin, former professor at the Vatican's Pontifical Biblical Institute who has been mentioned several times earlier, wrote in his book, Hostage to the Devil, that demonic possession is not some fake story about human orgies involving the Devil, which results in happy endings. Instead, he explained that when a person willingly chooses to tune into Satan and his Demons, they will have a high price to pay—their soul. Martin said that God is the only way an individual can counteract Satan's powers. According to his work, Martin claimed there were between 800 to 1,300 major Exorcisms, as well as many thousands of minor Exorcisms performed by Catholic Priests annually around the globe. That is a lot of demonic activity. These numbers coincide with the numbers of Alien Abductions, which are also reported annually.

Martin contended that in order to become possessed, one must open their mind and accept whatever entity happens to come in. It some cases, a person can completely be possessed and have no direct indication as to the Demon living within them. Others who are possessed may encounter paranormal phenomena such as objects flying around rooms, strange noises, doors opening and closing, electronic appliance interference, an inability to stay in the presence of anything Christian, and strange odors.

The only way a Demon, or what Martin terms an Alien "Presence," can be cast from a possessed individual is in the name and by the authority and power of Jesus Christ. As we have already discovered in this chapter, the mere calling out of the name of Jesus also happens to be the only known avenue at present to completely stop an Alien Abduction in process and to keep future abductions from ever happening again. The name of Jesus wields great power. Their response makes one more suspect that Demons and Aliens are the same because Jesus has the same effect on both of them— they vanish.

Demonic possession can come about through the use of psychedelic drugs, Ouija Boards, Yoga, Astral Flight, Chanting, Transcendental Meditation, Séances, and any other means that have the power to open the pathway to the human pineal gland. Those claiming to have seen Demons describe them as being about four feet tall, with a large head and big eyes. Some also report that these Demons have claw-like hands and are slender in their bodies, which are not proportionately sized with their heads. Others report tall, thin grotesque beings with bat-like wings and dark skin. The most unusual trait made reference to is the smell these beings produce, which is sulfuric. Descriptions of demonic encounters are almost identical to the entities reportedly witnessed during Alien Abductions. A descriptive commonality exists within the two, which cannot be dismissed as coincidental.

When a person takes on the huge task to expose the work of the Devil, they pay dearly, both physically and mentally for treading on his turf. I personally have found that to be the case while pursuing research for this book. It is apparent that others have suffered similar fates from their work in performing exorcisms against Demons. When called into this type of ministry, one must be prepared to fight the battle of their life, as everything around you and within you will be attacked. I mean everything! Satan's power to torture the body and mind is evident from this passage in the Book of Job:

"So went Satan forth from the presence of the Lord, and smote Job with sore boils from the sole of his foot unto his crown." (Job 2:7).

Like Job, our protection can only come through our unmovable faith in the power and grace of God, or we would be quickly extinguished by Satan and his army. Fighting the good fight in life means a person is fighting the powers of Satan continually. Being a Christian is really one of the hardest things a person will ever do in their life. Exposing the Devil for what he really is increases an individual's fight against him, ten-fold. The closer walk you have with God, the more Satan and his Demons attack. Remember that the lives of all of Jesus' Disciples ended in much tragedy, yet they continued to preach the Gospel and fought the good fight unto their deaths, for the crown of eternal life they would receive.

Satan uses emotions to attack humans by amplifying the electrical signals of the brain. The first response he attempts to generate within an individual is the feeling of fear, and the second response is anger. That is why God, through His

Holy Scripture, tells Christians, "not to fear anyone or anything except the Lord" and "be slow to anger."

"Now therefore fear the Lord, and serve him in sincerity and in truth; and put away the gods which your fathers served on the other side of the flood, and in Egypt; and serve ye the Lord." (Joshua 24:14.)

"Let us hear the conclusion of the whole matter: Fear God, and keep his commandments: for this is the whole duty of man." (Ecclesiastes 12:13).

"And fear not them which kill the body, but are not able to kill the soul: but rather fear him which is able to destroy both soul and body in hell." (Matthew 10:28).

"Cease from anger, and forsake wrath: fret not thyself in any wise to do evil." (Psalms 37:8).

"He that is slow to anger is better than the mighty; and he that ruleth his spirit than he that taketh a city." (Proverbs 16:32).

"Be not hasty in thy spirit to be angry: for anger resteth in the bosom of fools." (Ecclesiastes 7:9).

"Wherefore, my beloved brethren, let every man be swift to hear, slow to speak, slow to wrath." (James 1:19).

The emotions of fear and anger draw demonic activity to a person. Once this cycle begins, it starts to manifest into a vicious cycle around and within the person.

Satan and his Demons are able to sense the negative energy generated by fear and anger within the person's body. When this happens, they set up camp around that person and begin to establish a constant negative force of attack. Their plan behind this increased attack is to break them to such a point that they will give in to Satan by cursing and blaming God for their apparent misfortunes. It is not that Satan forced the person to love him, but that he has deceitfully cut them off from God by allowing them to falsely accuse God for their dilemma, when, in fact, God had nothing to do with their circumstances.

There is no evil in God. Satan just sets people up to blame God. People complain constantly that they do not know why God let bad things happen, when it was not God, but Satan at work. Even bad weather is blamed as an act of God, when it should be considered an act of Satan, as Satan has power over the elements.

Until researchers of Aliens, Demons, Fairy Folk, and Biblical history tackle the aspects of an ongoing cover-up by an agency outside of all governments, our chances of securing the facts of these increasing visitations are nil. In the famous words of President Ronald Reagan,

"In our obsession with antagonisms of the moment, we often forget how much unites all members of humanity. Perhaps we need some outside, universal threat to make us realize this common bond. I occasionally think how quickly our differences would vanish if we were facing an alien threat from outside this world. And yet, I ask you, 'Is not an alien force already among us?'"

(42nd General assembly of the United Nations: September 21, 1987).

Was then-President Ronald Reagan telling the world at large that he knew for a fact alien life existed and what their capabilities were? One cannot help but wonder if this is true, because it was under his administration that the Anti-Missile Program named STAR WARS was developed. It was not in a race against the Soviet Union, because Reagan directly invited them to join the USA in its development. Both Bush Presidents and President Clinton continued the project. It remains the most expensive weapons system in the USA arsenal today, and is now called the National Missile Defense Program.

So just what is it that the powers-that-be want desperately to protect us from? If the Fallen Angels (Aliens) are already among us as Reagan so eloquently stated, then exactly who or what will be coming in the air in which we might need such high tech protection from? Hmm, could it be potentially devastating asteroids? Or could this Strategic Defense System (SDS) be protection for Satan's army from the prophesied wrath upon Earth prior to the Second Coming of Jesus Christ and His Mighty Angels at the future Battle of Armageddon? Are the Fallen Angels secretly preparing mankind to assist Satan in doing battle with the Saints—in other words, a Battle of the Children of Darkness against the Children of Light?

NASA's Space Probe of their Deep Impact Mission collided with Tempel 1, at 7:52 p.m. PDT on July 4, 2005. The space probe chased down the speeding comet 83 million miles away and fired an 820 pound projectile into its rocky nucleus. The 23,000 mph explosive missile hit its target and formed a huge crater on the surface of the comet. Was this a dress rehearsal? Is something coming in the sky that we need to attack with a vengeance?

Could this threatening object be the same thing as the one that Vatican officials are tracking, called "Wormwood," at their new Vatican Observatory that was strategically located in Arizona for that sole and secret purpose? Why else would the Vatican choose to name the object they are closely monitoring "Wormwood" unless it represents to them the prophesied object that will bring great destruction at the End of the Ages?

"And the third angel sounded, and there fell a great star from heaven, burning as it were a lamp, and it fell upon the third part of the rivers, and upon the fountains of waters; and the name of the star is called Wormwood: and the third part of the waters became wormwood; and many men died of the waters, because they were made bitter." (Revelation 8:10–11).

If top Vatican officials are aware of "Wormwood's" prophetic timing and are tracking its movement toward Earth, then they know that the Tribulation Period will begin soon. Possessing this arcane knowledge of a prophetic timeline before "Wormwood" hits the earth gives credibility as to why 115 Cardinals elected 78-year-old Ratzinger to be Pope. Then, he up and resigned to coincide with the nearing of the Tribulation time period in order to get their last and final Pope, (Francis I) 'Peter Romano II', in place to hand over the reins of the Roman Catholic Church's New World Religion to the Antichrist.

No wonder the newly formed Jewish Sanhedrin in Israel made their number one priority the rebuilding of the Temple. Their High Priest is about ready to make his grand entrance. That is why Pope Benedict XVI was and now Pope Francis I is meeting and aligning himself with Jewish officials and calling for them "to love and respect one another." This all makes perfect sense when you are privy to the whole story. Catholics and Jews have got to come together in order for the plan to work.

Therefore, a clandestine group has been set up by Satan to go after the very souls of mankind. How we, on the outside, approach their control over us is a major question. From what we have previously discovered, very few people ever get close enough to expose the truth about what is being hidden from the public at large. It is evident that their matrix of deception is a very large web with an enormous spider devouring every bit of UFO and demonic morsels of truth into its stomach. Even Steven Wright, in his video entitled Environmental Warfare, comments that President Woodrow Wilson once remarked about this clandestine group of men by saying,

"There is a power, so complete, so organized, so subtle, so watchful, so interlocked, so complete, so pervasive that prudent men better not speak above their breath when they speak in condemnation of it."

A deliberate cover-up by this same Brotherhood has been going on for a very long time and is being carried out in an effort to keep the masses blinded. Their goal is to create a New World Order where Satan will control everything. "You are mine," said the Spider to the Fly . . .

There is loads of evidence of a government cover-up within the classified UFO data collected by the CIA and NSA. This truth is evident due to all the blacked and whited out sections within NSA and CIA documents that have been reviewed under the Freedom of Information Act. Within these documents there exist UFOs over intercontinental ballistic missile sites of nuclear weapons; as well as, radar-visual observations from the ground, coming out of the oceans and from military aircraft. According to author and UFO researcher, Stanton T. Friedman, "Project Blue Book's "Special Report No. 14", included 3,201 UFO sightings where 21.5 percent were Unidentifiable and the Condon (University of Colorado) study found 30 percent of UFO cases it evaluated could not be identified." Friedman goes on to say, in his MUFON article, March 2018, "China SETI: Will it make first contact?", that there has been a recent release of data about a TOP SECRET American project to collect UFO data for the U.S. Air Force, including the expenditure of $22 million in secret." Anyone who does not believe something very sinister is taking place in the sky above us and underneath the oceans is fooling themselves. We are not alone on this planet.

Chapter Twenty-Eight
Animal Mutilations

Not only have humans been used for experiments during UFO abductions, so have animals. Research is ongoing that details facts about UFO sightings and animal mutilations. While abducted humans are usually returned alive following medical probing aboard UFOs, animals are returned to their pastures mutilated. From the incisions left on the animals' maimed bodies, it appears they have also been exposed to some unknown form of probing. Mutilations are by no means a small problem. Numerous animals have been discovered throughout the world with what appears to be surgical intervention using an unknown heating element.

Right before a mutilated animal is found by its owner, there is usually some type of UFO disturbance that is witnessed in the sky over the area of the mutilation site. Once the animal is discovered, its remains are sometimes investigated by veterinarians. In those cases reviewed by veterinarians, their reports indicate the animals are covered with strange cuts and incisions. Their examinations of the remains indicate that the animal's skin is typically burned along the edge of what appears to be surgical sites. The most unusual finding is the complete absence of blood within the animal's veins, muscles, and ligaments. If and when traces of blood are vaguely noted, it is coagulated.

The animals, in most of the cases, are surgically incised to remove the tongue, alimentary tract, larynx, pharynx, and salivary glands. Usually one or more of the ears and eyes are missing, along with all reproductive organs. Sometimes the entire heart and the sack around the heart have been removed. There have also been cases where a pregnant cow's calf has been taken. The cases that have been extensively reviewed point to the fact that the mutilated animals were not attacked by wild animals, as there were no signs of a struggle found at the sites.

The strangest after effect in all investigated cases is that other animals in the field will not come near the mutilated animal and will even stay away from the spot long after the animal has been removed. If the carcass of the animal is left to deteriorate at the site, no vulture will eat the remains and there is no smell of rotting flesh. In a few instances, ants were noted to be feeding on the carcasses; but when analyzed, they were discovered to be disoriented with most of them dead.

Animal mutilations have been occurring world-wide for sometime. In 2002, a report of a case in Canada noted that a six-year-old Charolais Bull had its left eye, left ear, testicles and rectum removed. The stomach was opened with a neat laser type incision that was oval shaped at about 14 inches by 9 inches. The skin from the incision site could not be located, but the flesh along the site was not damaged. Most odd was the fact that the samples of blood taken from this particular carcass revealed that only pure hemoglobin remained inside the bull. This type of professional procedure would take very sophisticated equipment to reduce blood to only hemoglobin out in the middle of a pasture. Many witnesses living in the area where the bull was later found reported lights in the skies the night the mutilation occurred.

There are a good number of mutilation cases documented between the years 1993 to 1997, which note bovine excision sites where pure hemoglobin was left inside several of the carcasses. These cases reportedly found the separation of blood to form hemoglobin occurring near the incision marks. To isolate hemoglobin from whole blood requires separating red blood corpuscles from lighter plasma components through centrifugation. The plasma is siphoned off, and ether is then added to the corpuscles causing the cells burst. The process of centrifugation then removes the busted cell covers, leaving a clear red solution of pure hemoglobin. It remains a mystery as to how this procedure could be carried out in fields around the world by unqualified professionals.

What would be the need for bovine hemoglobin? It just may be that the late Dr. Roger Leir, a podiatric surgeon, may have unknowingly stumbled upon the reason hemoglobin is so important to the mutilators. Leir had been successfully removing what he claimed were Alien implants from patients experiencing Alien Abductions. These implants had unique properties, according to the article entitled "Implant anomalies continue" by Dr. Roger Leir, MUFON UFO Journal, November 2002, pg.6. The article states that,

"Leir had the specimens analyzed by a pathologist who reported that they were made up of protein

coagulum (derived from clotted blood and consisting of pure protein), hemosiderin (oxygen-caring iron pigment related to hemoglobin), and keratin (the most superficial layer of the skin), which the pathologist reportedly found puzzling."

These implants are composed of some of the same body fluids and tissues found removed from mutilated animals. There has to be a connection between those performing the mutilation of animals and those abducting humans. Implants may very well be the link. Besides having its own form of electromagnetic field, the implants are a biological membrane that has formed over a metallic structure using a new form of science, we discussed earlier, called Nanotechnology. Proteins are capable of forming ordered structures. These proteins can be stuck to various metals and then crystallized to form what NASA's Ames Research Center in California calls "nanotemplates." These nano-templates can be used as a sensor, computer chip, or a transmitter. Whatever the case, someone is already using nanotechnology in what Dr. Roger Leir described as Alien implants.

The worse recorded cases on record of mutilations occurred in Argentina in 2002. Over 200 animals were reported to have been found dead in less than a couple of months. Veterinarians in Argentina could find no explanation for the deaths of any of these animals. Some people reported that the predators were in UFOs that had arrived by air. Even big rats were blamed for the mutilations. Others speculated that the animals may have been taken, slain elsewhere, and dropped back in the fields.

The investigation into the 200 mutilated cases revealed there were, indeed, common patterns. Most times, the left side of the animal's face was skinned to the bone beneath the eye. The tongue and vocal cords were removed. There were no traces of blood found inside or outside of the animals' bodies. The cause of all 200 animal deaths still remains a mystery. From 2002 until of this writing in 2006, these strange mutilations are still occurring in Argentina without any evidence as to whom or what is killing the animals.

There seems to be some form of strange anomaly going on around the world, and not only in Argentina, where some high tech professional is traveling from area to area killing animals and boldly bringing their carcasses back to the location, or near to the location, where the animals were first abducted. No tracks are ever found around any of the dead animals. As stated before, no other animals will come near the site where the mutilation has occurred. The carcasses are never bloated or giving off offending odors when discovered. Some of the animal's bodies appeared to have been dropped from above by the way their legs were found folded underneath them. Sheep, horses, and cattle are among the large numbers of animals found mutilated in their pastures across Argentina.

There is a similar behavioral reaction between animals refusing to go near mutilation sites and those exposed to Crop Circle formations. Animals refrain from entering Crop Circles, and if physically placed inside them against their will, they immediately exhibit signs of intense fear and distress. This same scenario in animal reaction happens near a mutilated site. It is as if animals, when exposed to these strange locations, are affected by an unseen force that humans cannot sense. Yet many cases exist of humans complaining that when they are near mutilated sites or within Crop Circles they tend to feel dizzy, disoriented, and nauseated.

An interesting feature in the Argentina mutilation cases was the discovery that along with strange lights in the sky, large tanks holding thousands of gallons of water were found dry with no sign indicating where the water went. There seems to be a unique correlation between water and unusual phenomena such as animal mutilations, Crop Circles, UFOs, Megalithic sites, Gothic Cathedrals, and Oracle sites. Crop Circles are sometimes discovered after beams of lights are witnessed in the sky. True Circles are always strategically located over areas where underground water exists. Like mutilations, Crop Circles occur randomly around the world, usually following UFO sightings. The skill of incisions, located on mutilated animals, is as remarkable as the skill and precision necessary to produce certain Crop Circle formations. Both abilities are highly perfected.

Samuel Adams wrote about finding one of his cows dead after a host of strange circumstances in his book Cattle Mutilations—An Elusive Prey. Adams writes that when he found the carcass, there was an odor that had a sweet, but nauseating, sulfuric smell around it. The odor caused him to become queasy as he got closer to the cow's dead body. He documented that the unusual smell in no way resembled that of a decaying carcass. Documentation of sulfuric smell is a reoccurring marker in many paranormal activities. It is found in Crop Circles, attributed to those who are said to be possessed by Demons, as well as Alien Abductions of humans and UFO close encounters. In all these circumstances humans report feeling sick or strange.

There exist documented cases where priests conducting exorcisms have noted that the demonically possessed tend to give off a strong musky and sulfuric odor that caused those in the room to become queasy, according to the late Malachi Martin in his book, Hostage to the Devil.

Additionally, there are many cases involving Alien Abductions and UFO close encounters in which humans mention encountering strange sulfuric smells. Sulfur is a nonmetallic yellow chemical element that the Bible calls Brimstone. Brimstone has always been used as a punishment by God against the wicked. No wonder those who have left the scenes of mutilations, Crop Circles, demonic activity, and UFO close encounters all have a sulfuric odor about them. Sulfuric odors conveniently tie them all together in one demonic pile.

Cattle mutilations have been documented by United States law enforcement officers as having been reported in forty-nine states since 1963. It has become an international problem, which is being blamed on everything from Satan worshippers to occult groups to wild animals. There have been over ten thousand reported cases of livestock mutilations since 1967 in the United States alone. These cases all have similar manifestations. The body parts and tissues that were removed are essentially the same in most all the cases. Sex organs, along with one or both eyes and ears, were often times cored out. The tongues were cut very deep into the throats and removed. Large oval incisions appeared on the jaw where the hide was stripped to the bone. The entire rectums were cored out, along with the surrounding tissues and muscles. All orifices of the body, along with reproductive organs, were surgically removed using great precision while leaving no trace of blood. The hide of the animals had been cut, but the hairs were not disturbed, as if something cut from the inside out.

Of the recorded autopsies performed by veterinarians, they have noted that temperatures exceeding 300 degrees Fahrenheit seem to have been applied to the bodies of the mutilated animals. The incisions appear to have been made by an instrument that utilized a laser-like application when applied to the animal's skin. As it cut, it may have been necessary for it to cauterize to prevent bleeding, unless the blood had already been removed from the body. This unknown procedure remains a mystery.

The first documented cases of mutilation began in the 1960's. A couple of cases are somewhat sketchy before that time period. Most all of the first reported cases involved witnesses who had seen UFO's in the area above or near the later discovered mutilated animal. This identical scenario has continued to occur in additional cases documented around the world. No one has yet gained a complete understanding of the strange phenomenon.

There have been many theories that a secret agency is performing medical examinations without the public's awareness. This secret program could be to check animals for cancer, Mad Cow Disease, or any other disease that could be directly affecting mankind without our knowledge. These covert operations are suspected as being carried out to avoid causing mass panic.

If this is the case, the clandestine group could go to stockyard sales and purchase animals for study. They could go to slaughter houses and get parts to test, or grow their own cows in governmental facilities to be used for medical experiments. It makes no sense to steal a farmer's animal, kill it, remove some organs, and return it to the pasture where they found it. What is reason for returning the animal? This feature only makes the situation more suspicious. Why would an investigative agency risk being shot out of the sky by an angry farmer? Most cults just kill a chicken to use in their services and do not return it. The theory of wild animals and rats being the cause of animal mutilations is purely ridiculous.

Mutilation cases have remained a mystery for well over 60 documented years. They are increasing and include all types of animals. The mystery surrounding mutilations is a strange phenomenon that cannot and must not be overlooked by those searching for answers to UFOs, Aliens, Crop Circles, Oracle sites, Megalithic Monuments, Fairies, and Fallen Spiritual Beings. Any way you slice it, all of the above give off the same sulfuric smell!!!

"The Lord trieth the righteous: but the wicked and him that loveth violence his soul hateth. Upon the wicked he shall rain snares, fire and brimstone, and an horrible tempest: this shall be the portion of their cup." (Psalms 11:5–6).

Chapter Twenty-Nine
Crop Circles

Could it be that the same entities that abduct humans, mutilate animals, travel in UFOs, and demonically possess humans, also create Crop Circles? It is very possible. The first recorded Crop Circle on file appeared in 1687. Interestingly, that Circle was believed to have been an act of the Devil. Before that time, Crop Circles were known as Fairy Rings, which were believed to have been made by the Fairy Folk.

Since the 1687 formation, Crop Circles have occurred around the world in fields of wheat, grass, rice paddies, potatoes, vegetable gardens, sugar cane, sunflowers, on ice, in sand, and in the snow. These geometrically placed Circles all have neatly formed edges, while inside the formations the particular crop or earth is twisted in a flat style upon the ground. The Circles seem to be demonstrating some sacred form of energy and intelligence. Gerald Hawkins, well known scientist and author, linked Crop Circles with the ratios of the diatonic musical scale in a 1992 article published in Science News.[20]

The strange phenomenon of Circles appearing from out of nowhere has been going on for ages. Circle formations have been known to be very prevalent near Megalithic Structures like Stonehenge. Over the course of the last several years, researchers have come to identify the differences between hoaxed Circles and those that are made through some unknown energy force. The real Crop Circle seems to be formed from the sky, directly above the formation. Their formation uses a type of electrical energy that produces microwaves, wilting the base of the plants and causing them to fall over without breaking.

Within a hoaxed Circle, the stalks are broken and crushed. In true Crop Circles, an unknown form of microwave energy produces tiny explosion holes in the plant stems causing them to wilt. This type of formation could be achieved from the sky using a tightly focused microwave laser beam to produce such an effect on plant stems.

Crop Circle locations like those of Oracles and Templar Cathedrals also appear to be strategically placed at known sites where telluric energy sources and underground water are intersecting. Those involved in the formation of true Circles equally seek out earth energy lines. This choice in location may be based on the fact that earth ley lines move in harmony with the earth's tectonic plates and produce electromagnetic fields. All real Crop Circles are geometrically placed, perfectly, on these lines. Ley lines were termed 'Dragon Lines' by the Chinese centuries ago. When these 'Dragon Lines' cross each other, their energy spirals into a vortex. If several lines cross at a given point, called a node, it produces a massive vortex of energy. The Hartmann Grid, located at Avebury in England, is where 12 lines meet and go down into the Earth. This is a place where Megalithic Stone Structures were built in ancient times, and is where many Crop Circles appear today.

True Crop Circle formations originate from using a form of Sacred Harmonic Geometry and are architecturally intellectual in their designs. In other words, their designs are literally speaking and communicating theories of sacred geometry, music, astronomy, astrology, physics, and engineering, all at the same time. This harmonic phenomenon is highly sophisticated and has only recently been understood because of the advancements in computer technology. A Crop Circle is in no way a chaotic structure formed through some freak action of nature, as debunkers have claimed. Genuine Circles contain a form of sacred geometry that scientifically incorporates the vital numbers of 5, 6, 7, 8 and, more recently, 9 into their formations; meaning they are becoming more and more mathematically complex over time. It is as if the Circle Creators are trying to impart secret knowledge to mankind in order to advance our boundary of mathematical and geometrical comprehension.

Because of such a projection of knowledge from an unknown source that is occurring, the extensive lists of correlations that exist between Megalithic Structures, Oracle Sites, Templar Cathedrals, and Crop Circles cannot be ignored. Within all these features, a type of sacred and Hidden Mystery has been included in their construction. The knowledge of sacred geometry ties back to the lineage of Cain, who was the first born from the wicked seed of Satan. His lineage, because of their earthly bodies being fused/mixed with a spiritually Fallen Angel, gained knowledge of the elements to such a degree that they were able to originate advanced methods of architectural sciences in an attempt to increase mankind's enlightenment before the Flood.

This ongoing sinful relationship between mankind and Satan's Fallen Angels was why Jehovah sent the Flood. Satan and his cohorts were deceptively leading mankind astray in an attempt to make them believe they were gods themselves who did not need to worship the Creator. With this pagan ideology, Satan was condemning the majority of the human population to eternal death, and Jehovah wanted this to stop. Our generation is renewing Satan's secret knowledge by slowly fusing it in with the scientific discoveries of the present.

Within Crop Circle formations, a trained person can detect a force upon their body if standing in areas where the earth currents cross. From the sacred harmonic tune of the King's Chamber within the Great Pyramid, to the electrical sensations felt at Megalithic Structures with their alignments to Oracle sites, Crop Circles and Gothic Cathedrals equally possess the direct ability to affect the human body and enhance one's reception of Satan. Like the Megalithic Structures, Crop Circles produce strange sensations upon the human body. Some people report experiencing weakness, dizziness, nausea, electric static with their hair standing on end, racing heart beats, fainting, general body aches, hallucinations, time standing still, missing time, astral flight and the feeling of an unseen spiritual presence.

It is a scientific fact that the human body emits electrical energy. This energy appears to be interacting with the force inside the Crop Circle, just as the body does when one enters and stands at precise locations within Megalithic Structures. Certain geometrical designs of particular Crop formations have been known to invoke sickness upon all who enter within them.

At other times, formations of a different design seem to have a healing effect on everyone who enters in. Other strange phenomena that has been documented as occurring inside Circles includes batteries going dead, strange glowing objects appearing in photos, and compasses spinning out of control.

The most interesting finding about Crop Circles is that they have a profound effect on the pineal gland. This is the same gland connected to the Crown Chakra of the human body and its seven Kundalini sites. These seven sites match the earthly pilgrimage route of the Templar to the Oracles on which the Gothic Cathedrals were placed, and, in turn, mirror the seven planets, moon and sun that will be in perfect alignment to them on July 28, 2019. The Crown Chakra is where esoteric religions believe enlightenment is transmitted and stored.

Willfully opening the pineal gland ('Third Eye') allows enlightenment from the Serpent at the base of the spine to travel upward and to come forth. It is through this Kundalini ritual that the Serpent speaks to those who seek his illumination by willingly receiving his Dragon energy. One has the choice in life whether to allow their body and soul to receive the Serpent in exchange for his power of enlightenment. Choosing Satan over Jehovah allows the person to bask in the Serpent's Hidden Mysteries, but it will cost that person their eternity in Paradise with Jehovah. The penalty of everlasting punishment in Hell is what few think of when they are eager to receive Satan's rewards of earthly treasures here and now. Unfortunately, for their decision there will be an eternal payday.

Crop Circles have been scientifically proven to have a profound effect upon the human body. According to one research study, a 72-year-old woman and a 54-year-old man had their hormone levels measured by Ann Smithells of

Biotech Health, located in Petersfield, Hampshire. Their levels were measured using the 'Bioenergetics Stress Testing System' before they entered a designated Crop Circle located at Windmill Hill, in Hampshire. The two participants were tested at 12:00 noon. They then entered the formation at 2:30 p.m. and were retested at 4:30 p.m. after leaving the Circle. The tests showed a significant increase in both their melatonin levels, as well as increased thyroid hormones in the man.

Melatonin, remember, is the hormone produced by the pineal gland. The strange feelings and sensations reported by numerous visitors to Crop Circles could have come from similar changes in their body's hormonal levels. The pineal gland produces more melatonin if a person stays in darkness. The gland stops producing melatonin by shrinking when exposed to light. It appears, from the above research, that although it was daylight, the Crop Circle affected the human body as if it had been in a state of darkness.

There are some people who carry high levels of melatonin and they tend to have more psychic insight and knowledge than normal subjects. If melatonin is given at increased levels to the normal population, many people experience hallucinations, horrific nightmares, vivid dreams, and feelings of possession. These hormonal effects are the key reason Secret Societies and cults hold their rituals in darkness. They believe from this Darkness Comes Light (wisdom).

Additional research upon the plants flattened and weaved within Crop Circles has produced even more strange and unexplainable anomalies. It has been discovered that when plants removed from inside the formations are ingested in the diet of humans, their consumption produces strange sensations upon the body. These sensations include extreme nervousness, highly alert states, an inability to sleep, intense anxiety, rapid pounding heartbeat, stomach fluttering, loss of appetite, tingling sensations and, at times, disorientation.

People who suffer from known food allergies exhibit many of the same physical complaints as those who ingest plants from inside Crop Circles. What could have happened genetically to produce an allergic effect in a person who would normally be able to eat wheat without symptoms, and then suddenly become allergic to wheat inside Crop Circles? The problem resides in Genetically Manufactured (Modified) Organisms (GMO) that is being produced in laboratories around the world, as well as inside Crop Circles.

It was Starlink patented GMO Corn that inadvertently was used to make taco shells for a fast food chain that caused major sickness in the humans that consumed it. These allergic reactions by consumers might explain that when the genetic makeup of something edible is altered from its originally created state, it is not digestibly the same. Even worse, Monsanto owns 11,000 U.S. seed patents, and the majority of their modified plants will not produce seeds. These high-tech hybrids are called 'frankenseeds' because they are genetically bred to grow over huge areas of the country. This enables the patent holder to sell to a huge market while the original seeds in their possession, which were created by God, are allowed to become extinct.

On top of all this, the phenomena producing Crop Circles is also genetically altering our food chain. When crops are gathered in fields where Circles have appeared, the grain is harvested together with no regard that some were inside the formation. Because of this, people around the world have been consuming altered grain in a variety of products. If the body cannot digest these altered grains, then they will sicken the person or lodge in various organs, as they cannot be properly broken down. This potentially can cause diseases like cancer, simply because the liver's detoxification of the body is compromised through something it does not recognize. So far, the Food and Drug Administration has yet to investigate just what effect genetically-altered grain has on humans or any other living organism.

Crop Circle formations tend to resemble what some call a mandala. Mandalas are symbols used to induce meditative states. These particular Crop Circles are said to emit harmonic vibrations, which stimulate the brain into a relaxed and altered state of consciousness. The brain's reaction to these formations might be due to Extremely Low Frequency (ELF) waves being emitted from the Circle by what appears to resemble microwave radiation. These identical electromagnetic Extremely Low Frequency (ELF) waves are being developed by our government in the HAARP project as possible psychological warfare tactics. Tesla was the first to publicly reveal that these ELF waves have the capacity to control the human brain.

There have been documented cases where loss of time happened to a person while they were within a Circle. This same phenomenon reportedly occurs during Alien Abductions, where abductees complain that time elapsed that they could not account for. The similarities between the two must mean some unknown force has the capability to manipulate our time and space dimension. If that is true, then the unknown force has to be coming from another dimension above that which is perceivable by the human brain.

Another strange anomaly reported to occur inside formations is the uncontrollable oscillation of a compass. This is the same malfunction described by pilots who encounter strange compass readings when flying over the 'Devil's Triangle' in the Atlantic Ocean. Many researchers believe this same phenomenon, which produces wild oscillating of compasses and the failure of electronic devices, has caused planes and ships to become lost and perish at sea. These strange compass movements seem to be the result of a blast of alternating positive and negative energy.

A fluctuation in energy fields would cause a compass to behave irrationally and all electrical systems to fail. Because the human body is also electrical, the change in a force field could produce disorientation, which would further complicate matters. These same reactions hold true in regard to Crop Circles. When compasses behave in a strange manner within a Crop Circle, the people inside them report becoming disoriented as well.

There are several cases where animals demonstrated great fear near Crop formations and would not enter inside them. During observation of the animals, they began to develop a high level of agitation. Because of the fact that dogs can sense when a person is about to have a seizure, which is the result of a change in the electrical stimulation of the human brain, there exists a possibility that a dog could also sense the electrical activity going on inside the formation.

Animals will go to the edge of the Circle but will not enter in it. They will not go near a mutilated animal, eat the dead carcass, or graze on the spot after the dead animal has been removed. It is as if they can sense that something strange and out of the ordinary has occurred. In reports where animals were in the Circle as the Circle was forming, they are found to be completely flattened and/or dehydrated (mummified). For days, the dead animal within the Crop Design does not smell or decompose, just like those in the mutilated cases.

Many Crop Circles around the world are sometimes formed without being discovered unless accidentally spotted from an airplane. These formations require one to be looking down on the earth to see the designs that are not visible from the landscape. This is reminiscent of the Nazca Lines, located in Peru, which were only discovered after the invention of flight. Even the full beauty of a Crop Circle cannot be appreciated unless it is viewed from the air, just like the Nazca Lines

Crop Circle Researcher Nancy Talbott claims she actually witnessed a Circle being formed. The published account occurred on Monday, August 21, 2001, at 3:15 a.m. in Hoeven, Holland. Talbott stated that,

"About 3:15 a.m., a brilliant intense white column, or tube, of light—about 8 inches to a foot in diameter from my vantage point—flashed down from the sky to the ground, illuminating my bedroom and the sky as brilliantly as if from helicopter searchlights. My room was so bright I can't, in retrospect, understand how I could so very clearly see the "tube" of light outside—its' distinct edges—but I could for about a full second and there seemed to be a slight bluish tinge along the sides of the tube."21

Talbott, along with another witness at the house, went outside to where the beam had hit the ground, which was about 15 feet inside a bean field. There they discovered the newly formed Crop Circle. Both were convinced that the "power and precision of the light tubes" were deliberately placed there on purpose.

A powerful energy phenomena is present before Crop Circles appear, according to Eltjo Haselhoff, Ph.D. Dr. Haselhoff, a member of the Dutch Center for Crop Circle Studies, stated that,

"There is evidence that some sort of electromagnetic energy is directly involved with the creation of Crop Circles. This was scientifically confirmed by the peer reviewed scientific journal on plant physiology and biophysics, Physiologia Plantarum. This research confirmed that the plants inside a crop circle were affected by an electromagnetic force that created the circle. Plants and the seeds within the circle undergo biological modifications which change their chemical makeup."22

Electrically induced alterations in plants should be a major concern for consumers. The seeds from these altered plants have already entered the food chain and are more than likely causing unexplained physical illness in humans or animals that may be consuming them. Genetically and chemically altered food, such as modified food starch, etc. are increasing daily in edible products around the world and have not been thoroughly tested. These modified foods may be producing a slew of stomach ailments to unbeknownst consumers. Next time you are in any drugstore, notice the vast array of stomach medications and how fast some of them seem to sell out.

The issues of safety surrounding the digestibility of altered foods and supplements are worth thinking about the next time you eat something that does not agree with your stomach. If you find yourself traveling from doctor to doctor with each of them seemingly to fail miserably at being unable to confirm why you are sick, then you may want to check out what you are eating. Most doctors choose the option to prescribe gastrointestinal pills that have a whole host of side effects, while never discovering the root of the problem as to why your body got really sick in the first place. The majority of pills just mask the symptoms, as you continue to eat and get sicker.

What the consumer needs to understand here is that all modified foods are potential dangers lurking within the food chain. Modified corn starch and modified wheat starch, which are increasing as ingredients in a host of foods on grocery store shelves, are genetically modified foods that have proteins from other organisms spliced into them. Check your food labels if you are experiencing digestive difficulties. You will be surprised how, right under your nose, the foods you have grown to love and trust have been changed and that there is not any good ole' corn syrup being used in the majority of processed products any more. What is worse is the fact that nobody warned you of the dangers.

With the advancements in the science of biogenetics, scientists are in heavy pursuit to be the first to combine genes from different sources and produce a better product.

These improvements include, among other things, tomatoes with added frog genes so tomatoes can grow in the snow. The frog gene keeps the tomato from freezing. Or take the grape tomato, which combines both a fruit and vegetable species into a tiny, sweet, grape-tasting tomato. Genetically modified combinations are endless, but like the Crop Circle's altered seeds and plants, there may be a physical price to pay if one is allergic or if the human body is unable to digest these mutations.

The world at large is witnessing the creative explosion of the ancient science of Alchemy and its transmutation upon the genes of all biological entities. What this means is that with our understanding and mapping of genetic blueprints, any living thing can now be altered or mixed. Today, the science of biogenetics is boldly attempting to redefine and perfect Eden without the slightest knowledge of the outcome. Combinations of human genes with pigs, cows, rats, monkeys, etc., are well underway. No one has the power to foresee what the consequences of these combinations will be in the long run. It appears our ancestors in Babylon and Egypt knew how to mix as their gods had animal heads with human bodies and human heads on animal bodies that can be seen in their paintings and sculptures. Apparently, we are just now acquiring the capability of mixing, which our ancestors perfected a long time ago using the Sacred Sciences.

The 'mammon' driven concept of big business is: "Be the first to produce or sell it and then let someone else worry about the consequences later." Regardless of the potential for disaster, the march is on and moving at a fast pace toward attempting to perfect mankind, along with the environment. If you saw the movie The Island of Dr.

Moreau, you may have thought the plot of all his evil genetic mixing between plants and animals was scientifically impossible—just look out. The days of designer jeans are quickly being replaced by designer babies, designer tomatoes, designer pets, and one day, a possible redesigned you. Satan's secret knowledge is reaching its pinnacle by enabling mankind to believe he has the power to create the perfect world. The Time is close at Hand!

Further investigation regarding altered seeds collected from within Crop Circles was reviewed in Dr. Eltjo Haselhoff's book entitled, The Deeping Complexity of Crop Circles—Scientific Research and Urban Legends. Dr. Haselhoff explained in his research that rats will not eat the seeds harvested from Crop Circles. When presented with a Crop Circle seed and a control seed, the rats always, 100% of the time, chose the control/normal seed. Haselhoff also related that bread made from the seeds of a Crop Circle plant will give human subjects a very bad aftertaste following its consumption. He also discovered:

"When Crop Circle Wheat Seeds were planted along with control wheat seeds, rabbits in these fields ate the sprouts from the control wheat, but would not touch the Crop Circle Wheat."[23]

From Haselhoff's studies, animals seem to be more aware than humans about the seriousness of ingesting the altered seeds of Satan. Mankind should take note from our furry friends that something very bad is going awry with the food chain, right under our noses. Animals are no doubt more sensitive to the deceitful manipulation of the elements by satanic forces than humans are. We definitely do not have the keen sense needed to tell the difference between what is safe and what is rotten until we eat of the poisonous fruit. Then, it may be too late.

Through temptations, mankind becomes a victim to the sins of Satan. Humanity has yet to learn that the desires of the flesh are the evil seeds that grow within to bring forth eternal death and destruction. Satan's main objective has always been to destroy mankind's heart, soul, mind, and body. It is the greatest ongoing war of all time—that between flesh and spirit.

As we have already learned, Crop Circles have been witnessed and recorded for a very long period of time. In this generation alone, there have been over 10,000 Circles reported in a total of 26 countries. The majority of these Circles occurred in Southern England near the ancient Megalithic Structures. The Circles are formed as a result of the sacred knowledge of geometry, harmonics, and vibration. Author George Leonard (1978) in his book, The Silent Pulse, stated,

"Every Particle in the physical universe takes its characteristics from the pitch and patterns and overtones of its particular frequencies–it is singing."

All true Crop Circles seem to incorporate these same geometric harmonic patterns into their designs. Dr. Linda G. Corley of Houma, Louisiana, interviewed the late Lt. Col. Jesse A. Marcel in 1981 regarding the debris he handled from the 1947 crash of a UFO near Roswell, New Mexico. Marcel described symbols on a beam found at the crash site. Dr. Corley took those symbols and compared them to hieroglyphs recorded on The Rosetta Stone, as well as symbols found in Ancient Egypt, Greece, and Rome. She translated her findings from those ancient sources using Latin. According to Dr. Corley, the beam Marcel saw at the UFO crash site said something like the following:

"To go sail, fly, move—from a point in time or carry away from some place—toward first the point or goal at which anything arrives—to be, exist, live, take place, happen, and occur—the mouth singing."24

The musical scale, with a perfect harmonic pitch, is a hidden mystery of sacred geometry. That is why music has always been referred to as the 'universal language.' It is this sacred language, in its purest form that produces the harmonics and vibrations felt within the Megalithic Structures, Oracle Sites, Gothic Cathedrals, Tesla Technology, Alien Abductions, UFO Encounters, and Crop Circles. Each of these anomalies generates some form of electromagnetism, ultra sound waves, strange humming and trilling noises, as well as interference with electrical equipment. Each one is also capable of producing an altered state of consciousness through direct stimulation of the pineal gland. They are the tools of Satan's 'Craft.'

Crop Circles offer a world of scientific knowledge; therefore, top members of governments around the world are very interested in these formations. These governmental agencies attempt to pretend to the general public that they are not concerned with Circle anomalies, all the while discreetly doing undercover investigations. This became evident when it was released that the government helped in financing the 2002 film Signs, which featured veteran actor Mel Gibson. The government did this while openly preaching to the general public that Crop Circles are a hoax and not worth the government's time and money to investigate. Was and is Mel Gibson a puppet to the Illuminati's Plan to indoctrinate the masses with certain esoteric information in order to slowly raise the veil from our eyes?

Mel Gibson, months after Signs was released as a huge Box Office smash, undertook a project that he says he paid for out of his own pocket. Claiming to be a devout Roman Catholic, Gibson produced the controversial movie, The Passion of the Christ. His particular rendition of the Last Days of Jesus on Earth is different in some very important aspects from what the Holy Bible portrays about them through the Gospels. Gibson used visions from mystic Roman Catholic nuns, Anne Catherine Emmerich (Germany) and Mary of Agreda, to 'mix' with the Christian version in order to make his movie. Emmerich's work, The Dolorous Passion of Our Lord and Savior Jesus Christ, claims that "Jesus quivered and writhed like a worm as he was being beaten." Mary of Agreda, in her writings, said she could leave her body and teach people in foreign lands. Yet Gibson used their visions to make his movie because, according to The New Yorker, (9/15/03), he said, "They supplied me with stuff I never would have thought of."

There are a lot of things in the movie that no one would have thought of unless they were members of mystical societies—'those with eyes to see.' For example, Gibson depicts Satan tempting Jesus and moving freely through the crowds as a Black Madonna who has the features of a male and female combined—a hermaphrodite. The face of Satan in the movie resembles, to an uncanny degree, the hermaphrodite painting of Leonardo da Vinci's Mona Lisa, which he painted to symbolize the Masonic principle of successful alchemic mixing of opposites known as the 'The Great Work.' On top of this, Gibson shows Satan carrying a grotesque looking child in his arms that looks like 'a little old man child.' This symbolization is a direct reflection of the Black Madonna (Isis) carrying her son Horus, who was Cloned from his father Osiris. Gibson is revealing that something very old, which has existed through the ages, will be reborn in a child's body. Was this scene informing 'those with eyes to see' that the child is really the Devil, who will be re-born from Jesus' blood, like the Templar who revealed in their Grail Legend that King Arthur, 'the once and future king,' would live again in the flesh? This correlation to the Holy Grail legends might be why Mel Gibson wears a Templar Cross around his neck. (See Book Page, April 2004, for his photo wearing two Templar crosses.)

In the movie, Gibson has Satan carrying this 'old man child' through the scenes where Jesus' blood is splattering. If you slow the frames down in various parts of the movie, you will see blood splattered between frames as if sending a blood subliminal message. If your eyes are fast enough you can actually see the splattered blood happen while the scenes are moving at normal speed. Was Gibson sprinkling viewers with blood or subliminally sending your brain a hidden message about Jesus' blood?

Gibson's movie also claims that Mary Magdalene was a prostitute. The Gospels of the Holy Bible teach that Jesus cast seven devils from her. Never do they mention her as the prostitute that Jesus defended against the Pharisees when he drew a line with his finger in the sand, as the movie portrays. Was Gibson trying to send a message that if Magdalene was a prostitute that she would have had sexual relations with Jesus, too? The Knights Templar believed that she and Jesus had children, and to this day that lineage is referred to as the Holy Royal Merovingian bloodline.

In the movie, Jesus was played by Jim Caviezel. According to Mel Gibson, he was chosen not only because he, too, is Roman Catholic, but because his particular facial features assisted Gibson in attempting to recreate the face depicted on the Holy Shroud of Turin. Walking around in such a holy image may be why Caviezel was struck by lightning three times. Especially since he was parading around in the image of Jesus and mocking him, like in the following blooper scenes that were cut from the movie. These cut scenes were gathered for The Morning News on March 2, 2004, by Interloper Paul Ford, and appeared in print under the headline, The Passion of the Christ: Blooper Reel.

"Jesus hangs on the cross, bloodied, in agony.

Take 3
Jesus: My God, my God, why hast thou—
[laughing]
Off Camera: [laughter] Forsaken!

Take 4
Jesus: Thanks! Okay. My God, my God, why hast thou—[starts giggling]
Off Camera: [laughter]

Take 10
Jesus: I got it. I got it. Hold on. My God, my God, why hast thou—argh!
[takes breath] Forsaken. Forsaken. Forsaken. Forsaken.

Sabachthani, sabachthani, sabachthani, Okay.

Take 12
Jesus: Hey! I can see my house from here.

Take 14

Jesus: My God! Why have you— [Caviezel is struck by lightning.] Off Camera: Cut"!

Not respecting the image of Jesus is an abomination! If all that is not enough to open your eyes, notice at the very beginning of the movie that it is produced by I Con, whose trademark is an 'All Seeing Eye'. (Also see Gibson's profile on the front cover of Book Page, April 2004, as he imitates that same trademark showing his profile and only one of his eyes).

The so-called anti-Semitic rouse that occurred over the movie's release may have been a planned controversy. Though it seemed to point fingers, in reality, what really happened was that the opposition, the Khazar Jews, got airtime to justify that their ancestors—the Pharisees, Sadducees, Scribes and Essenes—did not crucify Jesus. Was the movie really propaganda strategically used as a dialogue to make Christians more sympathetic to the Jews and blame the Romans entirely for what really happened to Jesus? Modern Jews, as we have already discovered, are actively seeking unity with the Roman Catholic Church by declaring that Jesus was a divine prophet. Did Gibson indirectly assist in this unification of Jew and Catholic? Remember that Gibson was used in similar propaganda financed by the government in the so-called science fiction movie Signs. It also mixed a little truth of the real and ongoing phenomena of Crop Circles in with the esoteric, just like The Passion of the Christ did in order to spark dialogue and change.

The above form of covert operation used against an unsuspecting public is an example of what we have already discovered is known as 'Double Speak,' which is used extensively by the Illuminati. This elusive manner of communication is intentionally designed to give the ignorant public a false impression of one thing, while those initiated into the Hidden Mysteries know it secretly means the opposite of what is being played out in the open. Secret Societies use 'Double Speak' as a code, so that only those initiated will understand their true message. Wherever newly formed Circles are discovered, the military is busily checking them out. In some cases, the military has even threatened the public to stay away from a particular formation by sealing off the area. It is those particular Circles that offer an enormous amount of sacred communication through their unique designs that the government is most interested in. Apparently, there is fear within the top ranks of the Illuminati that their sacred information will get into the wrong hands, and that someone will expose the true nature about what is really going on.

Various researchers have speculated that an international group above the heads of all national governments is behind the feeding of disinformation to the general public regarding various anomalies. The Trilateral Commission is just one example of that type of group. The Commission is a secret group of elite financiers that was formed by David Rockefeller. David is the grandson of the late John David Rockefeller, Sr., who helped J.P. Morgan break Nikola Tesla. It was Laurance Rockefeller, also a descendent of

John David Rockefeller, Sr., who funded the Crop Circle studies that announced the possible discovery of a new form of energy. This energy is more than likely that which was harnessed by Tesla in the late 1800's. There is speculation that this energy has been secretly used in underground operations by the elite Brotherhood since that time. Apparently, the time has finally come to slowly begin its introduction to the world.

A joint effort between countries regarding UFO investigations has been going on for some time. The Canadians, Americans, and Russians were all concerned about UFOs, according to the Top Secret memo, "Project Magnet," written in 1952 by Wilbert Smith, Senior Radio Engineer in the Canadian Department of Transport. Smith's work was recovered from the archives at the University of Ottawa by researcher Nick Balaskas. These files show that UFOs are the highest classified subject within the U.S. government. The reports state emphatically that UFOs exist, but that the government does not know what they are.

There is a suggestion that those investigating the phenomenon believe UFOs involve the use of electromagnetic radiation, magnetic domain resonance, and magnetic wave motion. The draft even implies that these aspects of magnetism are a possible key to a new type of energy. This same magnetic energy has been used in the formation of Crop Circles, thereby providing a link between UFOs and Crop Circle formations. It is also the new energy that Laurence Rockefeller proclaims was recently discovered, when in reality, it is what Nikola Tesla had harnessed back in the late 1800's.

Another highly classified report demonstrating the United States Government's interest in UFOs was the Project Grudge Report. This report regarding UFO investigations was prepared by the U.S. Air Force during August of 1949, two years after the UFO Crash at Roswell, New Mexico. Project Grudge was a Top Secret Technical Report (NO 102-AC49/15–100) that was put together by Air Material Command Headquarters located at Wright-Patterson Air Force Base in Dayton, Ohio. The report was declassified on July 23, 1997. The most disturbing aspect of the entire report was that our own U.S. Air Force had recommended using the mystery of unsolved UFOs as a means to induce psychological warfare upon an unsuspecting public.

Are the geometric designs of Crop Circles delivering intelligent information to those schooled in the sacred arts? Over the last ten years, the Circles have increased in their architectural complexity. The Circles have been delivering coded messages in respect, some say, to DNA Strands, Cell Division/Fission, Chakra Points of the Kabala, Ptolemy's Theory of Musical Chords, Grids of the Earth, Seal of Solomon, Pentagrams, Celtic Crosses, Celtic Beltane Wheels, Planet locations within the Solar System, Sun, Serpents, Ouroboros (the Dragon swallowing its own tail symbolizing regeneration/fission), the Buddhist Wheel of Dharma, Nine-Fold Sacred Geometry and many more New Age Symbols. Over time there has also been a noted shift from 3rd-Dimensional to 4th-Dimensional space designs of the Crop Circles.

With each passing year, Crop Circles are becoming more complex, and are now incorporating the 'Natural Law of Nine-Fold Geometry.' The achievement of a Nine-Fold Geometrical design constructed within the 4thDimensional plane connects Circle formations to the old Hermetic Principle of 'As Above, So Below.' The only difference, in this new Hermetic Principle from that of the old principle is that in 4th-Dimensional, the design above the ground is reflected in the identical design below the ground. Imagine a ball buried half way in the ground—half above and a matching half below. This concept means that the Crop Circle makers are using the same principles of sacred knowledge as that of the ancient Egyptians, who acquired it from Hermes, 'messenger of the gods.' This highly advanced sacred principle continues to be manifested in Crop Circles—'As Before, So Today.'

The ever-increasing Crop Circle Phenomenon involves much mystery. The non-hoaxed Circles are strategically located on aquifers, near wells and ponds, as well as on top of underground streams. These placements are unique in that all water has properties that can be magnetized to create a low electromagnetic field. The potential to turn the location into a natural conductor of electrical energy is then possible. This form of energy is exactly what Nikola Tesla proclaimed could be freely harnessed back in the early 1900's. The ground inside the Crop Circle is magnetized easily using the iron in the soil.

Little balls of iron have been discovered inside Crop Circles, as well as at mutilated animal sites. Implanted objects removed surgically by the late Dr. Roger Leir from humans claiming Alien Abductions also have magnetic properties. Darrel Sims, who once worked with Leir on implant analysis, discovered that the implants were highly magnetic and in the shape of shiny balls with an irregular surface so that tissue would adhere to them. These strange and unusual similarities seem to tie the makers of Crop Circles to animal mutilation sites and Alien implants.

Magnetized Circles cause compasses to spin out of control, drain batteries, and manifest white spots called Orbs in developed film taken inside the Circle. These particular Circles also cause engines to die in planes flying over the formations, produce a slowing of time, and generate an altered state of consciousness. Crop Circle manifestations are therefore uniquely similar to the same phenomena that is recorded in UFO encounters, animal mutilations, and incidents occurring in the Bermuda Triangle (Devil's Triangle).

Many Crop Circles appear to be produced by an unseen force through the use of a beam or magnetic sphere that incorporates an electromagnetic frequency near the microwave level. It is a scientific fact that if an object vibrates at 2 Hertz below the frequency of the human eye, the eye cannot detect it. If it is detected, the object will appear as an apparition. This might account for how Crop Circles are formed in daylight and are not detected until after the formation appears in its completed stage. Some of the largest and most extravagant Crop Circles have appeared near areas where large groups of people were gathered during daylight hours. No one noticed anything unusual at these sites until someone saw the completed Circle.

Circle formations appearing at night have included reports of strange lights in that area before the designs were discovered. These balls and beams of light could be the heat waves from the electromagnetic energy being used to form the Circles. These beams seem to come from above and are many times associated with a UFO being sighted.

Researchers have come to the conclusion, in most cases, that the Circles are speaking or singing to mankind through the energy source that produces the formations. According to author J.J. Hurtak, in his work The Keys of Enoch, he states that light would one day be understood as a language. Hurtak believed that Enoch's teachings revealed that highly intelligent symbols would one day be used by the 'Light Beings' to change mankind from their present spiritual development into that of another. These 'Light Beings,' Hurtak wrote, would give mankind a new science that would explain the nature of the universe right before the end of time. These keys of knowledge, according to his interpretation of Enoch's teachings, would have the power to open the minds (pineal glands) of all humanity so everyone at a given moment could connect to the light that explains the 'Nature of All Things.' Circle formations are, indeed, symbols of the light of Lucifer. Enoch taught that the light of Lucifer would appear near the 'End of Time.' This generation is witnessing the manifestation of Enoch's prophecy.

When the pineal gland is stimulated, the human body immediately undergoes changes at the hormonal level, and mind manipulation can quickly occur. If the masses ever lose biological control over their pineal glands by an unseen force, the keys of Satan's light, with its unprecedented knowledge toward evil, will immediately be manifested within them. Unfortunately, when mankind loses the power to choose, their souls are snatched into eternal Hell by the Light Bearer—Lucifer. If a person is not caught up in the 'Rapture of the Church' and are left behind to endure God's

Great Wrath with the Antichrist, they will be subconsciously moved to receive the 'Mark of the Beast.' When this happens, their soul will never see Paradise in Heaven.

This scenario may explain why The Book of Revelation records that the 144,000 saved on Earth during the Tribulation period, who had previously not heard of Jesus, will be sealed in their foreheads so that Satan cannot gain control of their pineal glands before they have heard the truth. If you have heard of Jesus before the Tribulation, this seal will not be available to you, as you had the ability to choose before Satan manipulated the elements to take that choice away from you. Make your choice to serve Jesus now, while you still have the chance. Doing so assures you a place at the 'Rapture' with the 'Saints of God,' thereby totally allowing you to avoid Satan's Trap during God's Great Wrath on Earth.

The Circle makers do not like hoaxers who are attempting to emulate and copy their work. In 1991, symbols written in some unknown language were formed on Milk Hill, in England, expressing the Circle designers' displeasure with hoaxers. The language used to communicate their message was researched and discovered to be post-Augustan Latin. Augustan Latin was what the Knights Templar used as their alphabet for communicating secret codes to members of the Order. A team of scholars translated the words, using the Templar codes, as meaning, "I Oppose Acts of Craft and Cunning." Augustan Latin is an interesting link between Crop Circles and the Knights Templar.

Like the Circle Makers, the Templar used sacred geometry as a key to manipulate the elements through Alchemy and gain greater understanding of nature and the universe. The Templar believed, like the Megalithic Builders, that through this geometric harmony the knowledge of heaven could be attained on earth. Acquiring heavenly powers would then allow the unraveling of the mystical and hidden chemical makeup of the body.

Our generation has unraveled the blueprint of human DNA. Biogenetic labs are working diligently to determine what changes to the DNA might result in the eradication of sickness and disease, as well as the body's ability to regenerate itself. With little regard to the understanding of the soul, the biogenetic science of Cloning, with its perceived perfection of the human race, is being planned as the new wave of the future. DNA is a form of digital coding. Harnessing the understanding of this code offers unlimited potential to improving the body's biological processes. In essence, biogenetics seeks to rewrite the language of God in a vain attempt to produce a perfected human body.

The search for the Holy Grail is almost over. Buried in the DNA code is the origin of life and the future of cellular immortality. The human DNA is a barcode, and everything biologically about an individual has a designated place on that code. Unfortunately, there has been no gene found, so far, for the human spirit, the soul. The quest to be the first to redesign the body seems to be the only goal. That may be okay if the body never dies, but if one thinks they can Clone themselves or be raised from the dead through Cloning, then the issue of the soul becomes a major complication.

We are, no doubt, the generation that will attempt to use Satan's counterfeit keys to manipulate nature. His keys of enlightenment over the elements to obtain immortality of the body are the same quest Gilgamesh sought after the Flood, as has every Secret Society throughout history. Crop Circles are the communication tools being used to inspire humanity to seek more and more of the keys to secure mass enlightenment, which Enoch spoke of.

Researchers have discovered that our solar system is harmonically set at more than 40 octaves. Forty octaves is the gap of frequency between what is sound and what becomes light. A beam of light can be sent at a frequency that humans cannot hear. This ultrasonic frequency of light can also be directed like a laser beam. The laser beam has the ability to produce a heating effect that is capable of dehydrating whatever it touches. This dehydrating process might offer an additional explanation as to the wilting effect that occurs in plants found inside Crop Circles. Dehydration may also be what causes those who report Alien Abductions to be experiencing electrolyte imbalances within their bodies. According to the late Dr. Roger Leir (see MUFON UFO Journal 415 Nov. 2002: pg.6) in his article entitled, Implant anomalies continue, two of the persons he removed Alien implants from had some unusual characteristics not seen before. Dr. Leir noted:

"It seemed that each of them had been subjected to a large and intense amount of ultraviolet light in the areas where the objects were located. Based on the lifestyle of the individuals, there seemed to be no explanation for this."

Proof that beams of light have the ability to carry information has been documented. Recently, researchers at the University of Southampton's Optoelectronics Research Centre in the U.K. that were led by Jingyu Zhang, actually recorded a 300KB digital text file onto nanostructured quartz glass in 5D using an ultrafast intense pulse laser called a femtolaser. These encoded crystals have an unlimited lifetime and are virtually indestructible. It was back on February 15, 2002, when the issue of Advanced Materials, declared that researchers at the University of Toronto had found a way to "nudge" nature into making photonic crystals. Photonic crystals allow researchers to control the flow of light. According to Professor Ted Sargent,

"Light can carry much more information than electronic switches and internet routers. The photonic integrated circuit is the holy grail of the optical communications industry."

Sargent goes on to explain, in the article, that the process is similar to a conductor of an orchestra who does not play the instruments, but is the driving force behind the rhythm and their particular placement within the music. From this advancement in optics, one can only imagine the amount of communication that is capable of being directed through light. Crop Circle designers appear to be using light to produce geometric symbols as their mode of communication with mankind. The problem with all this is not their high-tech style of communication, but what the Circle Makers are saying.

Isabelle Kingston, a spiritual Channeler, says the architects of Crop Circles are the 'Watchers' (Silva 2002). The 'Watchers,' remember, are the Biblical Fallen Angels and Satan. Kingston interprets the communications hidden in Circles as a plan the 'Watchers' are using to change mankind's consciousness into accepting a New World

Order. The plan, she relates, promotes Britain as its center, where a Prince will arise and offer mankind transition from the old order to a New Order. She contends that Crop Circles are coded with keys to entice all of humanity into accepting the 'Watchers' coming Prince and his New World Order of enlightenment.

These 'Watchers,' according to Kingston, have told her that a new energy will be discovered and made available to the world. The entities have informed her about a grid system that will be set up where the antennas of mankind will be tuned into being of one accord. It would appear from their communication with Kingston that mankind's pineal glands will be forced open through the use of this new form of energy that will possess the capability to render humanity totally receptive without a fight.

This is reminiscent of Tesla's Technology and Nanotechnology, in which our bodies are rendered unable to fight against what our brains are being programmed from a distance to do. It simply means that we will be biologically stripped of our ability to choose. At that point, the brain, unless sealed by God, will be automatically tuned to accept the Prince—Satan incarnate—as Messiah.

The manipulation of our minds and the re-patterning of our DNA will assist in overriding the body's ability to choose between God and Satan. Up until this point in our history of existence, mankind has been governed by the 'Law of Choice.' This 'Law of Choice' was allowed by our Creator even after Adam and Eve had eaten of the Tree of Knowledge. In the beginning, Adam and Eve did not know evil. The Serpent tempted Eve and she became the victim to

Satan's evil agenda. He told her that by eating with him she would be likening unto God, knowing good and evil.

Satan's Plan is evolving. In this generation, the finalé to his plan is to manipulate our freedom of choice so mankind chooses evil all the time because he cannot distinguish between right and wrong. Doing your own selfish thing, as long as you are tolerant of others, is quickly becoming the accepted way of the world. The Bible warns about Satan's tactics and mankind's failure to acknowledge good where Scripture warns,

"Woe unto them that call evil good, and good evil; that put darkness for light, and light for darkness; that put bitter for sweet, and sweet for bitter! Woe unto them that are wise in their own eyes, and prudent in their own sight!" (Isaiah 5:20–21).

The Devil and his Demons are preparing the world to accept 'good as evil and evil as good' through deception and manipulation of the mind. This is the reason why the so-called Aliens have not landed for a complete takeover of the world yet. They know that as long as mankind has the ability to choose, they cannot totally control the masses. If a person chooses to cry out to Jesus during an Alien Abduction, the abduction permanently stops. It is only when the capability to choose is restrained that mankind, as a whole, could potentially fall into complete demonic possession.

With advances in sciences and energy technology, Satan's Plan of mind control is only steps away from implementation. God knew that when this time came that mankind would be vulnerable and could not fight back if we lost the biological ability to choose. The loss of free will at the 'End of the Age' is why the Bible declares,

"And except those days should be shortened, there should no flesh be saved: but for the elect's sake those days shall be shortened." (Matthew 24:22).

Each day the world is moving closer to the prophesied time when the human mind will not have the capacity to distinguish truth. Our flesh will fail us. As a Christian, it is imperative that you protect your pineal gland from all forms of possible stimulation. That means never voluntarily participating in meditation, which promotes a vibratory harmonic hum like using the word, "OM." Stay away from Transcendental Meditation and Astral Flight, as well as any occult therapies that promote relaxation by encouraging you to open up to the light.

Do not participate in repetitious chanting or singing of verses over and over, even though they may appear religious in nature. Do not attempt to channel spirits from the dead or use Tarot cards. Avoid Yoga or any activity that coils the body into a cobra position. The cobra position allows greater access to your pineal gland to be easily stimulated. Do not play with White and Black Magic or any 'Craft' of the occult world. I promise that if you do, in the end you will get burned forever.

Demonic possession is no laughing matter. Do not assume it is all a bunch of fairy tales. Fairy tales, as we have already discovered, may, in fact, be true. Do not let Satan's temptations get the best of you. It is vital to put God first and foremost in your life, just like the First Commandment says, so that in the end you will be shielded from Satan's control. The promise of the 'Rapture of the Church' will be the one and only event that will save Christians right before the 'End of the Age' from Satan's final grip to control their mind. To miss the Rapture means you have been left behind with no bodily defense against the powers of Satan. That will be the ultimate nightmare! Without a way to protect your pineal gland, you are toast.

Crop Circles are a manifestation of geometrically encoded intelligent designs being sent from the heavens. The Bible mentions that there will be more and more signs in the heavens as prophesied to occur at the 'End of the Age.' Could Crop Circles, in actuality, be some form of these prophetic signs? As Crop Circles continue, they seem to be deceptively offering more and more knowledge toward the advancement of geometrical science, as if teaching the observers. It is important to be aware that Satan and his wicked seed might be the culprits behind these Circles, as they are busily working their 'Craft' in order to get a grip on the souls of mankind. Do not turn a blind eye; instead, open your eyes and see the evil plan going on in broad daylight for what it is. Warn your family and friends about these deceptive and innovative scientific tactics of Satan. Explain to those you love how the Devil's plan is to deceptively steal mankind's souls from an eternity with Jehovah God, the one and only true Father and Creator.

Part 6
Satan in the Flesh- The False Messiah

Chapter Thirty
"666-Is it Possible?"

Rabbi Goren, who at one time served as chief Rabbi of Israel's Defense Forces, professed to the world that he knew the location of the lost Ark of the Covenant. In November 1981, Rabbi Goren told Newsweek in an interview the following:

"The secret of the location of the Ark will be revealed just prior to the building of the Third Temple."

The Ark of the Covenant and its contents have eluded historians. The search for the famous Ark has sent many archeologists in circles over the years, in a vain attempt to locate it.

The Ark and the items it contained are but some of the relics that were believed to have come into the hands of the Knights Templar as part of the treasure they stole from the destroyed Temple during the Crusades. These Temple treasures are secretly reported to be buried in an old Enochian Chamber under the original Temple site, which was first constructed by the Megalithic Builders in ancient times before the Flood.

These antediluvian chambers, according to legend, are Arch Vaulted rooms hewn from stone deep within the earth. Their locations are secret to only a chosen few who have been selected to guard the treasures that are stored there. Interestingly enough, this same arch technology, which was used by the Megalithic Builders to build the vaulted rooms, exists today in masonry.

The true meaning behind Arch chambers is secretly celebrated within the Arch Degree of Freemasonry. Third Degree Master Masons must be 'exalted' to the Holy Royal Arch Degree, which is an extension to their degree that represents the completion of the 'ordeal.' Only about one-fifth of Master Masons become exalted. It is with the attainment of the Arch Degree that one is taught the 'ineffable name' of the Masonic God known to Masons around the world as 'The Great Architect of the Universe' (TGAOTU). The Name is revealed as Jahbulon. Each syllable of the name, which uniquely forms a trinity, stands for 3 different gods: JAH (Jahovah/Yaweh, the God of the Hebrews), BUL (Baal, the Canaanite God considered to be the devil), and ON (Osiris, The Egyptian God of the Dead).

This name of God, which is worshipped by Masonry, is a counterfeit of the 'True Nature' of the Christian Trinity, which consists of God, the Father; Jesus, the Son; and the Holy Spirit. Worshipping, as well as giving praise and oaths to Jahbulon, are in direct violation of the Biblical Commandment of Exodus 20:3, which cannot be stated enough,

"Thou shalt have no other gods before me."

If the Ark of the Covenant is being housed within the Enochian Chambers, then it is not under the control of Christians, but men who worship Jahbulon. So how did these men get possession of the Ark? Over the course of history, there have been many proposed scenarios as to what actually happened to the Ark of the Covenant. It is mentioned in II Chronicles 8:11, where King Solomon states that his wife, who was the Pharaoh's daughter, could not enter into areas where the Ark had been.

"And Solomon brought up the daughter of Pharaoh out of the city of David unto the house that he had built for her: for he said, My wife shall not dwell in the house of David king of Israel, because the places are holy, whereunto the ark of the Lord hath come."

The daughter of Pharaoh was a mixed seed of Satan who did not believe in Jehovah, and Solomon knew this. He could not leave well enough alone like he had been instructed by God and his father, King David. Solomon's disobedience in choosing to worship other gods caused Jehovah to leave the Temple. At this point, there is some belief that the Ark was taken to Heaven in order to keep it out of the hands of the wicked, while others believe since it was only a replica of what was in Heaven, that it is still secretly hidden on Earth.

John, the Revelator, records that during his vision of Heaven he saw the Ark:

"And the temple of God was opened in heaven, and there was seen in his temple the ark of his testament: and there were lightnings, and voices, and thunderings, and an earthquake, and great hail." (Revelation 11:19).

There remains a question as to whether John's vision was of the Heavenly Ark or the one that God instructed Moses to build during the Exodus of the Hebrew Children from Egypt. Either way, the Ark will be seen again at the End of the Ages.

Reference to the Ark of the Covenant that was built during the days of Moses is mentioned years after the death of Solomon. Scripture records,

"And [Josiah] said unto the Levites that taught all Israel, which were holy unto the Lord, Put the holy ark in the house which Solomon the son of David King of Israel did build; it shall not be a burden upon your shoulders: serve now the Lord your God, and his people Israel." (II Chronicles 35:3).

Jeremiah the Prophet was in Jerusalem during the reign of Josiah. He also foretold and witnessed the destruction of the Temple where the Ark was housed. It is not surprising to find that the final mention of the earthly Ark in Scripture is by Jeremiah, when he stated,

"And it shall come to pass, when ye be multiplied and increased in the land, in those days, saith the Lord, they shall say no more, The ark of the covenant of the Lord: neither shall it come to mind: neither shall they remember it; neither shall they visit it; neither shall that be done any more." (Jeremiah 3:16).

Later, in the Book of Ezekiel, Jeremiah gives instructions about the Temple, but never mentions the Ark again. When the Temple was destroyed, Scripture does not list the Ark as an item that was carried off to another country. Some Jewish legends suggest that Jeremiah took the Ark before the Babylonians destroyed the Temple and hid it in a cave in Mount Pisgah, Jordan.

The late archeologist Ron Wyatt believed Jeremiah hid the Ark in Jeremiah's Grotto near Mt. Moriah, which is also called Golgotha. Wyatt claimed to have discovered the Temple treasure on January 6, 1982, in an underground Arch-vaulted stone chamber hidden deep within the earth, which was located directly below the surface where Jesus was reportedly crucified. He further claimed he was told by high ranking Israeli officials to keep his discovery quiet for security reasons, as they were already aware of the Ark's location. These officials had to be part of the secret Brotherhood overseeing the security of the Enochian Arched Chambers to have been privy to the Ark's location. Furthermore, these officials were not aware that Wyatt had been digging in that area, because he had not gotten permission from authorities. They made it clear to Wyatt that the Ark was being kept secret until the right time to unveil its location.

The unveiling of the Ark is a vital part of a secret plan that will correlate with the Antichrist walking around in the rebuilt Temple of Jesus' flesh. Wyatt even admitted that when he returned to the site at a later date that the chamber had been cleaned; so someone other than himself was aware of the location. Wyatt's untimely death due to cancer stole from him the opportunity to see the Ark's location exposed. But, Wyatt did leave behind his scientific analysis of Jesus' blood he took directly from the Ark's Mercy Seat. Once it was spun and reconstituted Jesus' blood was very much alive and not dead. Israeli scientist had done this for Wyatt without knowing it was Jesus' Holy blood. The unique blood showed only 1 chromosome for the Father and the normal 23 chromosomes for the mother. This means it was different than any other blood in history because the father was God, himself. Because the blood is alive it can be cloned. So blood on the Shroud of Turin, like the Mercy Seat, can, also, be reconstituted and cloned because it is alive and not dead blood, either. The blood from the Ark and Shroud prove Jesus was the son of God and is why they will, both, be used to beguile the masses to accept the Antichrist who is walking in the very flesh of Jesus.

Additional stories about the Ark being stolen from the Temple before it was destroyed in ancient times by the Babylonians have been circulated. Some Ethiopian historians and archeologists believe there is evidence to suggest that Prince Menelik I stole the Ark. Menelik I was the son of Solomon and the Queen of Sheba. As a son of Solomon, historians record that he was raised by the king. When Solomon started worshipping, wrongly, to appease his many wives of the Canaanite religions, Menelik became displeased and wished to return to his mother's land of Ethiopia.

Solomon wanted Menelik to have a copy of the Ark to take with him, because he would not get to return and worship the real one. Ethiopian history suggests that Menelik and a group of priests switched the replica with the real one and took it to Ethiopia for safe keeping. In accordance with this legend, all Ethiopian churches have maintained replicas of the Ark in their Holy of Holies throughout recorded history.

The legend further contends that the Ark was to be returned to Israel when Israel gave up idol worship and solely accepted Jehovah as their one and only God. Because Israel became 'a nation born in a day' on May 15, 1948, as the Bible had prophesied, and then won the Six Day War in 1967 to remove itself from under the control of the Gentile nations, there has been an ongoing effort to return the black Jews of Ethiopia, which some claim to be descendants of King Solomon, and the Ark to their true homeland, Israel.

The original contents of the Temple will be of utmost importance to the World Leader who will come in the name of peace and proclaim himself as the Messiah. This world dictator will have to be able to produce the Ark as proof of who he says he is. His blood must match that which was poured on the Mercy Seat of the Ark, as well as the blood that exists on the Shroud of Turin, on the Face Napkin, and on the Spear of Destiny. Some, if not all, of these items are already in the possession of the Roman Catholic Church. To successfully deceive the world, the Antichrist will have to make it appear that he is, indeed, capable of fulfilling the prophecy of John the Revelator's vision of the second coming of the Messiah. Any deviation would immediately expose him as a fraud.

Prince Mengesha Sevoum, former Governor General of Ethiopia, stated on national television in the fall of 1988 that he knew the Ark of the Covenant was protected in Ethiopia. He even released photos of his trip to visit the Ark in 1965. Those accompanying Sevoum on that trip included Queen Elizabeth II and her husband, Prince Phillip, along with Emperor Haile Selassie. According to various reports, the Ark of the Covenant is said to be housed in Aksum beneath the ancient Church of Zion of Mary. Aksum is located in the northern section of Ethiopia.

It is an interesting fact to learn that Queen Elizabeth II was invited to be included in the viewing of this particular Ark. There is much speculation about a hidden plan that predicts from the Queen's lineage will come 'the Prince that will rule the nations.' If that is the plan, then the location of the Ark would be of major importance to her and her future heir to the throne. The Royal Family is overly interested in sacred relics and strange phenomena. They keep their interest in these subjects hidden from public knowledge.

According to the book Forbidden Archeology, written by Michael Cremo, he states that the basement of the British Museum is filled with "forbidden discoveries" that most people dare not speak about for fear of ridicule by the "scientific community." Britain has many secrets all her own.

The Antichrist must be privy to the location of the Ark of the Covenant, so that the Temple can be set up for him to enter in and stop the daily sacrifices. British royalty is presently leading the way for the rise of this Dragon King—Satan, incarnate. He will be worshipped as the Messiah of the New Age, which has been his ultimate agenda since the Garden of Eden.

In years past, head Dragon kings were called Pendragons among the British Celtic lands. The last Pendragon on record was Cadwaladr of Gwynedd, who reigned from 654 to 664 A.D. The family of Pendragons is where the famous Red Dragon of the Wales Dynasty (which is a part of the British throne) originated. This bizarre lineage known as the Pendragons initially came from descendants of the ancient kings that ruled by succession in Mesopotamia and Egypt. In the earliest of days, they were merely called Dragons. The anointed ones were referred to as head Dragons or Pendragons. Their mark came from their blood lineage to Cain. The Pendragons were recorded as being half man and half god. Their fathers were the 'Watchers'—Satan and his Fallen Angels. These descendants of the 'Watchers' were said to possess the sacred and divine blood of their spiritual fathers. This bloodline, they boldly claimed, gave them the power to rule over normal human beings.

In 1982, Sir Iain Moncrieffe, Her Majesty the Queen's Albany Herald of Arms, stated that Charles, the Prince of Wales, claimed a royal descent from the House of Dracula. Moncrieffe stated,

"Today, perhaps the most famous of His Royal Highness's Romanian relations is Prince Vlad Dracula the Impaler, an ancestral uncle who took the surname of Dracula because his father Prince Vlad Dracula was proud to be a Knight of the Dragon."25

It appears that there is great pride in Royalty claiming direct descent from the Dragon bloodline. The promoters of this form of genealogy attempt to make commoners believe that the Dragon bloodline was the one that included Jesus. As you will recall, Jesus came from the lineage of Seth, not the lineage of Cain. Cain was the first Serpent King.

According to Sir Moncrieffe, in 1982, not only did Charles add the House of Dracula to his lineage, but Diana, Princess of Wales, incorporated into her lineage a descent from Melusine's House of Lusignan. This provided their son, Prince William, born in 1982, of the Royal House of Windsor, a connection to Melusine's dynasty from the Kings of Cyprus and Jerusalem through his mother, as well as a connection to the Dragon Kings through his father, Charles.

One should wonder what on earth possessed Charles and Diana to deceitfully manipulate their genealogical heritages against historical evidence and records that prove otherwise.

Why would it be important for Prince William to be from the lineage of the Dragon Kings? Equally disturbing is why it would be so important for him to be from the lineage of Melusine, who was claimed to be the daughter of Satan? This modification in Prince William's pedigree is an attempt to prove that he has the blood of the lineage of Cain flowing through his veins.

Again, remember, the promoters of this genealogical pedigree profess that the Grail Bloodline started with Cain and included Jesus. We know that is not the case, but every bit of Grail history has been written in a deceitful attempt to tie Jesus to Cain. Jesus never had the blood of Satan running through his veins. Cain's lineage was tainted by Satan and his Fallen Angels. Seth, of whom Jesus is descended, was Adam and Eve's child whose lineage remained pure. The truth regarding Jesus' real ancestry is quickly being changed within the pages of New Age propaganda. It is a very deceitful agenda taking place daily in book stores around the world.

Melusine, who Princess Diana added to her lineage and claimed to be descended from, was the Lady of the Fountain, according to Grail Lore. Melusine is portrayed as holding the key to the doorway of light. This mythological doorway symbolized a state of living in this world, but not being from this world. It is a condition of being undead; a body of this world with the soul of one not from this world.

The state of one being undead is best described as an image in the Book of Revelation, where John recorded what the Holy Spirit told him regarding the beast that would appear at the 'End of the Age,'

"And deceiveth them that dwell on the earth by the means of those miracles which he had power to do in the sight of the beast; saying to them that dwell on the earth, that they should make an image to the beast, which had the wound by a sword, and did live. And he had power to give life unto the image of the beast, that the image of the beast should both speak, and cause that as many as would not worship the image of the beast should be killed . . . Here is wisdom. Let him that hath understanding count the number of the beast: for it is the number of a man; and his number is Six hundred three-score and six." (Revelation 13:14–15, 18).

In these Scriptures, John wrote down that the Holy Spirit used the word "image" four times and the word "beast" five times to describe the Antichrist. The Greek translation for the word image is 'ikon.' It is the only word used as a translation for 'image' in all the New Testament. It means 'a quasiform of life; a life that seems to be artificial-like but in an iconic image.' This iconic form of flesh is alive but without a neshama; a soul.

A Clone would be an example of an artificial life. Born without a soul, through fission, a Clone would not be eternal or immortal, but continually living in an undead state. A Cloned body would be a perfect vehicle for Satan to take a ride in. He could totally inhabit a Cloned body, as there is no soul to compete with. In a normal body, Satan can only attempt to possess the body if the soul allows it to happen. With competition of the person's soul, Satan must contend with the fact at any given moment he can be exorcised out by a Priest, as well as through that individual's choice for him to leave, therefore losing control of the body.

Being the Antichrist requires Satan to find a vehicle that no human can remove him from. The only possibility for this scenario to happen is through a Cloned body that has no soul. The soul or spirit of the body, genetically, cannot be replicated. It leaves the body at death and exists only within the original host; it cannot be duplicated.

According to the book of Genesis, man has a living soul. The Talmud, a collection of texts and commentaries on Jewish religious law, calls the living soul the 'neshama.' Without the 'neshama' a man was considered to be not quite human. In the Talmud there are ancient references to creatures called 'Beasts' that lacked a 'neshama' to make them human. These beasts, called rulers of the field, were described as being in the image of a man. If Satan were to inhabit the Cloned body of Jesus, he would be living in a human body with no 'neshama.' He would truly fulfill prophecy by being a beast in the image of a man. That beast would possess the blood of Jesus, whose blood is considered by many to be a spark of the divine, and immediately be heralded as the Messiah. He would fulfill the Dragon King's Blood Lineage of being half-man and half-god—the beast the New Age is waiting for.

Could all of the above be the reason the Melusine and Dragon lineages are so important to Britain's Royal Family that they would go to such great length to validate fictitious pedigrees? Let us take an in-depth look at just what the Royal Family may be up to. Her Majesty, Queen Elizabeth II, has expressed the need for a universal teacher who will have wisdom to cater to the world's needs. She has openly stated that this leader should not be locked into the agenda of any one country or cult. He would need to be able to move as he so desired with cooperation from the world. She believes, for this man to be the leader of the world, he must be tolerant of genetic engineering, sex, abortion, homosexuality, population control, globalization of leadership, economics, and religion under a New World Order. Using these various platforms, in Elizabeth's opinion, will allow the universal leader to masterfully gain the approval of the world and bring all of humanity under the goal of internationalism. This universal agenda is an effort to darken mankind's intellect through promotion of social behavior over faith, thus making the world politically correct toward Satan.

Why is the Queen of England so interested in this future leader who will change the world to its destined New Order? Could she be privy to some knowledge hidden within the sacred mysteries regarding the coming of the Prince? Is she, herself, a pawn who is directly preparing the way for the world to accept this Prince? It is a well-known fact that Queen Elizabeth's father, King George VI, was a devoted Mason and member of the elite Brotherhood.

When Philip Mountbatten, Prince Philip of Greece, asked King George VI for his daughter's hand in marriage, the King made it plain that whoever married his daughter had to maintain the tradition of Freemasonry. Philip promised to join the Order of Freemasonry and with that sole commitment, King George gave Elizabeth's hand in marriage. When Philip joined the Masonic Order, Queen Elizabeth II took the Crown of England six months later.

The Royal Couple's first son, Prince Charles, was born in 1948. He is in line for the throne at his mother's death, as King. Throughout the majority of his life, Charles remained a bachelor because he was upset that his mother would not let him marry Camilla, the girl of his dreams. All the while he was getting older and much speculation was flying as to why he was still a bachelor. It appears the Queen did not want her son to marry until a certain plan and a specific time was in place. With so much gossip among the Commoners, it later appeared that Charles was forced into a marriage with a youthful Diana Spencer.

In truth, it was really a planned and timely arrangement of sorts hidden from public knowledge. Diana gave birth to two children before the couple divorced: Prince William, the future king, and Prince Harry. The Royal Couple's marriage was strained from the very beginning. In January 1982, a little over 3 months into her pregnancy with William, Diana attempted to take her and the unborn baby's life by throwing herself down a flight of stairs. The reason for this was blamed publicly on Charles' insensitive and unsympathetic nature, as well as the Queen's bombardment of the Press to promote the royal birth. Diana told friends that she felt she was just being used as a birthing chamber. How right she was!!

Charles and Diana were married at St. Paul's Cathedral, on July 29, 1981. Prince William was born June 21, 1982. Nine months prior to William's birth would have made September or October of 1981 the possible month of his conception. Buckingham Palace announced the Princess of Wales was expecting on November 5, 1981. The Royal couple's honeymoon ended late September of 1981 in Scotland, later, home to Dolly, the first Cloned mammal ever made public. Diana's first travel as Princess was with Charles in October 1981 on a three-day engagement to Wales, a principality within Britain with an equally strange history.

The flag of Wales has two equal horizontal stripes, white above green, with a large red Dragon centered on it. The flag was given the symbol of the famous red Dragon by Pendragon, Vortigern of Powys, in 418 A.D. The red Dragon, traditionally called Draconarius, was from an original military banner of the Sarmatians. The Sarmatians were cousins to the Black Sea Megalithic Builders/'Grooved Ware People.' You will recall that these Builders are historically recorded as the highly intelligent people who came to Sumer, in Mesopotamia, and started the first large civilization explosion after the Flood. The Sarmatians wore body armor that gave them the appearance of lizards. They, like their cousins from the Black Sea area, worshipped the Serpent.

It is interesting that while on this trip to Wales, Diana possibly conceived the future Prince William. As we shall soon discover, it may have been part of a very ancient plan. Prince William was born on Monday, June 21, 1982. The year 1982 is significant because it was when clairvoyant Isabelle Kingston says she received information about a coming period of enlightenment. As you will recall from the previous chapter, she stated that the 'Watchers' who form the Crop Circles told her about a Prince that would arise in Britain and bring about the New World Order. Through this Prince, a new energy would be found that would open up the mind (pineal glands) of all humanity into a 'New Age of Enlightenment.'

Could William be that prophesized People's Prince mentioned in Ezekial? Those that practice astrology claim that William's birth was on the day of an eclipse under a king's star, meaning planets were in a particular degree in Leo, therefore destining him to become a famous leader.

Prince William was born at 9:03 pm in St. Mary's Hospital, located at Paddington, London. He was the first of the royal family who will one day be king to ever be born in a hospital. William's pedigree includes being a descendent of James I of England/James VI of Scotland on both paternal and maternal lineages. This is the same King James who commissioned the printing of the original King James Version of the Bible. William, therefore, is the most British heir to the throne since the reign of James I.

Prince William has an unusual variety of lengthy names, which includes: Prince William Arthur Philip Louis Mountbatten, Windsor of Wales—given by the Queen. William was christened as William Arthur Philip Louis. His real name is even longer: Prince William Arthur Philip

Louis-Schlesweig-Holstein-Sandeburg-Glucksburg-Saxe-Coburg-Gotha-Battenberg. The Royal House changed their German names of Saxe-Coburg-Gotha-Battenberg to the House of Windsor and Mountbatten to make their ancestry deceitfully appear to be more anglicized. The fact is that they were of German descent, which meant that they might have assisted in the atrocities against what I believe were targeted sects of the Jewish people under Hitler's reign.

It is a known fact that their family members had been close friends with Hitler's family. Maybe that is why Prince Harry, brother of William, felt comfortable dressing in Nazi attire while attending a party during 2005. Unfortunately for Harry, pictures were taken and given to the press, who ran tabloid stories about British royalty still being Nazis. The negative publicity led to Harry being scolded by Prince Charles, who made him publicly apologize for his insensitive actions.

There is a hidden agenda behind the madness of the British royalty having so many names. These various name changes over the years have been to deceitfully ensure control of their blue blood status. Also, designating to a person a wide variety of names makes it almost impossible to establish the correct number of that person's name. On top of this, if they are chosen to be king, they can choose any name they want just like the Popes of Rome do; i.e. Joseph Ratzinger, Pope Benedict XVI.

Names have so much power and reveal prophecy 'to those with eyes to see.' For example, with Ratzinger, I saw 'Nazi Ratzi,' and in his choice of the name Benedict, I got the vibe of Benedict Arnold—traitor; which is what he really was because he resigned as Pope. According to the Associated Press Article, New pope selected, April 20, 2005, Ratzinger chose the name Benedict in an effort to soften his image as a doctrinal hardliner, as the Last Pope named Benedict XV is credited in settling animosity between traditionalists and modernists and whose dream was a reunion with Orthodox Christians. This might really explain Ratzinger's choice as 'Benedict' for his name; as Ratzinger sought unification of religions under the banner of a New World Religion. Names not only have Gemetria but can sometimes reveal a true sense of what is going on. Just like in Pope Francis I's case, his name is from St. Francis of Assisi whose real name was Pietro (Peter). This fulfilled St. Malachy's prophecy.

All in all, names do add up to certain numbers. Numbers and names contain vibrational frequencies that produce energy fields. The sound of one's name becomes more important than its spelling. For example, Prince William might choose to be called King William V; but he can

choose another name as king, just like his great-grandfather, Albert, who chose the name King George VI. There is a justifiable reason for Prince William's variety of names because it is part of an ancient plan to keep who he really is very quiet until he takes the throne as King. According to Revelation 13 the Beast must come to power before his name, which is given to him by the dragon, will equal 666.
On August 4, 1982, William was baptized in the Music Room at Buckingham Palace by the Archbishop of Canterbury, Dr. Robert Alexander Kennedy Runcie. The ceremonial Lily Font, used for past christenings of the Royal Family, was on this particular occasion filled with water from the River Jordan. This water was from the same River Jordan where John the Baptist baptized Jesus Christ over 2000 years ago.

William being baptized at the Palace instead of a Chapel, as well as, the water from the River Jordan being used is very much out of character regarding Royal christenings. Those that have been privy to write about the event claim that following the baptism, William 'howled.' It is my opinion that children cry, while wolves howl. What an unusual use of terminology found written by several authors (See Graham/Archer, Hoey) regarding William's strange reaction.

It is a known fact that Priests who attempt to exorcise Demons from possessed people report when the possessed are dashed with Holy Water, they will howl. They do not cry, they howl. Also, the fact that William's baptism was such a small ceremony by Royal standards for a future king makes one even more suspicious.

Diana and Charles' selection of William's godparents was strategic. Included in the group was Sir Laurens van der Post. Post was a philosopher schooled in the Mystical. He also served as Charles' spiritual advisor and mentor. Even though Post died during the adolescent years of William's life, his appointment was for the sole purpose to impart sacred mysteries and philosophy to the young prince.

According to Simone Simmons in her book, Diana The Last Word, William sought extensively to know his future from Diana's medium, Rita Rogers. Diana had already had his astrological chart done and told Simmons that William, "was born under a king's star," which according to Simmons meant, "that he had planets at a particular degree in Leo and was destined for great things." More intriguing in Simmons book is the fact that Diana described William as her "little wise old man." Diana proclaimed to Simmons that even as a teenager William sounded older than his years due to his possession of so much wisdom. Let us take a moment here to reflect. Where have we seen 'a child as an old man' portrayed? It was in Mel Gibson's movie The Passion of The Christ and in Grail Lore about King Arthur, who dies as an old man but will be re-born as a child to rule again as 'the once and future king.' Very interesting!

Before William was 8 years old, he was already being tracked by an electronic tracking bracelet and panic button surveillance systems. These high-tech gadgets were items most people around the world had never heard of until recently. Yet William was wearing them many, many years ago. Apparently, this little fellow was quite a bit more important to the Royal Family than previous or even present members of the family are. Today, his bracelet has been replaced by a bio-chip tracking device implanted in his body that is monitored 24 hours a day by satellite. The future king's location is known at all times.

On June 3, 1991, William was hit in the forehead with a golf club by a friend at the prep school Ludgrove, located in Berkshire, where he had been from the time he was 8 years old. The injury was very serious and caused a depressed fracture to his skull with the possibility of brain damage. It reportedly took doctors 70 minutes to operate to correct the indention in his skull by pulling the depressed bones out and smoothing them off. There appears to be no sign of any scarring from the operation on William's head wound. His head healed, and he suffered no brain damage. The seriousness of the event was downplayed by the Royal family. If modern surgical intervention had not been readily available, William would have died of a deadly wound.

Prince William chose to study art history and environmental geography at the University of St. Andrews, in Scotland. This university is located about an hour's drive from Edinburgh. The City of Edinburgh is famous because of Rosslyn Chapel, built by the Knights Templar, and Roslin Institute, home of the first Cloned sheep, Dolly. While in school, William had a private selection of friends, but still does not have a so-called steady girlfriend. As a young lad, he was schooled at Eaton, an all-boys institution, before graduating in 2005 with a Masters of Arts from the University of St. Andrews.

On January 9, 2006, William began his long-anticipated military training at Sandhurst. The Prince is left-handed, stands around 6'2" and weighed over 160+ pounds. He accepted his Royal Title when he turned 21 years of age and is hailed to as 'His Royal Highness Prince William of Wales.'

During his school years, William abbreviated his name with the initials W.O.W. These same initials are also being used to market to the world's youth a modern form of repetitious/chant Christian Worship Music—the feel-good and not the condemnation kind. One can only wonder with all these songs possessing a repetitious nature if someone might be behind such innocently appearing madness, using it to open up the pineal glands of youth everywhere and instead of God rushing in, Satan is. This 'Agenda' could be identical to what we discovered in a previous chapter involving the Masons in their Permanent Instruction, which targeted youthful priests in order to one day redirect the Catholic Church to accept the Antichrist 'in the Lord's vineyard.' The quickest way to change a nation is to brainwash its youth, the future leaders.

Youth has its innocence; but it is there that our minds are fashioned and shaped. For most of Prince William's young life, he openly stated that he did not want to inherit the throne as 'His Majesty King William V.' I am sure the tragedy of his parents' divorce, his mother's untimely death, and his father marrying an adulteress have played a role in him making such a statement. Over the years, he has mellowed to the thought. Unless the monarchy is abolished, which some have proposed as a real possibility, being King is his destiny by birth.

Prince William is a very handsome man who is smart, has great charisma, and studies hard at becoming a leader. He is in the 'perfect image' to become the universal leader his grandmother, Queen Elizabeth II, is preparing the world for.

William was once asked by a reporter to describe himself. He told the reporter, "I'm so used to me, that I don't really think about me. I just am." This is somewhat of a very strange response coming from a man of such royalty. It is interesting to note that William's response is very similar to the phrase, "I Am that I Am." Jesus used similar phrases to publicly describe Himself to the Pharisees and to His disciple, John the Revelator.

"Jesus said unto them, Verily, verily, I say unto you, Before Abraham was, I am." (John 8:58).

" . . . Fear not I am the first and the last: I am he that liveth, and was dead; and, behold, I am alive for evermore, Amen; and have the keys of hell and of death." (Revelation 1:17–18).

In the Book of Exodus we also read that Jehovah used those same words to describe himself:

"And God said unto Moses, I AM THAT I AM: and he said unto the children of Israel, I AM hath sent me unto you." (Exodus 3:14).

William was born on the summer solstice; when the sun stands still and produces the longest day of the year. June 21st is the time the Constellations change from Gemini, the Twins, to Cancer. The coming world Prince will, no doubt, be a twin in the image of Jesus. The evil twin is reflected in the image of the first and will be born in that first image by copying/Cloning the original. Copying the image of Jesus follows true to the sacred teachings of the Hermetic Principle 'As Above, So Below.' The Antichrist will accomplish this sacred principle through the use of a Cloned body to mirror Jesus, who is in Heaven.

In Astrology, the Gemini Twins represent the stars Castor and Pollux, the mortal and immortal twins. On Astrological charts, the twins are pictured holding thyrsus wands in their hands, which, in ancient times, were the symbol of initiation into the sacred mysteries. The summer solstice is marked by the moment the sun passes into Cancer on June 21. Prince William was born during this moment and can claim the gates between both astrological signs.

The Gate of Cancer is known as the 'Gate of Birth.' This is a suitable phrase for a constellation that has been designated for initiations by Secret Orders into the sacred mysteries. The Gate of Cancer is also visualized by initiates as their birth into a higher realm. The Masonic Lodge places the Constellation of Cancer at the central point of the Lodge. It is at this central point that the powers of the four elements meet and rise into a higher state called Quintessence. In esoteric teaching, Quintessence refers to gaining access to higher realms. It is referred to as the highest plane of being, where one is not subject to the normal elemental laws of gravity, time, space, dimension, etc. In essence, it is a gateway in an attempt to be equal to God.

The Portal/Gate of Birth, according to esoteric lore, is the sign of incarnation where the spirit descends into matter. In other words, during the Gate of Cancer, there would open a spiritual door to allow the Archangel Satan to easily descend into a Cloned body that has no soul. Esoteric Astrology teaches that Cancer is the gateway between 'Heaven and Earth.' It is through the Gate of Cancer that spirits are permitted to descend into the material realm at the moment of incarnation.

This, again, incorporates the Hermetic Principle where the 'upper is reflected in the lower.' The lower can only be an image of the upper, as the upper was created by God. The lower, a copy or Clone, is all that can be created by man, through the use of Satan's hidden mysteries. Mankind can perform transmutations of God's Creation with Satan's help, but he will never be able to create. Because Satan cannot create a body for himself, he has to copy one; and what better body to copy than the temple of Jesus.

According to the teachings of Freemasonry, the top most 'keystone' in the Royal Arch represents the Astrological sign Cancer. This lost key is what Freemasonry is desperately searching for. It represents immortality of the flesh - the key to the Tree of Life. The Royal Arch is topped by the keystone of Cancer (Birth), while at its base is a coffin, the symbol of death. Death is attributed to the zodiacal Gate of Capricorn, the Goat (Satan). Cancer is ruled by the moon, while Capricorn is ruled by Saturn. These two zodiac signs symbolize the Portals of Birth and Death. Cancer is also the symbol of eternal - that which cannot die.

The major star in Capricorn is Sirius. When Sirius is finally transformed into the key of Cancer, the elite Brotherhood are taught an entrance will open between the dimensions of Heaven, Hell, and Earth. This will allow a dead person to be reborn when Sirius gives birth—the phoenix rises from the ashes. Sirius, represented as a five-pointed star/pentagram, becomes the sacred key that will open the way for Satan to be born in the flesh.

In Egyptian texts, Osiris became the constellation of Orion, and Isis, his wife, who was also known as the original Black Madonna with child, became Sirius. She gave birth to her son Horus through a form of fission from the cells of her dead husband, Osiris. Horus was portrayed as being part human and part reptilian—a Dragon King. The eye of Horus is the same as the 'All Seeing Eye' recorded throughout Egyptian Hieroglyphics. It is also the very same Eye that appears on the United States of America's One Dollar Bill. Take a good look at the eye in the Pyramid on the back of a dollar, and notice how reptilian it appears. Remember, Hitler called it the 'Cyclops Eye,' the reptilian 'Third Eye' of the pineal gland, that when stimulated, connected to the 'All Seeing Eye' for illumination. This same 'All Seeing Eye' is a major symbol of Freemasonry, as it represents their God known as Jahbulon, the 'Great Architect of the Universe.' As the reader will recall, the 'On' in Jahbulon represents Horus's father, Osiris.

Diana was the name of the moon goddess that ruled Cancer. Cults call Diana, the Queen of Heaven. She was worshipped second to her husband, Zeus. What a coincidence that Diana just happened to also be the name of the mother of Prince William. Even Princess Diana's own brother, Earl Spencer, made a point at her funeral that Diana was named after this ancient goddess. The moon goddess Diana, in mythology, is referred to many times as the wheat/corn goddess, Ceres. The corn goddess is linked to the Constellation of Virgo, the Black Madonna. The Virgo Constellation is the same one so honored by the Masonic builders of Washington, D.C., as well as their ancestors, the Knights Templar and Megalithic Builders. According to Astrology, Virgo symbolizes contact between the human plane and the spiritual realm. The Black Madonna is always pictured with her son Horus. Horus was born from the seed of his dead father, Osiris—a regeneration process known as Cloning.

Princess Diana was manipulated into marrying Prince Charles by powers she had no idea were involved. She was appropriately set up to be with him when she was 19 years of age. Diana turned 20 on July 1st, twentyeight days before their marriage took place in London's St. Paul's Cathedral on July 29, 1981. The number 19 is that special number of years between each full moon's appearing on the summer solstice. Because of this astrological event, the Illuminati would choose, as part of their on-going satanic rituals that had been practiced for centuries, a woman the age of 19, who must be a virgin, to give birth to the future Antichrist. As a prominent member of the Illuminati, Prince Charles became a key player in this secret ritual. He was aware that Diana had been hand-picked at the age of 19 to finally bring the ancient ritual of preparing for the birth of the Antichrist into reality.

Charles and the Illuminati knew when the predestined time would be for the Antichrist to be born. That is why he never married Camilla, as she would be too old to fulfill the secret agenda when the time was to be right. Instead, Diana was chosen to fulfill the plan and that is the only reason Charles married her. It is evident, from all accounts of those close to Diana, that Charles pursued her heavily and then treated her like an unloved piece of property when they married. He never quit loving Camilla, but he had to fulfill the Illuminati's plan before he could have her.

Diana became the incubator for the Illuminati's Cloned seed. Charles never loved Diana; he knew she was only a pawn in the scheme of the agenda—a mere sacrificial lamb.

According to the NBC Special, Princess Diana—The Secret Tapes, hosted by Jane Pauley, March 5, 2004, at 10:00 p.m., Diana made comments on tape that, "I felt like I was going to a slaughter, told I could not turn back, and I knew Charles did not love me, all before I was married." Right after these comments, the NBC station took a 30 second break to allow a commercial. Would you believe it was a commercial advertising Mel Gibson's The Passion of the Christ, which interestingly enough showed scenes from the movie of Jesus' mother, Mary? Could the timing of this advertisement at 10:27 p.m. EST during a show about Diana have been anymore esoterically and subliminally planned? I think not. After this commercial, Diana told on the tapes that her wedding night was, in her own words, "Strange, very strange, and I cried myself to sleep I was so unhappy." She even elaborated that all Prince Charles did on their wedding trip was read strange books on African Black magic and psychology.

As soon as William was born, Diana and Charles' marriage fell apart completely; as if it really was ever together. Charles began actively pursuing Camilla, who was already married at the time. He had done his part in bringing William into the world, as planned by the Brotherhood. Charles knew once the satanic plan was in place that he could have the love of his life, Camilla, and be free to one day marry her, which he did in 2005. That is why on Charles and Camilla's wedding day, she wore wheat in her hair.

As we have already learned earlier, in Chapter 22, the symbol of wheat is architecturally a mixing of the spiritual with the mortal and prides itself on public display as a sign of regeneration, rebirth, reincarnation and unification of opposites. Charles and Camilla's royal wedding had also been keenly scheduled for April 8th, the same day as a hybrid Solar Eclipse, the only total Solar Eclipse for 2005 that would be taking place.

A Solar Eclipse can only be observed during a New Moon. Mystical teachings cite that when the Sun and Moon combine, it creates a dimension of oneness. A hybrid Solar Eclipse leaves a ring around the moon before it moves into total eclipse, which looks identical to the 'All-Seeing Eye' of pagan Egyptian and Sumerian origin. The number eight, which was also selected for the date of their marriage, represents regeneration and materialistic goals.

Unfortunately, Pope John Paul II died, and his funeral was scheduled on April 8th for exactly the same reasons Charles and Camilla's wedding had been carefully planned for that day—a Solar Eclipse. It is an interesting fact that Pope John Paul was both born on a Solar Eclipse and then buried on a solar eclipse day just as St. Malachy's prophecy of the Popes predicted. I wonder what the odds were for this to have happened. One thing is for certain, the Pontiff's funeral took precedence over the Royal Wedding, which was moved to the very next day, April 9, 2005. This accommodative date change is interesting to note because the Church of England will not allow their King to marry a Roman Catholic, as they feel they are in direct opposition with each other; yet the Royal wedding was rescheduled in observance of the Pope's funeral.

Maybe there is not as much hostility going on between the Roman Catholics and Protestants as is promoted by the media to be. It may very well be that this so-called estrangement between these two religions is nothing more than a Hegelian ploy to deceive people. This technique, so masterfully carried out by them, is to ensure no one knows what is really going on until the veil of deception is lifted and it is too late for anyone to escape. Remember that the Order of the Illuminati was formed with no allegiance to anything or anyone. Their only goal is world dominion, and they will use every avenue available in order to meet their New World Order objective.

It is evident that in the early days of Charles and Diana's marriage that Diana became aware of the Illuminati's evil plan, and she became very ill. She tried to commit suicide on several occasions. The emotional strain of knowing she was part of such an ill-fated scheme caused her to become bulimic. As mentioned before, Diana tried to kill herself and her unborn son, William, by throwing herself down a flight of stairs. Her psychological wellbeing was surely in question.

Something was creating havoc within Diana other than just not having a loving husband. There is speculation that she knew the baby she was carrying was not Charles' real son and that she was being used as a birth chamber to produce the Antichrist. To ensure Diana went along with the plan after her suicide attempts, she was given appropriate drugs to secure her willingness to accept her role in the agenda.

The Illuminati's plan took complete control of Diana's life. She was taken to the hospital to have her baby, something that the Royal Family had not been accustomed to. The real reason for the hospital, which is hidden from public knowledge, was that she could be induced into labor so that Prince William would be born at a certain time. The timing was like that of Masonic astrological foundation charts, where certain planetary alignments must occur to bring the spiritual realm to the physical realm. William arrived as planned, during the summer solstice, at 9:03 p.m. on Monday, June 21, 1982, in the private Lindo Wing of St. Mary's Hospital, located on Paddington, in west London. Even the name of the hospital, St. Mary's, has esoteric meaning.

The commoners were told that the Princess had been placed at the hospital for a variety of reasons, which included (1) the Royal family was changing to the modern way of giving birth, (2) in the event of complications the mother and baby would be at the hospital, and (3) that the delivery would not interfere with Prince Charles' Polo matches. What a deceptive joke!

The Windsor Bloodline is engrossed in the study of Astrology and the sacred mysteries. They knew the child that had been implanted into Diana had to be born, like Horus, at the peak of the sun's power. Astrological timing meant everything. All of the events surrounding the conception and birth of William were not a coincidence.

The birth of the Antichrist had to occur on schedule as part of the ancient plan, and at a time when Satan could inhabit a body without a soul. Diana, I believe, was artificially inseminated while in Wales. I also think that she was led to believe, at first, that her egg and Charles' sperm, which she was receiving, had been biogenetically perfected to ensure a healthy baby boy would be born to eventually rule as king. She knew it was her duty to try and have a son, so she easily bought into the lie. Once she figured out the real reason for the strange artificial insemination procedures, it was too late, so she attempted suicide to kill herself and the baby before it was born.

It is no wonder that Diana referred to the Windsor Family as "Lizards", which is correct, because they are Royal Serpents from the lineage of Cain. She is allegedly to have told friends, in confidence, that she was part of something that would shake the foundations of the world. Diana had thought about telling her secret revelation to the world when she was suddenly killed in the car crash in Paris. Her accidental death can only serve to remind one of the untimely deaths of Marilyn Monroe and Diana's own bodyguard, Sergeant Barry Mannakee. Mannakee was killed in a suspicious motorcycle accident that James Hewitt, one of Diana's lovers, claimed was arranged, more than likely because Diana probably had told him too many secrets.

Monroe, like Diana, had also planned to tell an Illuminati secret and was killed before she could release it to the world. Was it a coincidence that pop star Elton John was asked by Prince William to sing at his mother's funeral? Elton, a professed homosexual, revised his smash hit "Candle in the Wind," which was originally about Marilyn Monroe, to a new version in honor of Diana. No wonder Elton John was knighted by the Queen and now goes by Sir Elton John; do what they ask and the world is yours. His song served to let every elite member of the Brotherhood know that revealing secrets are punishable by death; like Monroe, so goes Diana. Therefore, the plot thickens; not one of these planned events was a coincidence.

The date of Prince William's birth was equally a carefully planned event. June 21st is the summer solstice, which holds great significance in all the Megalithic structures built around the world. The Pyramids of the Mayan culture were built to display the summer solstice with half the Pyramid covered in light and half covered in darkness. This arrangement of darkness and light still produces the appearance of a Serpent on the side of the Pyramid. This image of a Serpent seems to travel down the side of the Pyramid, from the sky to the earth, each year on the 21st of June. To the Megalithic Builders, the summer solstice was a time of hermetic celebration. To the Mayans, it was a time when the Serpent returned to earth.

Regarding the rise of the Antichrist at the End of the Ages. Dr. Jack Van Impe, world renowned prophecy teacher, stated that,

"A generation is 51.4 years. According to Matthew 1:17, it states there were 42 generations from Abraham to Christ. From Abraham to Jesus Christ is a total of 2,160 years. If you divide 2,160 by 42 then you get 51.4 years as a generation."26

Israel, according to Dr. Van Impe, is the key to understanding the time regarding the 'End of the Age.' Israel removed all Gentile control in the Six Day War on 6/10/1967 and after U.N. Resolution 242 on 11/11/67. Gentile removal was prophesized in the Bible to occur during the last generation of the people who would not see death. Dr. Van Impe says that when you add one generation that will not pass until Christ returns to this prophecy about Israel, you get a span of dates from 10/10/2018 to 3/11/2019 as the possible dates for the 'End of the Age.'

"Seventy weeks are determined upon thy people and upon thy holy city, to finish the transgression, and to make an end of sins, and to make reconciliation for iniquity, and to bring in everlasting righteousness, and to seal up the vision and prophecy, and to anoint the most Holy. Know therefore and understand, that from the going forth of the commandment to restore and to build Jerusalem unto the Messiah the Prince shall be seven weeks, and threescore and two weeks: the street shall be built again, and the wall, even in troublous times. And after threescore and two weeks shall Messiah be cut off, but not for himself: and the people of the prince that shall come shall destroy the city and the sanctuary; and the end thereof shall be with a flood, and unto the end of the war desolations are determined. And he shall confirm the covenant with many for one week: and in he midst of the week he shall cause the sacrifice and the oblation to cease, and for the overspreading of abominations he shall make it desolate, even until the consummation, and that determined shall be poured upon the desolate." (Daniel 9:24–27).

" . . . many shall run to and fro, and knowledge shall be increased . . . it shall be for a time, times, and an half; and when he shall have accomplished to scatter the power of the holy people, all these things shall be finished . . . And from the time that the daily sacrifice shall be taken away, and the abomination that maketh desolate set up, there shall be a thousand two hundred and ninety days." (Daniel 12:4, 7, 11).

We are living in the generation when the Antichrist will come to power. Although the Bible teaches that no one knows the hour or the day of the 'Rapture of the Church,' according to Dr. Jack Van Impe, we can calculate the possible year of the Revelation based on an understanding of the length of a generation. The Revelation is the date when Jesus Christ returns to fight the Antichrist at the Battle of Armageddon. The time, as you can see, has to be very near for the 'Rapture of the Church,' as it precedes the Battle of Armageddon during the same generation.

"Verily I say unto you, This generation shall not pass, till all these things be fulfilled . . . But of that day and hour knoweth no man, no, not the angels of heaven, but my Father only. But as the days of Noe (Noah) were, so shall also the coming of the Son of man be . . . Then shall two be in the field; the one shall be taken, and the other left. Two women shall be grinding at the mill; the one shall be taken, and the other left . . . Therefore be ye also ready: for in such an hour as ye think not the Son of man cometh." (Matthew 24:34, 36, 37, 40, 41, 44, Parenthetical comment mine).

"Now this I say, brethren, that flesh and blood cannot inherit the kingdom of God; neither doth corruption inherit incorruption. Behold, I shew you a mystery; We shall not all sleep, but we shall all be changed, In a moment, in the twinkling of an eye, at the last trump: for the trumpet shall sound, and the dead shall de raised incorruptible, and we shall be changed." (1 Corinthians 15:50–52).

So what has all this generational time line of the Antichrist, Rapture, Tribulation, and Second Coming of Jesus got to do with Prince William? Plenty! In 2002, William turned 20 years of age. In 2018, he will be 36 years old. It has been reported by Brian Hoey in his book, Prince William, that Queen Elizabeth II (Queen B) and Prince Charles (the Dragon) are equally determined that nothing is going to stand in William's way and that slowly they will have him ready to take over as king.

Dr. Van Impe's "End of the Age" dates correlate with yet another strange occurrence that was strategically planned to also come to pass in the year 2019. The reader will recall that the Megalithic Builders established seven great Oracle sites in seven places on earth upon which the Knights Templar later built seven of their most famous Gothic Cathedrals. These seven places were called the Earth's Chakras, just like the human body is believed by mystics to have seven Chakras. The Sun Oracle was located at the Cathedral of Notre de Chartres, the Moon Oracle at Romanesque Cathedral, Mercury Oracle at Toulouse, Venus Oracle at Orleans, Mars Oracle at Notre Dame de Paris, Jupiter Oracle at Notre Dame Cathedral in Amiens, and the Saturn Oracle at Rosslyn Chapel.

These seven Oracle sites correspond to a certain sequence in our planets. The initiates of the sacred mysteries traveled these routes from Iberia to Scotland like one would a giant labyrinth to mirror 'Heaven on Earth.' The Druids, a Dragon cult, called this pilgrimage their 'Lactodorum'—the great North Road of the celestial heavens known as the Milky Way. They believed walking this labyrinth aligned their spiritual side with their half human side.

The illuminated masters of the mystery schools at Chartres taught that the planetary alignments with their seven major Oracle Sites would one day in the future herald a main event known as the Apocalypse. At the moment the terrestrial alignments of these Seven Cathedrals/Oracles match their celestial alignments of corresponding planets within the heavens, the Apocalypse is set to occur.

Apocalypse is the Greek translation for the word "Revelation." According to Biblical Prophecy, the Revelation will occur when Jesus Christ returns at His Second Coming to fight the Battle at Armageddon against the Antichrist. As we have already mentioned, these seven earthly Oracles are scheduled to align perfectly with their matching planets on July 28, 2019.

If the established time line for the Apocalypse is that close then the Antichrist has to already be alive and walking among us. With this in mind, it is vitally important for us to take an observant look at the image of Prince William. He stands 6'2" and weighs more than 175 pounds. William's physical features do, in fact, resemble those of the crucified man believed by many to be Jesus on the famous Shroud of Turin.

The Shroud of Turin was examined, and a variety of cloth samples, which included sections of blood stains, were removed from the Shroud in 1969 and again in 1973 by a team of scientists. During the time period of 1978–1981, a newly formed Shroud of Turin Research Project (STURP) Committee also took additional blood samples from the Holy Shroud. From that time on, many other researchers have carried out extensive analysis of the Shroud, with some claiming that it is authentic and some claiming it is not. The controversy ended on Easter 2017 when Pope Francis I informed the world the latest research totally proved the Shroud of Turin was from the time of Jesus and it was real; not a hoax.

As mentioned before, the Shroud of Turin is purported to be the burial cloth that wrapped the crucified body of our Lord, Jesus Christ, and is presently owned by the Vatican and housed in Turin, Italy. It is the most extensively researched relic in all of history. Research on the Shroud might still be ongoing, but it is not a fake.

Author David Rorvik wrote "In His Image: The Cloning of a Man" in 1978. He first promoted his book as based on a true case, but later recounted his claim when the general public went into an uproar over the implications he unveiled about human Cloning. His book sparked the Cloning debate that still continues today, even though Cloning is rapidly moving ahead as an accepted form of science in many countries. What part did Rorvik play in bringing this subject to light and exposing it to the public? Was Rorvik a puppet of the Illuminati like Mel Gibson was in the movie Signs and with his so-called out of pocket production The Passion of the Christ, or was he like Sir Elton John with his re-written Candle in the Wind? One thing is for certain; Rorvik's claim that a real man had been cloned was treated in a manner similar to earlier reports about UFO sightings.

To prepare the world for the real presence of UFOs, the famed radio event entitled The War of the Worlds was released over the radio waves like a real live broadcast in order to make people think the Earth was being attacked by Martians. When the general public reacted to it in mass panic and fear, they were told that the event was faked and that UFOs did not exist. Immediately following the broadcast, the National Security Agency was formed by General Dwight D. Eisenhower to keep up with all UFO data without the public's knowledge. Records that are just now being released under the Freedom of Information Act state that President Eisenhower was justified in his actions because he thought the public would panic if they were told the truth.

There can be no doubt that Rorvik's book was allowed by the powers-that-be to introduce the world to the occult science of fission and transmutation called Cloning. Just as in the staged Martian attack, when the people panicked, Rorvik's so-called non-fiction book was professed to the public as fiction, although it had been written and released from the publisher and author in the beginning as factual. Even still, his book began hot debates about Cloning. Unbeknownst to most of the world, all the while this debate has been stirring the public, the Cloning process was going full speed ahead underground; just as it had been since the days of Hitler. Rorvik's book was used to break the ice regarding the potential reality that Cloning was not just a mere product of science fiction. Simple achievements related to Cloning have been gradually released since that time to the public in order to indoctrinate them into full acceptance of Human replication.

Once the powers-that-be felt there was a reduction in panic over the Cloning issue, the world was quickly introduced to Dolly, who was already born. Waiting until after her birth to announce her to the world insured the public could not go into an uproar and terminate the pregnancy of the sheep carrying Dolly before she was born. The Brotherhood knew it would be easier for the general public to accept her once they saw her alive. Also, the public's acceptance of the first Cloned sheep meant that the road was better prepared for the first Cloned human. I personally find it interesting that the powers-that-be chose the Cloning of a sheep to release their achievement to the world. Sheep in the Holy Bible are identified with the 'Chosen People' of God. Also, Jesus is referred to as the sacrificial lamb. What better way for the Illuminati to tell their initiates that the Lamb (Jesus) had already been successfully Cloned than through their announcement to the world about Dolly. On top of all this, Satan has always been portrayed by the Bible as a wolf hiding behind sheep skin. In the end, that is exactly what Satan is planning to deceitfully do—walk among men in the skin Cloned from the Lamb of God.

The Cloning of a human being is really a very simple procedure. First, you need a cell of the individual to be Cloned. That cell can come from a living or dead person. For example, the blood samples removed from the Shroud of Turin by trained scientists contained red blood corpuscles, hemoglobin, heme, protein, bilirubin serum, white blood cells, albumin, and possible pericardial fluid. From these blood stains, scientists were able to secure cells, as well as DNA samples.

The DNA samples, when analyzed, proved that the person on the Shroud was a male. Those same cells, which housed the DNA that was analyzed, have the potential to be used to Clone another human being identical to the man on the Shroud. Each individual human cell is a holographic image of the complete body. Once the cell is coaxed into dividing through an electrical shock, it will grow into the exact image of the body from which it was originally taken—not a twin. Cloning of a human does not first require the unlocking of that individual's DNA blueprint. The only advantage of being able to unlock the DNA code would be to identify genetic factors or markers that might indicate an unusual blueprint, known as 'first matter,' if a body was part human and part god. As mentioned earlier, Ron Wyatt proved Jesus' blood was alive that he took from the Mercy Seat of the Ark of the Covenant when it was spun and reconstituted. The father had one chromosome…first matter.

As far back as the early 1960's, Professor Lorenzo Ferri, with permission from the Vatican, studied the height of the man on the Shroud. He estimated the height of Jesus to be around 6'2"—the same height as that of Prince William. Ferri also estimated the weight of Jesus to be about 175 pounds and William is about the same. Facial features appearing on the Shroud are remarkably similar to early paintings of Jesus and to those of Prince William. An excellent early painting of Jesus, for the reader to review, is one found in St. Catherine's Monastery, Sinai, from the 6th Century. It is reproduced in Grant R. Jeffrey's book, Jesus-The Great Debate.27 The facial dimensions of the Prince and Jesus are remarkably similar.

In lieu of the constrained time issue, Prince Charles is beginning to pave the way for his son, Prince William, to become the World Leader that Queen Elizabeth II has reportedly been preparing for. According to a news article that appeared on April 16, 2002, in the Times of India:

"The Prince of Wales (Charles) is to launch a multifaith campaign that is being seen as a move to take on an extended royal role following the death of the Queen Mother. He has held a summit for Britain's religious leaders at St. James's Palace to combat a 'dangerous' breakdown of tolerance in society. He will make public their proposed solution on the eve of the Queen's golden jubilee address to parliament, flanked by a Cardinal, two Archbishops, and a chief rabbi. The multi-faith campaign coincides with plans to increase his royal profile."28

In 2002, Prince Charles began holding monthly meetings with Britain's Prime Minister. Most significant has been his increase in attending public engagements occurring in

Scotland, home to Rosslyn Chapel and Roslin Institute. Prince Charles is not only an heir to the throne, but the eventual governor of the Church of England, as is his son William. He is very much for the uniting of Christians, Roman Catholics, Jews and Muslims. His religious movement is funded by the Prince's Trust Fund. His formal meetings have included religious leaders of Muslim, Hindu, Buddhist, Jain, and Christian faiths. These meetings regarding interfaith relations are the groundwork for the One World Religious Order, which will be ruled by the coming Antichrist.

It is vital that the Antichrist pulls together all the religions of the world under One New Religious Order. Prince Charles is working diligently to prepare the way for the coming Prince, just as the Vatican has been doing under their leadership of Pope Francis I. In Britain the English Law of 1701, called the 'Act of Settlement,' was modified to allow a Roman Catholic to either marry the future king or for the future king to be Roman Catholic without losing his line of succession to the throne. These changes make sense and are not just a coincidence. Maybe that is why the Royal family did not mind burying Princess Diana with a Roman Catholic rosary in her hand? This simple gesture had the power to promote unification between England and the Pope. Also, the fact that Charles and Camilla relinquished their wedding day to Pope John Paul II's burial further promoted unification between the Church of England and the Vatican.

The Antichrist, according to Saint Malachy's Prophecy of the Popes, must have the Roman Catholic Pope serving as his False Prophet in order to unite the world's religions. When Pope John Paul II first entertained all the religions from around the world, he indicated that the Catholic Church would be heading the way toward unification. He clearly made a straightforward statement to those in the Orthodox religion about Peter being the head and that the Orthodox would have to unite under Roman Catholic authority. These comments of Pope John Paul II happened on the same day lightening hit St. Peter's Basilica. The Antichrist must involve the Roman Catholic Religion's willingness to accept all other religions under their umbrella of tolerance in order to successfully pull off being recognized by the masses as the Messiah.

As mentioned earlier, Saint Malachy predicted the 112th Pope will call himself Peter Romano II after the First Peter. No other Pope in history has ever chosen the name of Peter because they felt they were not worthy to be known by the same name as the church's so-called founder. But, Pope Francis I, now, also, wears the fisherman's signet ring of Peter that he uses to sign all his documents. So, according to Malachy, Pope Francis I as Peter will soon become 'the Defector' just as the first Peter denied Jesus three times. The Antichrist will use him as his False Prophet, thereby securing the New World Religion guided by the Roman Catholic Church.

Prince Charles is a member of the Order of the Garter, which are the elite Knights of the Illuminati. They are the controllers who are chosen to implement and complete the plan for the New World Order. The Knights of the Garter are the leaders of the Committee of 300. The Committee of 300 is the legislative group of the Illuminati. These men pretend to be Christians by holding meetings in St. George's Chapel, but in reality, they are said to practice Satanism. The Order of the Garter is secretly called 'The

Foundation' and is believed to be the precursor to an establishment called the 'Circle of the Round Table.' The Order of the Garter is the world's oldest order of chivalry.

Prince Charles was initiated into the Order on June 17, 1968. He serves with 23 other companion Knights and their two leaders, which are broken down into two groups of 13 members. These diabolical men oversee covens of satanic worshippers and control the Aristocrats of the world. According to Texe Marrs' book Circle of Intrigue, these men are waiting for King Arthur to take his place among them so they can reinvent the Arthurian legend of Camelot and become King Arthur's Knights of the Round Table. King Arthur arrived because on June 16, 2008, William became the 1000th Knight and also 'Royal Knight Companion'.

William's father, Prince Charles, is also a product of the 13th Illuminati Bloodline and a very powerful Luciferian, according to Fritz Springmeier in his book, Bloodlines of the Illuminati. Family members of this 13th Holy Merovingian Illuminati Lineage consider themselves divine beings who are direct descendants of Lucifer through Cain's bloodline. The 13th Illuminati Bloodline is the bloodline through which Satanists teach that the Antichrist will be born. This bloodline is said to have mixed the Holy Blood of Jesus with the Spirit of Satan to create the Antichrist. When Prince Charles married Diana, Luciferian covens were alerted to prepare for the birth of the Antichrist.

Could William really be Harry Potter's Half Blood Prince (half human/half divine), who was brought to life using the hermetic Sorcerer's Stone (Philosopher's Stone) hidden within the Chamber of Secrets (Enochian Chambers holding relics below the destroyed Temple that the Templar seized), which was taken Prisoner of Azkaban (Knights Templar killed and imprisoned for heresy during the Inquisition) only to arise as the Order of the Phoenix (Freemasonry arising from the ashes of the Templar) to produce the long awaited Half Blood Prince (a Chimeric Clone) from the Goblet of Fire (the Holy Grail)? Yes! Harry Potter's author has been preparing readers and moviegoers for Satan's big event using the infamous Illuminati language of 'Double Speak'; no doubt, she, too, is an Illuminati puppet used to indoctrinate the world to Satan's Plan, just like Rorvik, Gibson, Sir Elton John, and many others.

From Revelation 13:18, we find a way to prove who the Antichrist will be:

"Here is wisdom. Let him that hath understanding count the number of the beast: for it is the number of a man; and his number is Six hundred threescore and six."

Therefore, the Antichrist's name will numerically equal 666. Does Prince William have a possible connection to that unique number? We shall find out.

The number of the Antichrist, 666, has intrigued humans for centuries. It is an interesting fact that the Apostle John, who wrote the Book of Revelation and was writing to a Greek reading public, chose to use the number 666 (an elaborate symbolism of Gematria) instead of a Greek translation of the Antichrist's name. The letters of both the Hebrew and Greek alphabets stood for numbers, which became the basis of Gematria.

Gematria is a method of finding hidden meanings underlying the surface of a written text by turning a word into a number and then finding the word from the total sum. It appears that Gematria, giving letters numbers, can be used with any alphabet, including English, according to author Frank Allnut. In his book, Antichrist—After the Omen, he states,

"In English this can be accomplished by assigning letters the value of their consecutive ranking such as A=1, B=2, C=3, D=4, Z=26."29

The particular system used by Allnut is called the Roman Thesis System of Assigning Letters to Numerical Values. As an example, let us use Prince William's name and replace Prince with a possible leadership title since he does not want to be king. We will give him the position of the leadership of the future combined American and European Union (AEU).

Therefore, William's name and future identifying title for this combined Union could appear as:

AEU = 27 + William = 79 + Arthur = 86 + Philip = 70 + Louis = 76 + Mountbatten = 145 + Windsor = 102 + of = 21 + Wales = 60.

Therefore: 27+79+86+70+76+145+102+21+60 = TOTAL 666.

According to Dr. Jack Van Impe on his television show that aired 10/17/04 at 10:00 p.m. EST called Jack Van Impe Presents, he stated that the English alphabet can be assigned multiples of 6 where " A=6, B=12 to Z=156. Interestingly enough, Computer=666 and Mark of the Beast=666."

Using Dr. Van Impe's formula, I found that Prince William's initials:

W=138+A=6+P=96+L=12+M=78+W=138+W=138:
Also,

TOTAL 666.

The fact that William has been given such a variety of names as well as all the family names that have been added and deleted over time, could be to secretly hide the numerical value of his name from public calculations. This poses a problem, as there could be a number of endless calculations possible for a person with so many name variations. On top of all this, he can choose any title, number, or name when he becomes king. The above two examples are just simple ones; even so, they did yield something worth noting—the unique prophesized number of the beast—666.

An entire book could be written on various calculations using many forms of Gematria to give numerical values to William's lengthy names and possible future titles. The fact that so many names and changes have gone on within the 13th Illuminati Holy Merovingian Bloodline is not a coincidence, but a plan of deception to hide Satan's identity as long as possible. In lieu of this scheme, let us turn our attention to some other identifying factors.

Prince William's birthday offers some interesting facts when using a form of modern numerology. Modern

Numerology, according to the book Man, Myth and Magic, states:

"Modern numerology is where you calculate your number from your birth number. It is found by adding up the day, month, and year. This number is believed to reveal the mould in which the mysterious worship of fate cast you at your birth; what you are destined to be. Your birth number should harmonize with your name. The number 1 is the # of God; 2 is the # of his arch-opponent, the Devil."30

Prince William's Birthday: 6/21/1982

Add, 6+2+1+1+9+8+2 = 29; then 2+9= 11; and 1+1=2
Therefore: Prince William is a 2.

Based on information provided by Man, Myth and Magic, on interpreting an individual's birth number,

"The number 2 is the evil and ominous #, the # of woman and the devil, passive and receptive. The Birth number is meant to show your basic, underlying characteristics, 'the foundation on which you stand' or 'the reason for which you came on earth.'"31

Again, we discover another interesting correlation. William's birthday number does, in fact, match the number of his name. They both are indicative of demonic connotations.

The Crest/Coat of Arms that is unique to Prince William is embossed with a Lion and Unicorn. To make it distinctively his, William added red scallops from his late mother's Crest. This was considered a highly and unusual move on his part, because most men who are to become king take a symbol from their father's Crest.

Of course, if Charles is not his real father, and William is a Clone from the Shroud of Turin, then it is understandable that he would take a symbol from the lineage of his mother's Crest. William, in a strange twist of theory, would be like Jesus, who took His lineage from His Virgin Mother, Mary, because Joseph was not truly His real father, even though both Mary and Joseph were descendants of the lineage of David from Adam's son Seth. Mary's lineage from King David was the purest thru Nathan as we have already discovered clearly recorded in Luke 3: 23-38.

The scallop shell that William selected from his mother's Crest has a long history in Grail Lore. This particular seashell was identified with the goddess Aphrodite, who was believed to have been born from sea foam. Her birth is referred to as the birth of Venus.

Aphrodite (Venus) was considered a sacred harlot and love goddess identical to the Egyptian Black Madonna, who we know gave birth to her son Horus using cells artificially inseminated from his dead father. Just like the Serpent swallowing its tail, Aphrodite (Venus) gave birth to a re-generated being. She underwent a sacred union with Hermes that produced 'The Great Work' in Alchemy known as a hermaphrodite.

A hermaphrodite, as we have already discovered, is a hybrid/Chimera that can only be reproduced over and over through Cloning without the sexual act between a man and a woman. With a mixture of both, you have no need for anyone else; in other words, you have achieved the 'Spirit of Cain,' that of Self Love. That is why Aphrodite, in Grail legend, was considered the May Queen—the goddess of the circle symbolized as the Serpent swallowing its own tail, known to us already as Ouroboros, 'Fiery King of the Underworld.' Ouroboros kept swallowing his own tail to continue to reincarnate himself as the same being over and over, thereby achieving an unnatural and unholy immortality of the flesh. It was only through the persona of Aphrodite that such Arthurian legends believed that mankind would one day be able to regenerate themselves like Ouroboros to avoid death and live forever in their manmade Camelot (Eden) on Earth.

Aphrodite is just another name for Melusine, who the late Diana deceitfully had incorporated into her ancestry. Melusine, according to Grail Lore, was the daughter of Satan. She is portrayed in these legends as a priestess who came from the waters of the fountain of youth. Scallop shells were her symbol because she was considered a mermaid—part human and part fish (god/reptilian). Scalloped edges have been used throughout the ages by artists in many portraits, but the most famous is the grail cup skirt design in a portrait of Mary Magdalene by Caravaggio.

The scallop shell is believed to be the collector of divine nectar from the sacred waters of the fountain of youth. This sacred fluid, according to legend, was menstrual enzymes collected from a virgin woman. These enzymes were believed to cause the body to regenerate as they were composed of fluid directly from the pineal gland. These fluids were called the 'ambrosia of immortality.'

Recently, scientists have confirmed that controlling certain enzymes within the body is the key to cellular immortality. The scallop shell is symbolized as the key to obtaining the fountain of youth. The Sacred Science of unlocking the fountain of youth is not new, as it was written about around 2000 B.C. According to a Sanskrit song called Sama Veda, it tells how to collect the body's sacred enzymatic fluids to achieve immortality.

Even Secret Societies with their history of Hidden Mysteries include references to the scallop shell. Rosslyn Chapel, the most holy site of the Templar, has a beautifully carved scallop shell at its location. It was placed there to symbolize the pilgrim's final destination to enlightenment. Reaching Rosslyn was considered the ultimate achievement in opening one's Crown Chakra where the dew cup of illumination resides.

The dew cup symbolized as a scallop shell and Holy Grail is what holds the fluid of the pineal gland. That is the reason the scallop shell is symbolized in stone at Rosslyn Chapel. Once the pilgrim/initiate encountered Rosslyn, they had gained the knowledge of the Serpent. The Serpent was now and forever living within them and was tuning them into his deceitful enlightenment regarding the Hidden Mysteries of immortality.

Charles and Diana are both descendants from the lineage of King James. King James was the first king to rule both England and Scotland. The Masonic rituals established at Rosslyn Chapel by William St. Clair became a magic movement during the reign of James VI of Scotland. James VI became King James I of England.

Diana Spencer was, according to King and Beveridge's book Princess Diana—The Hidden Evidence, a descendent 'queen' of the Judaic royal bloodline. The House of Spencer can be traced back to the Celtic Royal House of Dunkeld and Stewart (Stuart), which was the first true messianic royal dynasty of the Scots, as well as direct lineal descendants of the Merovingian bloodline. According to Sir Laurence Gardner, internationally known sovereign genealogist, historian and author of Bloodline of the Holy Grail, the Stuarts were the last ruling dynasty in Britain in which both primary strands of the Messianic bloodline were conjoined. It was the Stuarts who were removed from office by the German House of Hanover, which is now known as the House of Windsor. The only lines the House of Windsor can claim to the Merovingian strain is that King James I had a daughter named Elizabeth who married Frederick of Bohemia, and their daughter Sophia married Ernst August, the German Elector of Hanover.

History tells us that Scotland's Royal House of Stuart rose from the marital union of the hereditary lines springing from the Merovingian and from the Celtic Kings (Pendragon) of Britain. The Merovingian's claimed to be priest-kings with both supernatural ability and a royal bloodline stemming from earthly kings. They were the sorcerers who possessed extensive esoteric knowledge and magical powers. The Merovingian's built an underground chamber for the worship of the goddess Diana in Paris, France, during the 6th Century. This chamber was used for blood rituals and human sacrifices to the goddess. The site of the chamber was chosen because a legend thrived from ancient times that it had once been a battleground where kings, and anyone else who was killed there, would go straight to heaven.

The site of the ancient chamber built to worship Diana still exists today within the city limits of Paris. It is called the Pont de L'Alma tunnel. This is the same tunnel where Princess Diana died, when the Mercedes she was a passenger in hit the tunnel's 13th pillar. She literally bled to death in the ancient chamber that had been built to the ancient goddess Diana. The fact that the number 13 is the sacred number of Satan and the tunnel was an ancient sacrificial site of the Merovingian cannot be explained away as just another coincidence. Diana's death there was strategically planned.

Princess Diana's memorial at Althorp is a megalithically-inspired Greco Roman Temple. Her image is found centrally located on it as a cameo silhouette. If one stares at this image of her long enough, it begins to look identical to the image visible on a full moon, except more reversed, as if a mirrored reflection. This is way too unearthly to just be a mere coincidence, especially since the Greeks and Romans called 'Diana' their Moon Goddess. She was worshipped as a huge statue at Ephesus and was known as both the goddess of the moon and patroness of witches. The early Christians regarded her as a Demon, an entity of the Devil.

Princess Diana was buried in a designer black long sleeve wrap around dress that she had supposedly ordered some weeks earlier before her death and had never worn. In her hands was placed a Roman Catholic rosary, which was reported to have been a gift she had received from Mother Teresa. Diana and Mother Teresa had indeed met. But when she demanded to know from Mother Teresa, "where all the charitable contributions went, when the people for whom it was intended were reduced to living their last days in shreds," Mother Teresa refused to undergo an audit.

According to Simone Simmons book, Diana The Last Word, Diana asked,

"What is she doing with the money—sitting on it?' Diana had lost her respect. She further commented that there was no need for raising money for the Roman Catholic Church which was already the richest institution in the world."

Even still, Simmons noted in her book that Diana had thought about converting to Roman Catholicism. According to Simmons, Diana said to her, "It would have been embarrassing if the ex-wife and mother of future Supreme Governors of the Established Church of England, the country's officially sanctioned faith since Henry VIII's rejection of papal authority five centuries before, had 'gone to Rome.'"

Knowing all of this history, why on earth would the Royal family or even Diana's own family allow such paganism and controversial issues to forever become associated with the burial and memorial to Princess Diana? This all seems a bit out of line, especially if she was considered a member of the Church of England, which in the past had denounced the sovereignty of the Pope. Putting a rosary, the symbol of the Roman Catholic Church, into the dead hand of the mother of the next King of England (who will one day preside over the Protestant Church as Supreme Ruler) while she is dressed in black like the Black Madonna, has got to just about symbolically say it all, don't you think?

The Stuarts of Scotland, of which Princess Diana was a direct descendant more so than Prince Charles, were considered to be the Grail Dynasty. As we have previously discovered, the Grail Dynasty was from the mixed lineage of Cain, not the Seth lineage. Therefore, Jesus has no connection to the Grail Dynasty. The Coat of Arms of the Grail Dynasty is known as the House of Unicorn. The Davidic Lion of Judah and the Franco-Judaic Unicorn are both incorporated in the Royal Coat of Arms for Scotland.

The unicorn is a unique symbol that represents the science of Alchemy. The legend of the unicorn is the combination of the genes of a male and female into one beast—a Chimera/hermaphrodite that is rich in the symbolism of opposites. The one-horned beast is said to represent supreme power, which is connected to gods and kings. The symbol of the unicorn literally depicts that a transforming has occurred where a human being has been spiritually purified and has liberated the god within himself. This transformation signified victory over one's intellectual darkness.

That transformation, to release the darkness of matter, is what Satan tempts a person with so they will willingly allow their soul to connect to his light during their pineal gland's opening. When this occurs, the initiate gladly accepts the ancient unicorn concept, which epitomizes that of a hermaphrodite, because Satan has clouded the initiate's mind by making the person believe that their transformation has resulted in a super human mixture of good and evil. Prince William's Coat of Arms embodies this super human union of good and evil by claiming rights to both the Unicorn and Lion dynasties.

The ABC Television Sunday Night Premiere Movie, "Prince William," which aired on September 29, 2002, was very informative and was promoted as the true story Prince William wanted to tell the world about himself. The documentary showed that Prince William was given a body guard, because it was feared that extremists may try to kill him. That seemed a rather strange concern as the movie did not disclose just who the Royal Family thought the extremists might be.

The term "extremist" is used to identify those who go to drastic measures to defend their beliefs. Christians have been recently labeled extremists by the politically correct, because they are not considered tolerant to the New World Order. Could the Royal Family fear that Prince William needs to be protected from Christians? There is no need for them to have this concern, as Christians already know what is going to happen to the Antichrist at Jesus' Second Coming. They will not take such matters into their own hands. Christians, therefore, are the least of their worries because they believe in the Scriptures of the Holy Bible, which instructs true believers regarding such matters.

"If any man have an ear, let him hear. He that leadeth into captivity shall go into captivity: he that killeth with the sword must be killed with the sword. Here is the patience and faith of the saints." (Revelation 13:9–10).

"Recompense to no man evil for evil. Provide things honest in the sight of all men. If it be possible, as much as lieth in you, live peaceably with all men. Dearly beloved, avenge not yourselves, but rather give place unto wrath: for it is written, Vengeance is mine; I will repay, saith the Lord. Therefore if thine enemy hunger, feed him; if he thirst, give him drink: for in so doing thou shalt heap coals of fire on his head. Be not overcome of evil, but overcome evil with good." (Romans 12:17–21).

In another segment of the movie, Prince William's character takes a photo of his late mother, Diana, and lays it next to a picture of Mary, the mother of Jesus. The scene shows him sitting at his personal computer where he takes a book next to the computer and opens it to a picture of Mary. He, then, places Diana's photo next to Mary's picture. In the picture of Mary it appears that Jesus' hands are near to Mary, but the movie frame cuts out the body of Jesus, who is on the left side of Mary in the picture. William puts the photo of Diana next to the right side of Mary and stares at the two, together. Then, William picks up Diana's photo and his fingers point toward Mary from the right side of the photo. Could it be a coincidence that his fingers are in the same position on the right side, of Diana's picture, as those of Jesus, on the left side, of Mary? Were the producers of the movie trying to imply that William and Diana are like Jesus and Mary? Were William's hand placements silently signifying that Mary was his real mother?

If Mary is his mother, then William is a Clone and he has the lineage of Mary's blood flowing through his veins. If this is the case, then the producers and the character portraying William were symbolically establishing awareness of William's Royal Blood Line to 'those with eyes to see,' to reveal that he is the one their ancient esoteric Plan calls the evil twin.

Other interesting facts contained in the movie included the Royal Family not wanting to give Diana a Royal Funeral. They acted as if she had been a mere peasant who was used to birth William, without any consideration that she had once been an important member of their Royal entourage and the future king's mother. William is shown intensely begging his father, Charles, and his grandmother, Queen Elizabeth II, for a Royal Funeral on behalf of the woman who gave birth to him. The need for the future king to have to beg the Royal Family seems a bit strange, indeed. Regardless of the fact that Charles had divorced Diana, she still was publicly considered William and Harry's mother.

From most accounts, Charles has always been somewhat distant as a father; yet, firm with his expectations of William. He appears more like a preprogrammed instructor who has been chosen to ensure William is totally protected and prepared for kingship years ago. He gave William an armored car with bullet proof glass and a tracking satellite sensor for his birthday. We can only assume or wonder if all the other Royal Family members have had this same magnitude of protection provided to them. William has openly said that he did not want to be king. Maybe he already knows he will never be King of England because he is really the 'Prince of this World,' who has a much bigger plan: to be worshipped as the Messiah— King of all mankind.

There have been many theories as to Princess Diana's tragic and untimely death. As mentioned earlier, on March 5, 2004, NBC began a special on Diana called Princess Diana: The Secret Tapes, which was hosted by anchorwoman Jane Pauley. On this show, several audio tapes of Diana's actual voice were revealed for the first time ever. Diana made some very unusual comments, which included:

"I always knew I would never be the next queen."

"I felt trapped and alienated from the world."

"I felt I was a lamb for slaughter."

Some researchers believe she was murdered because she seemed to be planning to marry Dodi Fayed, and she was possibly already pregnant with his child. The pregnancy would have infuriated those in the highest power who are behind the New World Order. A baby by Fayed would link the Arabic Muslims by kinship to the future world leader, William. This would have only complicated matters between Arabs and Jews, as it might rekindle the issues that divided Abraham's children, Ishmael and Isaac, regarding their inheritance to the Promised Land, especially if Diana's Royal Bloodline would directly link all her heirs to it. To avoid these issues and investigations into whether Diana was pregnant or not, her body was partially embalmed from the waist down, against French Law, thereby removing all evidence of any fetus.

On top of all of this strangeness, Diana's body was buried in a quarter-ton, lead-lined coffin in an unmarked location on a manmade island in the center of a lake at the Althorp Estate. A lead-lined coffin can stop all radiation, x-rays, etc., from reviewing or locating her body. Some believe that Diana was cremated to further limit any investigation into her tragic death or whether she was the real mother to William and not just an incubator to a Cloned cell that had no relationship to her or Prince Charles.

Even more revealing is Diana's Memorial Fountain that was built at Hyde Park. It is egg-shaped with a strange walkway penetrating the egg-shaped area. From the air the image looks just like a woman's egg floating in a petri dish while it is being pierced from one side. This image is identical to the image a scientist sees when cloning as he gently inserts a cell into a hallowed out female egg.

Simone Simmons, the Jewish author of Diana The Last Word, who claims to have been one of Diana's closest friends, states in her book (pg. 54) that the paternity of Diana's youngest son, Harry, was questioned. In response to these accusations, Simmons writes,

"Diana was told in no uncertain terms that her sons should have a blood test, and, of course, everything was as it should have been."

Notice the above deceptive play on words. Why did Simmons not say that the blood tests revealed without a doubt that William and Harry were Charles's sons? Instead, she said the test showed everything "as it should have been." This is a weird remark. Of course, if those administering the blood tests already knew that William was a Clone, then his blood results would have showed it "as it should have been." Also, Harry's blood would have been different "as it should have been" by linking him to his father, Prince Charles. Is the guarded statement "as it should have been" really trying to say something without letting the so-called 'cat out of the bag?'

Simmons would have been wise not to reveal any secrets that Diana might have shared with her regarding William's true lineage because it appears that anyone who goes against the wishes of 'The Firm' always ends up dead. Even Queen Elizabeth II is aware of the fact that there is someone very powerful out there running the show. No one knows that better than Paul Burrell, the late Princess Diana's personal butler. In his book, A Royal Duty, the Queen gave heed to him when she warned,

"Be careful, Paul. No one has been as close to a member of my family as you have. There are powers at work in this country about which we have no knowledge."

Apparently, nothing is allowed to stand in the way of fulfilling the wicked seed of Satan's diabolical plan.

The traffic cameras from the Ritz Hotel in Paris to the tunnel where Dodi and Princess Diana died were not working the night of their tragic car accident. It was the first time in the city's history that the traffic monitors had ever failed. At the exact time of the traffic monitor failures, all police communications went down in a radio frequency blackout. While all this was transpiring, Diana lay dying in the Paris tunnel, bleeding to death in the ancient Merovingian human sacrificial chamber built to the goddess Diana.

According to ongoing investigations, Diana had been driven to her death by a member of the French Secret Service. On February 26, 2006, David Leppard of The Sunday Times— Britain reported in his article, Diana driver was secret informer, that

"The chauffeur of the car in which Diana, Princess of Wales died was working for the French secret service, the British team reinvestigating her death has been told."

The monitors clearly were not working. Their untimely failure ensured police would not be sent to the accident in order that Diana would die on the sacred site. The entire event had to have been planned to the utmost degree so that Diana was sacrificed under the moon on the 31st day of August, which is celebrated by the Luciferian as Hecate's Day.

Hecate was queen of the ghosts and all manner of magic. Heralded by wolves, Hecate was said to journey through the night with a band of uncanny followers terrifying the unwary traveler due to her association with the underworld. The goddess Hecate is represented with three heads or three bodies joined back to back, and her powers included rejuvenation through the black science of Alchemy. She was goddess of the crossroads where energy and magical activities were said to occur. Crossroads meant ley lines where earth currents crossed each other to form powerful vortexes called Dragon nodes. These nodes were where Oracle sites were situated in ancient times. Princess Diana died on an ancient crossroad site. One has to wonder if she was wearing her favorite designer perfume by 'Hermes.' The Hermes logo is an old time hearse carriage being pulled by horses in black on an orange background—a symbol of death. It seems a little too coincidental that Diana's coffin was pulled in similar manner on a 1904 gun carriage by horses through the streets of London.

With Princess Diana no longer a threat, plans to make William a king quickly got underway. William is, now, His Royal Highness 'The Duke of Cambridge', His Royal Highness 'The Earl of Strathearn' and 'Baron Carrickfergus'. He is a member of the Privy Council of the United Kingdom and personal Aide-de-Camp to the Queen. William holds rank as a Lieutenant Commander in the Royal Navy, a Major of the British Army and Squadron

Leader for the Royal Air Force. He holds six Honorary Military appointments and three Fellowships. William is 'Bencher' for the Honourable Society of the 'Middle Temple'. The 'Middle Temple' is the western part of 'The Temple' which was once the headquarters of the Knights Templar before they were forced underground years ago. William is also a Knight of the 'Most Ancient and Most Noble Order of the Thistle'. As you can see, he has been inundated with secret order memberships, titles and appointments along with him being named the 1000th Knight to the Order of the Garter. This will provide to him their Knights of the Round Table as the stepping stone needed to project himself onto the world's stage as their re-created King Arthur, thereby fulfilling Satan's diabolical plan to become mankind's Messiah. That is why King Arthur is a common thread of wisdom among all Secret Societies.

Adolf Hitler knew that Jesus' blood was pure Aryan/God, which held an ancient code to the divine genetics of immortality. The Aryan race, described as part of Hitler's genetic studies, were touted as humans who had inherited traits of the gods because of their blonde hair, blue eyes, slender hands and feet, and elongated craniums. Prince William Arthur is blonde haired, blue eyed, slender in his features and has an elongated facial structure. He is genetically, on all accounts, the perfect specimen of Hitler's attempt at an Aryan race of god-men. William's name was chosen very carefully. It secretly tells it all, as William ends in the perfect choice of words about who he is genetically a Clone of—I AM. The title 'I AM' belongs to God. No wonder Diana called him 'Wills.' She could not bear the consequences of the rest of his name, which had been strategically planned for ages to counterfeit the real 'I AM.'

Diana even fought with Charles because he wanted to call him "Arthur'. In fact taking his name, 'William', 'Arthur', and removing what Diana called him, 'Will', actually leaves 'I AM' 'ARTHUR' in succession just as Charles wanted.

According to the Jewish Zohar I 25b-26a, the code found in a name's numerical value is hidden; but using the key that Shiloh and Moses are equal will break the code. It proclaims,

" . . . Until Shiloh cometh": this is Moses, the numerical value of the two names Shiloh and Moses being the same."

Therefore, for the two names to be of equal value there had to be a hidden code. I discovered using all Gematria codes that I could locate, not one of them scored the names of Moses and Shiloh as being numerically equal. In order to truly find the Antichrist, I searched for a possible code that mathematically gave Moses and Shiloh the same values. With much persistence through many trials, I was led to develop the following code:

"Dr. Joye's Gematria End Times Code"

IF:
A = 1
B = 2
C = 3
D = 4
E = 0
F = 5
G = 6
H = 7
I = 0
J = 8

K = 9
L/M = 10
N = 11
O = 0
P = 12
Q = 0
R = 13
S = 14
T = 15
U = 0
V = 16
W = 17
X = 18
Y = 19
Z = 20

THEN:
SHILOH =14+7+0+10+0+7= (38)
MOSES=10+0+14+0+14= (38) THEREFORE:
I=0
AM=11
KING=26
William=48
Arthur=49
Philip=41
Louis=24
Schlesweig=71 Holstein=57
Sandeburg=51
Glucksburg=63
Saxe=33
Coburg=24
Gotha=29
Mountbatten=80
Windsor=59

TOTAL 666

Additional names that other researchers have found that total '666' include: 'William V' and 'King William the Fifth Heir UK' in Hebrew. Unfortunately, what this all means is that until William is elected King and chooses his name and title, just like a pope does when the Cardinals elect him, we can only speculate his name and number. But one thing is for certain, I AM Arthur, Satan's King Arthur, has finally risen from the Holy Grail through cloning the blood of Jesus. Throughout historical literature, King Arthur has been proclaimed as the 'once and future king' (a Man as a Child) by those who believed that the Grail (Holy Blood) legends of Camelot were 'truth' hidden within allegory. Jesus, the carrier of divine blood, once lived, and now, through the hidden sciences of Satan, a replica of his body is able to return 2000 years later to reign as King of the material world; the very thing Satan offered him in the Wilderness, which he boldly turned down.

"Again, the devil taketh him up into an exceeding high mountain, and sheweth him all the kingdoms of the world, and the glory of them; And saith unto him, All these things will I give thee, if thou wilt fall down and worship me. Then, saith Jesus unto him, Get thee hence, Satan; for it is written, Thou shalt worship the Lord thy God, and him only shalt thou serve. Then the devil leaveth him, and, behold, angels came and ministered unto him." (Matthew 4: 8–11).

The sword in stone, known in Grail Lore as 'Excalibur,' is really the alchemical extraction of knowledge (DNA/Blood) from the stone (cut without human hands—Jesus) of the wise (God), which the sons of Satan hope will initiate the return of the Golden Age—their Camelot on Earth.

Unfortunately for anyone who chose to follow Satan and his Fallen Angels into such a deception, they will spend an eternity in Hell. God does not take lightly their vain attempt to create 'Heaven on Earth' by taking the image of God's Only Son and parading around in it to deceive the world so that the created is worshipped, rather than the Creator. This is the prophesied 'Abomination of Desolation.' It will be the most extreme form of idol worship ever carried out by mankind.

When this Clone/idol arrives in Jerusalem, as that genetically rebuilt Temple of God and proclaims himself God by sitting as a fake Messiah in the Holy of Holies, the most sacred spot in all of Planet Earth, you better believe that this will bring the 'REAL' KING OF KINGS AND LORD OF LORDS to Earth with a vengeance.

"And I saw heaven opened, and behold a white horse; and he that sat upon him was called Faithful and True, and in righteousness he doth judge and make war. His eyes were as a flame of fire, and on his head were many crowns; and he had a name written, that no man knew, but he himself. And he was clothed with a vesture dipped in blood: and his name is called The Word of God. And the armies which were in heaven followed him upon white horses, clothed in fine linen, white and clean. And out of his mouth goeth a sharp sword, that with it he should smite the nations: and he shall rule them with a rod of iron: and he treadeth the winepress of the fierceness and wrath of Almighty God. And he hath on his vesture and on his thigh a name written,

KING OF KING AND LORD OF LORDS. And
I saw an angel standing in the sun; and he cried with a loud voice, saying to all the fowls that fly in the midst of heaven,

Come and gather yourselves together unto the supper of the great God; That ye may eat the flesh of kings, and the flesh of captains, and the flesh of the mighty men, and the flesh of horses, and of them that sit on them, and the flesh of all men, both free and bond, both small and great. And I saw the beast, and the kings of the earth, and their armies, gathered together to make war against him that sat on the horse, and against his army. And the beast was taken, and with him the false prophet that wrought miracles before him, with which he deceived them that had received the mark of the beast, and them that worshipped his image. These both were cast alive into a lake of fire burning with brimstone. And the remnant were slain with the sword of him that sat upon the horse, which sword proceeded out of his mouth: and all the fowls were filled with their flesh." (Revelation 19:11–21).

I emphasize, once again, the 1st Commandment clearly states, "Thou Shalt Have No Other Gods before Me" (Exodus 20:3) and that includes not even a Cloned one. My hope in bringing this to light is that, "it will open your eyes and allow you not to fall victim to the greatest deception the world has ever known—A wolf in sheep's clothing."[32]

Chapter Thirty-One
ANTICHRIST-Prepare to Meet Satan

Prepare yourself to meet Satan in the flesh. He is alive and walking in a physical body among mankind. The Bible records that Jesus told his Disciples how important it would be for the final generation, at the 'End of the Ages,' to recognize Satan's Plan so they would not be deceived.

"And as he sat upon the Mount of Olives, the Disciples came unto him privately saying, Tell us, when shall these things be? And what shall be the sign of thy coming and the end of the world? And Jesus answered and said unto them, Take heed that no man deceive you. For many shall come in my name saying, I am Christ; and shall deceive many." (Matthew 24:3–5.)

"When ye therefore shall see the abomination of desolation, spoken of by Daniel the prophet, stand in the holy place, (whoso readth, let him understand:) Then let them which be in Judea flee into the mountains: Let him which is on the housetop not come down to take any thing out of his house: Neither let him which is in the field return back to take his clothes. And woe unto them that are with child, and to them that give suck in those days! But pray ye that your flight be not in the winter, neither on the Sabbath day: For then shall be great tribulation, such as was not since the beginning of the world to this time, no, nor ever shall be." (Matthew 24:15–21.)

"And when ye shall see Jerusalem compassed with armies, then know the desolation thereof is nigh." (Luke 21:20.)

A world government-like Empire is prophesied to arise during the End Times, before the 'Second Coming of Jesus.'

"And the ten horns which thou sawest are ten kings, which have received no kingdom as yet; but receive power as kings with the beast. These have one mind, and shall give their power and strength unto the beast . . . For God has put in their hearts to fulfill his will, and to agree, and give their kingdom unto the beast, until the words of God shall be fulfilled. And the woman which thou sawest is that great city, which reigneth over the kings of the earth." (Revelation 17: 12–13, 17–18).

This all-encompassing governmental body will be under the dictatorial leadership of the Antichrist.

"And he shall speak great words against the most High, and shall wear out the saints of the most high, and think to change times and laws: and they shall be given into his hand until a time and times and the dividing of time." (Daniel 7:25).

As we have already discovered, the Illuminati Brotherhood are pressing toward the achievement of that goal. The New World Order will be ushered in through a universal crisis. David Rockefeller, a member of these elite internationalists, made a resounding speech concerning the crisis needed to get nationalism to an international agenda. Rockefeller stated,

"We are on the verge of a global transformation. All we need is the right major crisis and the nations will accept the New World Order."33

A wide variety of global emergencies are being tried out to see what it will take to force people around the world to give up their love of nationalism for global protection. Threats of another world war, crashed UFO saucers, and the radio broadcast 'War of the Worlds' all share in the beginning toward the induction of panic on the world's masses. A major global emergency arose in 1999 with the Y-2K threats of massive computer failures around the world. Updated computers and new software programs quickly replaced old ones out of the deceptive propaganda that was used to promote global fear.

What the unsuspecting public failed to recognize was that with all their newly updated equipment came intense surveillance and loss of privacy. Intel Corporation produced the Pentium III processor that housed a secret number enabling all communication to be tracked from each person's computer worldwide. Microsoft also hid ID numbers in documents produced by any computer that used their software worldwide. E-Mail included hidden ID numbers, which have the power to identify the sender. Computer viruses are forcing more and more security systems to be put in place.

An even greater crisis was the terrorist attacks that occurred on September 11, 2001. These attacks affected the entire world in one way or another. Travel came to a halt, the stock markets declined, and the world economy suffered. The fear of further attacks has led many nations to incorporate a variety of new devices to be used as surveillance tools upon mankind. Some of these new devices include closed circuit cameras, identification technology, video monitoring of workers, background checks, implanted microchips, recording all forms of communication, databases for purchasing of items, infrared cameras, DNA Databases, Applied Digital Solutions Satellite Tracking Devices, Global Positioning Satellites (GPS), Echelon Communications Tracking Devices, Face-Off Technology for Facial identification, Iris Scans, Fingerprint scans, and much, much, more. The downing of only four U.S. jet airplanes quickly moved the world-at-large even closer to accepting the New World Order. The War on Terrorism began the effort of uniting countries toward a common goal.

A future crisis, such as a nuclear war or bio-terrorism, will be all that is needed to push the world into total acceptance of a united One World Government concept. Mankind will look desperately for a savior to save humanity from such an awful fate. That coming Prince will unfortunately be the Antichrist, who, along with his "New Age, One World Government," will offer a peaceful solution to the world's inhabitants that will seem to miraculously fall into place overnight.

The United States has been preparing for the day when the New World Order will be imposed. In the event of a national emergency, our president has been given executive powers to put the American people under Martial Law, which suspends our Constitution. The agency created to carry out the Presidential Order is called the Federal Emergency Management Agency (FEMA). They, along with the new Homeland Security Agency, will ensure all goes as planned. Executive Orders give the president the sole power to establish a dictatorship and join us with a One World Government. Nations all over the world have similar emergency systems set up to do exactly the same thing. Mankind will be herded so fast into joining the world government that they will not realize what hit them. Most citizens of America do not even know what an Executive Order is, much less the power it has at present over all our inalienable rights.

Executive Orders allow complete seizure of everything you own, including you. If you fail to cooperate, you will be labeled as politically incorrect and will be arrested or shot on site. Those who are arrested will be placed in detention centers, which have been built all over America, so they can be brainwashed toward the One World Agenda. Other resisters to the New Order will be terminated for committing hate crimes based solely on their resistance and lack of tolerance for the new way of the world. Once those that are against the New Order are removed, the plan will quickly be put into place as scheduled. This will allow the coming Prince of Darkness, Satan himself, to gain world power over "all kindreds, tongues, and nations."34

According to prophecy teacher and author Texe Marrs, America's former President, Bill Clinton, signed Executive Order (EO) 13107, Implementation of Human Rights Treaties, into law. This EO requires federal, state, and local governments to comply immediately with all United Nations Treaties, whether or not these treaties have been confirmed by the United States Senate as required by the Constitution. One of these treaties, the United Nations Treaty on Genocide, says that persuading someone to change his or her religion is a hate crime punishable by International Law. The EO 13107 is expected to be used by the Office of Religious Persecution Monitoring, which is set up under The International Religious Freedom Act that passed the U.S. Senate on October 10, 1998. It will eventually be used to arrest and imprison Christian missionaries and witnesses anywhere in the world who preach that all religions are not equal. The International Religious Freedom Act was designated to create the federal commission to monitor religion. It is chaired by a presidential-appointed Ambassador who serves as Special Advisor to the President, whose position is comparable to that of a director within the Executive Office of the President.

The person instrumental in facilitating the passage of Bills necessary to establish such an Office of Religious Persecution Monitoring was a Jewish attorney, Michael J. Horowitz. He is a senior fellow at the 'globalist' Hudson Institute in Washington D.C. Col. John R. Niemela (USAF-Ret.) openly exposed the objective behind the government's plan to monitor religious activities by stating,

"The blueprints that guide this law have been available for years, but most 'blinded' Christians ignore them. 'Protocol No. 14 of the elders of Zion' demand that no other religion should exist other than theirs, and, the 'Communist Manifesto No. 19' directs its members to infiltrate churches and replace revealed religion with other forms, discredit the Bible and inject Humanism." (Wisconsin Report 5-7-98).
It is interesting that once again we see the Khazar Jews, the seeds of Satan, who wrote The Protocols of the Learned Elders of Zion and Karl Marx, also a Khazar Jew and the Masonic brainchild behind the Communist Manifesto, promoting identical antichrist ideology in order to rid the world of Christianity. In fact, religious surveillance is

already being monitored within the United States by the United Nations Special Rapporteur of Religious Intolerance. This particular office was established in 1986 by the United Nations Commissioner on Human Rights. The particular standard that these officials apply to their so-called 'examination of religions' is the United Nations' 1981 'Declaration on the Elimination of All Forms of Intolerance and Discrimination Based on Religious Belief.' Christianity is the only religion that discriminates and will not tolerate sin because it believes in the 'Theory of Absoluteness' and not the 'Theory of Relativity' like the other religions. Einstein never meant to have his 'Theory of Relativity' be used outside the realm of Physics, and he would have been totally appalled that it is now being used to justify moral and ethical issues. Even so, the big guns of the United Nations are pointed straight at the elimination of Christianity based on that theory.

The establishment of a Religious Monitoring Office in the United States using United Nations directives is nothing more than a flagrant violation of United States Citizens' Rights. The very First Amendment of the United States of America's Constitution boldly states that "Congress shall make no law respecting an establishment of religion or prohibiting the free exercise thereof." Yet this is exactly what our Congress has done right under our noses with the applause of the Roman Catholic Church, the Anti-Defamation League (ADL), and a host of other Jewish Lobbyists. Now the United Nations has the power to control all religious activities on Planet Earth—a tool the future Antichrist will use to establish a One World Religion.

At present, Christians promoting God's 1st Commandment "to have no other gods before me" can be legally charged for breaking the law, as it is "considered a hate crime".35 An example of this occurred on October 10, 2004, when Philadelphia's 'hate crimes' promoters ordered 11 Christians to stop singing and preaching in Philadelphia's public streets during a huge "gay pride" event. The Christians refused. They were arrested and jailed for 22 hours, charged with 3 felonies and 5 misdemeanors, including "hate crimes," which, if they had been convicted of, would have added up to 47 years in prison with $90,000 fine for each person arrested. Interestingly enough, the news media blacked out the story. Philadelphia's District Attorney, Lynne Abraham, ordered the arrest. She serves on the national AntiDefamation League's (ADL) Board of Directors. The ADL/B'Nai B'Rith Jewish organization wants it to be illegal for Christians to preach the Gospel or condemn homosexuality.

It took until February 17, 2005, for these 11 Christians to be acquitted in Philadelphia, home of our nation's Liberty Bell. In the near future, groups wanting a New World Religion, such as the ADL, will help secure all religions under one umbrella by promoting the need for tolerance. Once this is established and the Antichrist comes to power, the law will no longer acquit Christians; instead, anyone found violating the New World Religion mandates will be severely punished; i.e. guillotine on courthouse square cutting your head off for all to see. Going against the Antichrist's so-called 'politically correct dictatorship' will be considered a hate crime that requires removing that person immediately from society.

The formation of the European Union was another planned move toward bringing all nations together under one leadership, including the United States of America, to eventually become an American/European Union (AEU). The United Nations Army, in the past, used soldiers from all the participating countries that made up the UN alliance. In the War against Iraq, the UN did not respond to the crisis as it should have. The United States and Britain's hands were seemingly forced to go after Saddam Hussein and Osama Bin Laden somewhat independently, even though the Twin Towers had been attacked by hijacked American planes piloted by Saudi Arabian citizens.

On top of all the 9-11 hysteria, our own government escorted Bin Laden's family out of the USA by way of a special flight, while all USA citizens and our planes were grounded. The FBI never questioned his family about where they thought Osama was at the time. In other words, America's Top Security let his family leave without detaining them or using them as a bargaining chip for his whereabouts. Even more bizarre is the fact that America had gone to war to help the Saudi Arabians keep their Muslim brother, Saddam Hussein, out of their country. For their pilots to attack America seems a little twisted; but then so does America, Christian capitol of the world, saving the Saudi Muslims from the Iraq Muslims when they consider us Infidels. Something just does not add up about 9-11.

The fact that our, then, President, George W. Bush, the day the Twin Towers were hit, called his Communication Specialist off vacation to meet him in Jacksonville, Florida, and fly with him to a children's school function in another city in Florida seems strange. Why would a Communications Specialist be needed for such a trivial guest appearance? Hey, but was it not conveniently wonderful that the Communication Specialist was along because when Air Force One went secretly air bound during this pinnacle of crisis on American soil it was the Communication Specialist who made contact with all the world's leaders? President George W. Bush could never have done this on his own, as he did not have the linguistic abilities that were needed for such a moment in history. Does this whole episode seem just a little too planned? Yes, and it was a lot bigger than mere partisan politics between Republicans and Democrats. It would have happened regardless who had been president because it was a universal order from the Illuminati. Both parties are controlled by them. Look at who they ran for President—Bush vs. Kerry—both blood brothers of the Order of Skull and Bones, the training ground for the Illuminati's puppets.

Whatever the truth is surrounding the attacks of 9–11; the event immediately lessened the United Nations' role in the ability to handle a world crisis involving terrorism, and in turn, opened the door for the European and American countries to begin forming another army. This army is in the beginning stages of producing a One World Army for a coming World Empire—a major plan of the Illuminati. Soldiers of those nations who refuse to fight under this banner of cooperation will be court-martialed, just like Americans were if they refused to wear the 'blue helmets' of the peace-keeping forces under the direction of the United Nations in times past. How is that possible, you might wonder, concerning soldiers from America?

To find the answer to that question, all you have to do is look at the United States Military flag with its pretty yellow fringe. That fringe is not just for decoration. It boldly symbolizes 'Maritime Law,' which, according to the Free Press International (2005), is under jurisdiction of the President and has no constitution, no laws, and no rules of court, and is not recognized by any nation. This Martial Law Flag "Pursuant to 4 U.S.C. chapter 1, 1, 2, & 3; Executive Order 10834, August 21, 1959; 24 F.R.6865, is under the control of the Commander-in-Chief of the Army and Navy. It is the flag in federal buildings everywhere. Why is it that no one is rushing out with banners saying, 'Remove the Yellow Fringe' but will instead instigate great controversy over a rebel symbol appearing on a southern flag?

Maybe the whole thing is being kept a little quiet so that America can be easily united under the New World Order without so-called constitutional issues, if you catch my drift, thereby bypassing all the hoopla that goes on with House and Senate hearings, which, by the way, they would have no jurisdiction over. How cleverly convenient! In reality, whether we like it or not, soldiers on the battlefields around the world have been fighting for the motives of the Globalist more so than just for America. This charade has been going on for a very long time.

The New World Order is quickly making its début, as the European Union has already established a One World Currency for all its members. As we have already mentioned, the timing seems to be perfect, since America, after all these years, changed its long-standing currency. And would you believe our money matches the design of EU's currency? How appropriate—theoretically, 'the chicken before the egg.' All of these so-called changes are being touted due to economic reasons and, according to some, to stop drug trafficking, money laundering and crime.

Will the newly designed money really help the United States economy, which is still faltering, or stop drug crimes, which seem to be at their highest? No. The real reason for the switch, at tax payers' expense, was to place a metallic bar in the money so that it can be tracked while in a person's possession—a violation to your personal rights. On a universal scale, new monetary exchange and international business deals are being put under an International Banking System so monetary equality in all countries will ignite the path toward a One World Economy.

A United World Empire, according to Biblical Prophecy as depicted in Daniel 2:42, 44; 7:7, 24; Revelation 12:3; 13:1; 17: 12 will consist of a ten-nation confederation and become the kingdom of the Antichrist.

"And as the toes of the feet were part of iron, and part of clay, so the kingdom shall be partly strong, and partly broken . . . And in the days of these kings shall the God of heaven set up a kingdom, which shall never be destroyed: and the kingdom shall not be left to other people, but it shall break in pieces and consume all these kingdoms, and it shall stand for ever . . . After this I saw in the night visions, and behold a fourth beast, dreadful and terrible, and strong exceedingly; and it had great iron teeth: it devoured and brake in pieces, and stamped the residue with the feet of it: and it was diverse from all the beasts that were before it; and it had ten horns . . . And the ten horns out of this kingdom are ten kings that shall arise . . ." (Daniel 2:42, 44; 7:7, 24).

"And there appeared another wonder in heaven: and behold a great red dragon, having seven heads and ten horns, and seven crowns upon the heads . . . And I stood upon the sand of the sea, and saw a beast rise up out of the sea, having seven heads and ten horns, and upon his horns ten crowns, and upon his heads the name of blasphemy . . . And the ten horns which thou sawest are ten kings, which have received no kingdom as yet; but receive power as kings one hour with the beast." (Revelation 12:3, 13:1; 17:12).

This United World Empire will soon rise to power with a magnitude equal to what it was in ancient times. A peace strategy to calm various degrees of crisis and the answers to a large majority of the world's problems will appear to be resolved by the leader of this empire. His move into power will be praised worldwide. Anyone failing to follow this initiative will be eliminated. Nothing will be allowed to stand in the way of Satan's greatest hour. He will finally become the World's greatest dictator, neatly packaged beneath the sheepskin of the Messiah.

The kingdoms made of Iron and Clay will fall, just like all the kingdoms before them—by the hand of God. The Gold kingdom of the Fallen Angels, the Silver kingdom of the Fallen Angels mating with humans to produce the Giants before the Flood, the Bronze race of the Demigods with the remnant of the Giants, the Iron race of Demigods mixing with pagans like the Canaanites, and the Clay and Iron race consisting of the mixing between the good seed of Abraham and Satan's evil lineages all will be destroyed. Scripture plainly states that mixing Fallen Angel genetics and mankind will not hold together; yet Satan, through the ages, has tried and tried to remake mankind to his pleasing.

According to veteran Ufologists Budd Hopkins and Dr. David Jacobs, the mixing of humans and Aliens are escalating. These two researchers have gathered information on this most disturbing feature that is presenting itself as part of the ongoing UFO phenomenon.

Their combined collection of reports identifies human looking Aliens that they have coined 'Transgenic Beings.' These strange entities seem to have mastered Alien paranormal abilities while functioning like mere humans on a daily basis. Hopkins and Jacobs are deeply concerned about what they have termed as "hybrid" (mixed) behavior patterns popping up in our society. It appears from their research that the Age of Clay and Iron is upon us and escalating.

In a book by Bill Chalker entitled, Hair of the Alien—DNA and other Forensic Evidence of Alien Abduction, the author releases some fascinating scientific findings for the first time in the history of Ufology. Chalker, who is a highly respected Australian ufologist, performed the first ever DNA testing on a hair sample, which an abductee found on his body after an Alien Abduction. Two phases of DNA analysis were performed on the blonde hair sample. The test revealed the hair came from the DNA of a rare Asian Mongoloid lineage—one of the rarest on Earth. Even stranger, the Mitochondrial DNA showed Chinese DNA, while the soft root tissue of the hair strand revealed the DNA of a Basque/Gaelic type DNA.

This was a most unusual discovery, as DNA should remain stable no matter where the hair strand was tested. The only available answer Chalker could find to explain this form of perfected DNA mixing would be that the individual was a Clone. The hair sample also showed total resistance to viruses that less than 1 percent of the human population harbors within their genetic structures and those who posses this rare gene are of Northeast European and Jewish descent. In this human population, their immunity to viruses appears to go back in time about 5000 years.

Satan is the Master at mixing because he cannot create anything. His Alchemical powers of re-making Eden on Earth are no doubt coming to fruition as it is more and more evident that we are the terminal generation that is prophesied. Regardless of that fact, Satan is going to fight God to the last second; but in the end, God, the Almighty Creator, will prevail. Jesus, the stone cut without hands, will be triumphant. Only those that have believed upon Him and who put 'no other gods before Him' will be the people allowed to reign with Jesus for all eternity. According to the interpretation of King Nebuchadnezzar's dream by Daniel the Prophet:

"And whereas thou sawest iron mixed with miry clay, they shall mingle themselves with the seed of men: but they shall not cleave one to another, even as iron is not mixed with clay . . . Forasmuch as thou sawest that the stone was cut out of the mountain without hands, and it brake in pieces the iron, the brass, the clay, the silver, and the gold; the great God hath made known to the king what shall come to pass hereafter: and the dream is certain, and the interpretation thereof sure." (Daniel 2:43, 45).

Regardless of what Satan already knows about what the future holds for him, his Secret Brotherhood of the International Community carefully continues designing their crisis situations in order to imprison the masses within their control. As we have already discovered, their deceptive games have a pre-planned solution before the staged tragedy occurs to ensure evil succeeds at a greater pace. It is the agenda of the elite Illuminated Ones to surround mankind with so much fear that they can easily be herded like sheep to the slaughter. The countdown began the moment Adam and Eve were removed from the Garden of Eden. Satan, from that time onward, has been after every soul he can get before Jehovah says, "Enough is enough," and confronts him at the Battle of Armageddon.

The souls of mankind are being fought over in a spiritual battle that rages on a daily basis. It is important that we wake up and take note of the choices that we are making moment by moment. Deception is being whirled at mankind from every direction so that we are increasingly being blinded to the real truth. You must remember Satan is the 'Master of Deception,' and he does not want you to see him for what he really is—the god of Hell and Brimstone.

The seeds of Satan are daily preparing our world for the rise of the Antichrist. The inhabitants of this world are being deceived and manipulated through a strategy known as the Hegelian Principle. This Principle deceives those not privy to what is really going on, and offers a solution to the crisis that the masses will jump at to stop the perceived emergency. An example of this concept is as follows. All Americans have had the freedom to own a gun. When a crisis is staged where kids start killing each other, the solution proposed is to have the American people agree to go along with getting rid of all personal guns. The Obama Administration pushed America closer than ever to giving up our guns. Now, during the Trump Administration, the push is being done by liberals using school shootings as the sole reason to give up our guns.

Since a good majority of the American public will not agree with this solution, the Hegelian Principle is then used. In an effort to seemingly compromise regarding a solution to this problem, the powers-that-be purpose to amend the solution to have all guns registered. Yet, before the crisis of kids killing kids, no one would have gone along with the need for fingerprints, background checks, and gun registration. The preplanned crisis along with an already decided solution deceptively pushed mankind a little closer to having no guns. Without guns, a country's citizenship cannot fight against a dictatorship.

The main objective of the Hegelian Principle is to deceptively get mankind to accept proposed directions by making them think the powers-that-be are meeting them halfway. It is like they instigate a war, knowing that they are the only gun dealer in town. They control both sides of the situation—the war and the guns. The Hegelian Principle is only intended to make someone think they have had a choice in a staged situation, unbeknownst that both sides of the controversy are controlled by the same group. So many people become innocent victims to these carefully contrived plots and are always on the losing end of the stick, though most times they do not even realize it.

In every country throughout history that has been forced or encouraged to give up their right to bear arms, that country was eventually ruled by a dictatorship that wreaked havoc upon its inhabitants, according to the booklet entitled Lethal Laws—"Gun Control" is the Key to Genocide by Simkin, Zelman & Rice. Yet in the beginning, all those countries were led into believing that giving up their guns would offer them total safety. In other words, they totally trusted in their government to look out for their best interest.

Daily, people's lives are being infiltrated with pre-planned mini-emergencies in an effort to make mankind hostage to the system of the controllers. Humanity is carefully being watched and manipulated by the 'Watchers'—Satan and his

Fallen Angels. These diabolical entities and their followers are alive and well in today's world. If you do not believe this, then step back and really take a good long look at all that is going on around you. You will be amazed how much has occurred right under your nose as you were hurrying along, engrossed in your own little world. What you will discover is that you have been accepting and overlooking things that at one point in your life you would not have agreed to.

In essence, you have become more and more tolerant of evil without realizing how far you have let it go. It is no laughing matter to jokingly say, "The Devil made me do it," because he probably did, and you went right along with him without thinking about your option to choose good over evil. You have become tolerant, and a tolerant generation is how the Antichrist will come to power.

Mystery Babylon, the great city of Jerusalem, will soon become the new home to Satan.

"And their dead bodies shall lie in the street of the great city, which spiritually is called Sodom and Egypt, where also our Lord was crucified." Revelation 11:8)

Every cult that came out of ancient Babylon was infiltrated with the seeds of Satan and their rebellious acts against the Laws of Jehovah. All sacred mysteries and Secret Societies can be traced back to the Tower of Babel, as well as to the lineage of Cain before the Flood. They have now positioned themselves in the Promised Land and await Satan, their Messiah.

The 'Great Work' will be promised by the seeds of Satan to all mankind as merely transmutation of oneself; the only drawback is that it involves selling your soul to the Devil. For most of humanity that will not be a problem, as no one wants to die. Just open your pineal gland and the Serpent is there waiting to enlighten you and gain possession of your soul so that the 'Triple Secret of the Great Work' can begin. The 'Triple Secret,' being the number 666, involves mankind's total acceptance of the Antichrist as their Messiah. Just remember, if you choose to follow Satan, you will spend eternity in Hell. Jehovah will destroy "Mystery Babylon" (Jerusalem) and all the paganism it stands for at the 'End of the Age.' John the Revelator recorded the vision he was shown regarding Mystery Babylon's fate in the final days:

" . . . Babylon the great is fallen, is fallen, and is become the habitation of devils, and the hold of every foul spirit, and a cage of every unclean and hateful bird." (Revelation 18:2).
It is important not to follow in the ways of Satan, because Jehovah will destroy all who do in the end. Your very soul is at stake every moment you breathe. All your thoughts and choices in life are recorded and you will be judged for your actions, unless you profess Jesus as your Lord and Savior. Scripture explains never to walk the path of sinners.

"My son, if sinners entice thee, consent thou not. If they say, come with us, let us lay wait for blood, let us lurk privily for the innocent without cause: Let us swallow them up alive as the grave; and whole, as those that go down into the pit: We shall find all precious substance, we shall fill our houses with spoil: Cast in thy lot among us; let us all have one purse: My son, walk not thou in the way with them; refrain thy foot from their path." (Proverbs 1:10–15).

"Blessed is the man that walketh not in the counsel of the ungodly, nor standeth in the way of sinners, nor sitteth in the seat of the scornful." (Psalms 1:1).

"This know also, that in the last days perilous times shall come. For men shall be lovers of their own selves, covetous, boasters, proud, blasphemers, disobedient to parents, unthankful, unholy, without natural affection, trucebreakers, false accusers, incontinent, fierce, despisers of those that are good, traitors, heady, high minded, lovers of pleasures more than lovers of God, having a form of godliness, but denying the power thereof; from such turn away." (2 Timothy 3:1–5).

If you choose to follow any of the paths of Satan and worship him over Jehovah, you will spend an eternity in Hell. A quest for enlightenment and divinity through the Hidden Mysteries of Satan are vehicles deceptively crafted to enslave your soul from God. The Bible explains that God will say these words to those that have followed after Satan, during the 'Great White Throne of Judgment:'

"Depart from me, ye cursed, into everlasting fire, prepared for the devil and his angels . . . And these shall go away into everlasting punishment: but the righteous into life eternal." (Matthew 25: 41, 46).

The Bible uses many names to describe Satan. The following is a list of those terrible names:

"Abaddon, accuser, adversary, Apollyon, Beelzebub, Belial, Devil, enemy, evil spirit, father of lies, great red dragon, liar, lying spirit, murderer, old serpent, power of darkness, prince of this world, power of the air, ruler of the darkness of this world, Satan, spirit that worketh in the children of disobedience, tempter, god of this world, unclean spirit, wicked one, son of the morning, beast, and Antichrist."

Satan and his Fallen Angels have been systematically attempting to destroy mankind's souls from the very beginning. There has been a seamless procession, down through the ages, of the same rituals to the same false gods, which continues to remain the 'Agenda' of today's Secret Societies. Satan has ingenious plans that are detailed and well designed for our present generation.

The Book of Job explains that God knows every one of Satan's evil works on earth. Also, notice that Satan is among those created by God, but not equal to God in the following Scripture:

"Now there was a day when the sons of God came to present themselves before the Lord, and Satan came also among them. And the Lord said unto Satan, Whence comest thou? Then Satan answered the Lord, and said, From going to and fro in the earth, and from walking up and down it." (Job 1:6–7).

The above verses of Scripture give us an understanding about the spirits of Demons coming from within the earth. Many reported cases over the centuries have included sightings of entities going into water, caves, Megalithic structures, mountains, and the ground. Satan and his angels exist in the spiritual realm. They possess the power that God created in all His spiritual beings. But they do not have power over Jehovah, the Creator.

Satanic power involves manipulating human consciousness through energy and thought vibrations. Some of these low frequency thought vibrations include hatred, fear, selfishness, and guilt. Demonic beings love to attack human emotions to break a person's spirit. They also enjoy attacks upon the human body through sickness, disease, and possession, in an effort to claim one's soul as the person begins to blame God for their unfortunate circumstances. In ancient times, all these forms of demonic activities were regarded as Satan's attempts at 'snatching one's soul.' Satan finds a person's 'Achilles' heel,' and in their weakened moment he can sometimes cause that person to give up on God and fall from grace.

Once a person turns their back on God, they have sinned. Satan wants mankind to follow in this selfish tradition, which began with his son, Cain. Scripture warns that committing sin is of the Devil:

"He that committeth sin is of the devil; for the devil sinneth from the beginning. For this purpose the Son of God was manifested, that he might destroy the works of the devil. Whosoever is born of God doth not commit sin; for his seed remaineth in him: and he cannot sin, because he is born of God. In this the Children of God are manifest, and the children of the devil: whosoever doeth not righteousness is not of God, neither he that loveth not his brother. For this is the message that ye heard from the beginning, that we should love one another. Not as Cain, who was of that wicked one, and slew his brother. And wherefore slew he him? Because his own works were evil, and his brother's righteous." (I John 3:8–12).

Satan's rise to power as the coming 'Prince of this World' will be the result of mankind's tolerance to evil and their acceptance of him as Savior. The control of the human mind and its biological activity will allow Satan to exercise power over mankind. He who has control of the mind has complete power over the body. A massive number of mind control programs are presently being developed around the world in a joint effort to suppress human consciousness.

These programs include electromagnetic devices, nanotechnology involving implanted nanorobots, vaccination programs to inject genetic markers in certain populations, food additives that produce lodged proteins that the body cannot assimilate, thereby setting up immune system deficiencies, and genetically altered foods that have an undesirable affect on the human DNA. As these programs are increasingly put into action, humanity will, in a sense, become sick and externally brainwashed to take their eyes off God.

The time is at hand for Satan to make his final move. Secret groups, similar to the U.S. Federal Emergency Management Agency, have been set up all over the world, along with newly constructed concentration camps deceitfully built as detention centers, to be used to imprison anyone who attempts to resist the plan for the New World Order. Those who fail to resist, on the other hand, are walking blindly into a path of destruction, which is being prepared for them by the 'Prince of this World.' The Antichrist is waiting in the wings. The earth is ripe for his dictatorship. No wonder John the Revelator wrote:

" . . . Woe to the inhabitants of the earth and of the sea! For the devil is comedown unto you, having great wrath, because he knoweth that he hath but a short time." (Revelation 12:12).

Part 7
The Omega ~
Your Wake-Up Call

Chapter Thirty-Two
Good versus Evil-Your Choice

Good seed and evil seed cannot successfully grow together, just like the old adage says, 'one bad apple can spoil the whole bunch.' It became mankind's fate, following the Garden of Eden, to have to choose between good or evil and, then, suffer the consequences. Pretending to be good but having an allegiance with Satan is not an acceptable path to Jehovah. No one can fool God by proficiency in the knowledge of Satan's esoteric Hidden Mysteries and secrets or by just good works. Jehovah knows all about each person's motives.

Since the wicked seeds of Satan and his Fallen Angels have been mixed within the various lineages of mankind, all the way down to the present Iron and Clay Race, the only way for a human being to claim salvation is through the grace and mercy of our Lord, Jesus Christ. In making this claim, a person must acknowledge that they are a sinner. They must openly confess that Jesus died for their sins and believe He rose from the dead to give them eternal life.

Mankind's only route to inherit eternal life is through the Cross of Jesus. This means that there are no dues or any special 'Craft' that a person must secretly participate in to obtain true spiritual immortality from God. On the other hand, choosing to play the so-called enlightenment game with Satan, by opening the mind's 'Third Eye' to receive his sacred knowledge, offers your soul a dead end.

Jehovah created Satan; Satan did not create Jehovah. Over the course of history, when Satan has gone head to head with Jehovah, he has lost. Satan did not have the power to keep Adam and Eve in the Garden of Eden. Satan did not have the power to stop the Israelites from crossing through the Red Sea unharmed. He did not have the power to stop David from killing the Giant, Goliath, who was a Chimera; part human and part Fallen Angel. Satan did not have the power to stop the Flood that was brought about because of the wickedness he had brought upon the earth's inhabitants and their offspring.

Most importantly, as Jesus hung on the Cross of Calvary, Satan could not kill Jesus as He bore the sins of all mankind. Jesus told His Father, Jehovah, at His precisely chosen moment, when to take His Spirit. Jesus said, "Father, into your hands I commend my spirit" (Luke 23:46).

At that moment, Jesus died. "Commend" means to entrust, committing to another with confidence. Satan did not have any power over Jesus; it was Jesus' decision to give up His spirit. Jesus was in total control as to when and exactly at what moment He would die. His bodily sacrifice was an all encompassing effort to save mankind. All we, as humans, have had to do from that day forward is ask for forgiveness of our sins and believe on Jesus as our Savior. Once we make the commitment to following Jesus, we are assured of eternal life forever.

Satan attempts to gain power over mankind through many different avenues. To protect oneself from evil, follow the instructions of the Apostle

Paul. In the Book of Ephesians, Paul writes,

"For we wrestle not against flesh and blood, but against principalities, against powers, against the rulers of darkness of this world, against spiritual wickedness in high places. Wherefore take unto you the whole armor of God, that ye may be able to withstand in the evil day, and having done all to stand. Stand therefore, having your loins girt about truth, and having on the breastplate of righteousness. And your feet shod with the preparation of the gospel of peace; above all, taking the shield of faith, wherewith, ye shall be able to quench all the fiery darts of the wicked. And take the helmet of salvation and the sword of the spirit, which is the word of God: Praying always with all prayer and supplication in the spirit, and watching therefore with all perseverance and supplication for all saints." (Ephesians 6:12–18).

Each individual has a choice in this life to either serve God or Satan. You, the reader, have been given the proof, throughout this book, that there has been, and still remains, a wicked parallel history devised by Satan for the continual deception of mankind. The knowledge of Satan's evil game is your personal wake-up call. You cannot continue yoking yourself together with men who practice the secret 'Craft' and expect to behold the glory of Heaven.

Jehovah will not coexist in your temple when your pineal gland is always tuned to Satan's channel of enlightenment. God will not dwell with those who worship the 'created more than the Creator.' He will leave your temple and He will never return. God has made it very clear that good and evil will never exist together in eternity. In God's eyes, there is no such thing as 'Yin and Yang' (Darkness and

Light) co-existing equally as a circle in perfect harmony. That is the backbone of Satan's Plan of deception. To enter into Jehovah's promise of eternal life, one must choose Jehovah solely, or He will "Spew thee out" (Revelation 3:16). Jehovah will never accept anyone into Heaven who is mixed up with Satan; only those who have called upon Jesus as their only Lord and Savior.

"Then shall he say also unto them on the left hand, Depart from me, ye cursed into everlasting fire, prepared for the devil and his angels. And these shall go away into everlasting punishment: but the righteous into life eternal." (Matthew 25:41, 46).

As we have discovered, the wicked seeds of Satan conceived an elaborate strategy to incorporate themselves into an undercover organization that would not be subjected to the ups and downs or the vagueness and uncertainties of political or social change, which might occur down through the ages. This organization is separate from society but in reality, controls all. Satanic manipulation of historical events through this covert organization has directly interfered with human development toward a relationship with Jesus Christ, the Son of God. This group of clandestine men has done more than any other organization known to mankind in out rightly setting up stumbling blocks that would condemn the soul's chance of spending eternal life with God, the Creator.

If you are caught up in this satanic web of deception of mixing good with evil, it is important to repent and come out of its grip before it is too late. You, and only you, control the true destiny of your soul by your personal choice. It is a great shame to have known the Will of God and then to intentionally turn away from Him like Satan, his Secret Brotherhoods, and the Fallen Angels have done.

"And many shall follow their pernicious ways; by reason of whom the way of truth shall be evil spoken of. For if God spared not the angels; that sinned, but cast them down to hell, and delivered them into chains of darkness, to be reserved unto judgment; And spared not the old world, but saved Noah the eighth person, a preacher of righteousness, bringing in the flood upon the world of the ungodly; The Lord knoweth how to deliver the godly out of temptations, and to reserve the unjust unto the day of judgment to be punished: But chiefly them that walk after the flesh in the lust of uncleanness, and despise government. Presumptuous are they, self-willed, they are not afraid to speak evil of dignities. For it had been better for them not to have known the way of righteousness, than, after they have known it, to turn from the holy commandment delivered to them (that of: 'Thou shalt have no other gods before me')." (II Peter 2:2, 4–5, 9, 21, Parenthetical comment mine).

The Book of Matthew reports that as we near the 'End of Time,' deception will be increased to such a level that even men of God could be deceived. Satan and his Angels know their time on earth is getting shorter, and they will begin using every form of evil technology available to try and trap man. Matthew records what Jesus told His Disciples on the Mount of Olives about the sign of his coming and of the end of the world,

"For there shall arise false Christs, and False Prophets, and shall shew great signs and wonders; insomuch that, if it were possible, they shall deceive the very elect. For as the lightning cometh out of the east, and shineth even unto the west; so shall also the coming of the Son of man be." (Matthew 24:24, 27).

Make your decision now as to where you want to spend eternity. Hell is a real place, where man will be tormented, have a memory, realize they are separated from God, and forever burn eternally with everyone else who chose to follow Satan and his Fallen Angels in their rebellion against God. Heaven, on the other hand, will be Paradise. It is a place of joy, love, peace, and eternal gifts from our Father, our Creator. It is important to remember that Heaven can only be enjoyed by those who choose to follow Jesus and pay homage to Him as the Son of the one and only God. If you make that choice to accept Jesus as your Lord and Savior, the Bible promises that the beauty of Heaven will be superior to anything your human eyes have ever beheld on Earth.

Jesus Christ is the only way to reach those beautiful Heavenly Gates. No one is ever good enough, because we, as human beings, are born in sin due to our ancestors, Adam and Eve, eating of the Tree of Knowledge against God's command. Salvation cannot be earned through the mastery of a so-called secret 'Craft' of Satan, pretending to be good by giving to charities, or even by just going to church. We are saved by grace through our faith alone. To be accepted by Jehovah, our Father, we must acknowledge His Son, Jesus, as our Personal Savior. The Book of John states,

"Jesus saith unto him, I am the way, the truth, and the life: no man cometh unto the Father, but by me." (John 14:6).

To be saved, you must openly believe and confess, before man, your love for Jesus. The Scriptures teach us:

"That if thou shalt confess with thy mouth the Lord Jesus, and shalt believe in thine heart that God hath raised him from the dead, thou shalt be saved." (Romans 10:9).

"Then Peter, filled with the Holy Ghost, said unto them, ye rulers of the people and elders of Israel . . . Be it known unto you all, and to all the people of Israel that . . . Jesus Christ of Nazareth, whom ye crucified, whom God raised from the dead . . . This is the stone which was set at nought of you builders, which is become the head of the corner. Neither is there salvation in any other: for there is none other name under heaven given among men, whereby we must be saved." (Acts 4:8–12).

Jesus promises all believers the reward for being faithful. The Book of Revelation reveals,

"And behold, I come quickly; and my reward is with me, to give every man according as his work shall be. I am Alpha and Omega, the beginning and the end, the first and the last. Blessed are they that do his commandments, that they may have right to the tree of life, and may enter in through the gates into the city." (Revelation 22:12–14).

Satan and his followers will be working overtime during the coming days to try and convince mankind that the way to eternal life is through the hidden sciences of enlightenment. As more and more Sumerian, Mesopotamian, Mayan, and Egyptian texts, which are linked to the lineage of Cain, are unearthed, Satan's alternative history, which has run parallel to Christian history, will be promoted as discoveries of the so-called real truth. The intent behind these discoveries will be to promote Satan's mixed religious practices of the Canaanite lineage over Jehovah's 'Chosen lineage of Seth.' Satan's secret way to enlightenment, found written on such discoveries, will be viewed as being tolerant and non-discriminating, while Jehovah's way will be considered outdated and very discriminating.

This new paradigm shift in world view will instigate changes regarding religious teachings in order for worshippers to become more accommodating to the acceptance of the Holy Grail Legend and to its deceptively crafted Holy Merovingian 13th Blood Line from Cain. This fallacious attempt is to try to historically erase the Christian lineage of Jesus from Seth and replace it with Cain's. Those behind this misleading plan will chastise the Christian faith by stating that Jehovah's Old Covenants have kept mankind in darkness, away from the full fruits of human possibility. Those behind the paradigm shift are pushing humanity toward a New World Religion.

The Devil is not an atheist by any means, nor is he opposed to religion. He personally knows God is very real and so do his Fallen Angels and Demons. Satan just wants everyone to follow his false religion and worship him instead of God. That is why pagan religion focuses on self and pride. Pride is what made Lucifer fall from Heaven in the first place.

"How art thou fallen from heaven, O Lucifer, son of the morning? how art thou cut down to the ground, which didst weaken the nations! For thou hast said in thine heart, I will ascend into heaven, I will exalt my throne above the stars of God: I will sit also upon the mount of the congregation, in the sides of the north: I will ascend above the heights of the clouds; I will be like the most High. Yet thou, shalt be brought down to hell, to the sides of the pit. They that see thee shall narrowly look upon thee, and consider thee, saying, Is this the man that made the earth to tremble, that did shake kingdoms; that made the world as a wilderness, and destroyed the cities thereof; that opened not the house of his prisoners? All the kings of the nations, even all of them lie in glory, every one in his own house. But thou are cast out of thy grave like an abominable branch, and as the raiment of those that are slain, thrust through with a sword, that go down to the stones of the pit; as a carcase trodden under feet. Thou shalt not be joined with them in burial because thou hast destroyed thy land, and slain thy people: the seed of evildoers shall never be renowned." (Isaiah 14:12–20).

Therefore, God will never allow intellectual pride to have a place in Heaven, because its fruit only produces bitterness, bondage, and poison. Do not allow yourself to be dazzled by the forces of evil, its supernatural powers (like fire falling from heaven) or promises of the things of this world (like wealth and great power). Satan's religion is a superficial faith that focuses on self-centeredness, the love of mammon, and the love of nature/Mother Earth over God, the Creator.

The Book of Romans warns mankind that by partaking in Satan's religion, which promotes things in the flesh, they are displeasing God and will suffer eternal death. On the other hand, if mankind seeks after the Spirit of God, they will live. Scripture is very clear about the differences between love of God and love of the flesh when it states,

"There is therefore now no condemnation to them which are in Christ Jesus, who walk not after the flesh, but after the Spirit. For the law of the Spirit of life in Christ Jesus hath made me free from the law of sin and death . . . For they that are after the flesh do mind the things of the flesh; but they that are after the Spirit the things of the Spirit. For to be carnally minded is death; but to be spiritually minded is life and peace . . . Therefore, brethren, we are debtors, not to the flesh, to live after the flesh. For if ye live after the flesh, ye shall die: but if ye through the Spirit do mortify the deeds of the body, ye shall live." (Romans 8:1–2, 5–6, 12–13).

Archeological discoveries will increasingly continue to prove that our present day technology does not even come close to the advanced sciences and knowledge that our ancestors achieved through their sacred mysteries. The coming 'One World Religion' will offer enlightenment to the flesh based on the 'Pillars of Destiny,' which will promise mankind a form of god-like status. This shift in thinking is part of the New Age agenda's focus on lifting the veil, which they preach, was put over our eyes by Jehovah. This way of thinking is slowly infiltrating our world through all forms of the media.

We are gradually being subliminally brainwashed to accept this paradigm shift without realizing that instead of worshipping God, we are tolerating the worship of Satan all around us. As we have already discovered, the Masonic movement has been quite successful in this tactic, saying one thing but meaning another. The Book of Proverbs warns about accepting the secret doctrine of wisdom, called 'Sophia' by the New Age gurus, when it says,

"Stolen waters are sweet, and bread eaten in secret is pleasant. But he knoweth not that the dead are there; and that her guests are in the depths of hell." (Proverbs 9:17–18).

Remaining a truly dedicated Christian during the coming years before the Apocalypse will increasingly become more and more difficult. Followers of Jehovah will be harassed and imprisoned by the world for being backward, blind to progress, politically incorrect, not tolerant, biased, standing in the way of progress, and a menace to the completion of the New World Order. Faithful Christians right now are the only thing standing in direct opposition to the New Age quest for immortality and their so-called inheritance of godlike status. Liberals are itching to Clone, legalize abortion, use aborted babies for flesh experiments, mix genetics of plants and species, stop the study of absoluteness, accept tolerance of allowing a person to do anything they want to do, respect their rights, and freedom of sexual expression—you name it. The only thing stopping them is the fact that right now there are too many Christians. The only way the seeds of Satan have in rendering this dilemma is to kill us, control us, or slowly brainwash us into accepting their line of thinking.

Satan's followers are even counterfeiting the born again experience of true Christians through their pagan practices of 'Third Eye' illumination involving the pineal gland. These gurus selling meditation and relaxation therapies to find the 'inner you' are making millions holding workshops in schools, the corporate world, and even in churches. Their techniques, whether experienced live or through a preprogrammed session for home use, are attempting to harness an energy that will force everyone to tune into Satan's transmissions of enlightenment. Once the masses are indoctrinated into willfully opening up their 'Third Eye,' the enlightened ones will schedule a planned event to ensure worldwide acceptance of Satan as the 'Savior of Mankind.'

"Even him, whose coming is after the working of Satan with all power and signs and lying wonders. And with all deceivableness of unrighteousness in them that perish; because they received not the love of the truth, that they might be saved. And for this cause God shall send them strong delusion, that they should believe a lie: That they all might be damned who believe not the truth, but had pleasure in unrighteousness." (II Thessalonians 2:9–12).

The Antichrist is waiting in the wings, and will soon offer miraculous signs and wonders to further mesmerize humanity without ever having to acknowledge the true Creator, Jehovah.

Those promoting Satan have secretly denounced Jesus Christ as their Lord, but will deceptively use the blood of Christ as a false plan of salvation. They are the Masters who took the Holy Blood from the Shroud of Turin, so protected by the Templar and the Vatican, to produce their Holy Grail for mankind's earthly regeneration. Their alchemical transmutation involving this sacred blood was used to produce a 'Cloned Chimera Beast' that will soon take the world's stage by storm. He will be the living example that will be used to promote the evil science of cellular fission as the key to earthly immortality. Satan will be so believable, walking among man in this Cloned image of Jesus, that few will recognize his counterfeit agenda. As the Antichrist, Satan will begin to rid the world of all who say he is not the risen Messiah, the Prince of Peace, and the Savior of Mankind.

The war between Satan and God started in Heaven and has continued from the beginning until now. From the moment Lucifer was cast from Heaven, he and his followers have been at war with all who have chosen to follow the Commandments of Jehovah and who believe in His Son, Jesus Christ. The Book of Revelation reveals,

"And there was war in heaven: Michael and his angels fought against the dragon; and the dragon fought and his angels. And prevailed not; neither was their place found any more in heaven. And the great dragon was cast out, that old serpent, called the Devil, and Satan, which deceiveth the whole world: he was cast out into the earth, and his angels were cast out with him. And I heard a loud voice saying in heaven, Now is come salvation, and strength, and the kingdom of our God, and the power of his Christ: for the accuser of our brethren is cast down, which accused them before our God day and night. And they overcame him by the blood of the Lamb, and by the word of their testimony; and they loved not their lives unto the death. Therefore rejoice, ye heavens, and ye that dwell in them. Woe to the inhabitants of the earth and of the sea! For the devil is come down unto you, having great wrath, because he knoweth that he hath but a short time. And when the dragon saw that he was cast unto the earth, he persecuted the woman which brought forth the man child. And to the woman were given two wings of a great eagle, that she might fly into the wilderness, into her place, where she is nourished for a time, and times, and a half a time, from the face of the serpent. And the serpent cast out of his mouth water as a flood after the woman, that he might cause her to be carried away of the flood. And the earth helped the woman, and the earth opened her mouth, and swallowed up the flood which the dragon cast out of his mouth. And the dragon was wroth with the woman and went to make war with the remnant of her seed, which keep the commandments of God, and have the testimony of Jesus Christ." (Revelation 12:7–17).

As Christians, we are the good seed that keep the commandments of God. We are and will continue to be the target of Satan and his Angels' rebellion against Jehovah. Throughout this book, we have seen how the war began in Eden, how it has traveled through history, both openly and secretly, and how in these last days it is raging and daily escalating. The process is like a woman in labor. As she nears delivery, the pangs increase and get closer and closer together.

Our generation is witnessing these birth pangs, which were prophesied to occur at the 'End of Time,' as they are getting closer and closer together. President Donald Trump is trying to bring a peace plan to the Middle East in hopes to slow the tensions between Israel and Palestine; as well as, defeat Isis. But, God's timetable for retribution is on the horizon so the stroke of midnight is drawing near for the final conflict between good and evil - the Battle of Armageddon. This enormous World War III will be a battle of religious nature. It will herald the Second Coming of our Lord, Jesus Christ. Jesus will fight and defeat the Antichrist, who will be deceptively posing as His Twin. The Battle of Armageddon will be both a physical and a spiritual war to completely rid the earth of Satan's false religions and the Secret Societies within which they have thrived.

God has provided, through His Word, the wisdom and understanding needed to prepare mankind for what we are experiencing in the world today. There is no reason for confusion regarding how world events will play out or what Satan's followers are really up to. After reading this book, you now have an understanding of what the Beast recorded in the Book of Revelation, known as the Antichrist, will act and look like. Open your eyes and embrace truth before it is too late.

I was once told a prophetic word from a minister of the Gospel who explained to me that God had given me great insight into His Word and that if I did not choose to share it with my fellow man I would become like the Dead Sea—nothing more coming in and nothing going out. The moment this man of God told me this, tears flooded down my face because I knew his words to me were true. Therefore, I have written this book in submission to my Savior's call in order to warn you, the reader, with the knowledge He has flowed into me before it is too late for you.

"So thou, O son of man, I have set thee a watchman unto the house of Israel; therefore thou shalt hear the word at my mouth, and warn them from me. When I say unto the wicked, O wicked man, thou shalt surely die; if thou dost not speak to warn the wicked from his way, that wicked man shall die in his iniquity; but his blood will I require at thine hand. Nevertheless, if thou warn the wicked of his way to turn from it; if he do not turn from his way, he shall die in his iniquity; but thou hast delivered thy soul. Therefore, O thou son of man, speak unto the house of Israel; Thus ye speak, saying, If our transgressions and our sins be upon us, and we pine away in them, how should we then live? Say unto them, As I live, saith the Lord God, I have no pleasure in the death of the wicked; but that the wicked turn from his way and live: turn ye, turn ye from your evil ways; for why will ye die, O house of Israel?" (Ezekiel 33:7–11).

If you think you have plenty of time and are not living in the final days before the Antichrist comes to rule and reign, then take heed. The Bible says the generation that will see these next ten signs come to pass are members of the terminal generation. The ten signs are as follows:

1. An Unprecedented Explosion of Knowledge.

2. The Invention and threat of Nuclear Warfare.

3. Israel Re-Born May 15, 1948, and Temple to be rebuilt (Sanhedrin reorganized on Jan. 12, 2005, and the Temple is their 1st priority).

4. Mockers of Christianity.

5. Jews of various ancestries return to Israel.

6. Jerusalem not governed by the Gentile nations–Six Day War - 1967.

7. International news media through satellite transmissions, which enables the Gospel to be preached to every nation, and in the near future will be used to transmit the two witnesses of Jesus, at the end of time, lying dead in the streets of Jerusalem in one hour.

8. Deception—Inability to distinguish the difference between good and evil. The Abomination of Desolation.

9. Floods/Famines/Pestilences/Earthquakes/Signs in the Heavens.

10. As it was in the days of Noah, so it shall be with the Second Coming of the Son of Man.

There is no question that these signs belong to our present generation and to none before, because once they are all fulfilled, the 'Battle of Armageddon' will ensue. You are definitely a member of the prophesied generation that will witness the 'End of the Age.' It is vital that you get your house in order and sweep out everything that has the sinful potential to force you to have to stand before God, the Creator, at His Great White Throne of Judgment.

The Book of Revelation clearly defines what this Final Day of Judgment before the Creator of All will be like:

"And the devil that deceived them was cast into the lake of fire and brimstone, where the beast and the false prophet are, and shall be tormented day and night forever and ever. And I saw a great white throne, and him that sat on it, from whose face the earth and the heaven fled away; and there was found no place for them. And I saw the dead, small and great, stand before God; and the books were opened: and another book was opened, which is the book of life: and the dead were judged out of those things which were written in the books, according to their works. And the sea gave up the dead which were in it; and death and hell delivered up the dead which were in them: and they were judged every man according to their works. And death and hell were cast into the lake of fire. This is the second death. And whosoever was not found written in the book of life was cast into the lake of fire." (Revelation 20: 10–15).

I leave you with a question that only you and you alone can answer. Now that you understand the consequences of falling victim to Satan's deception, "Is your name written in the Book of Life?" The choice is yours. Take time, right now, to understand this game of life you are living and ask

Jesus to come into your heart and save you. Make sure you are not playing along with your eyes closed concerning what is actually going on around you. You have been warned! There will be only one winner in the end, and that will be the team that is totally dedicated to following the Lord and Savior, Jesus Christ.

In other words, I believe it is like walking on water. Most people are afraid they will sink, so instead of stepping out onto the water in faith, they choose to stay in the materialistic boat that they can see and feel. As a Christian, you have to be different; you have to believe in Jesus. I am not going to stay in the boat. The answer lies in walking on the water, and I am going to walk on the water, just as Peter would have done if he had kept his eyes focused solely on Jesus. I invite you to do the same.

In closing, a lady whom I had just met one day following a long intensive prayer session at a local church went to hug me as I started to leave. As she turned to walk away, she looked back at me straight in the eyes and said prophetically, "I see a lighthouse when I look at you; you are a lighthouse."

At that time, I really did not totally understand the magnitude of what God had laid on her heart to tell me. Now I do. The road to where I am spiritually has meant spending many hours alone with the presence of God, researching and writing this book. Like a lighthouse standing alone on the hill, I pray that the light of Jesus will shine out over the water and lead you safely home to where you were created to be—in the arms of Jehovah your Creator.

As a soldier for our Lord and Savior, Jesus Christ, I look forward to you joining our Heavenly team and enjoying Eternity with us Forever!!!!!

"Not to oppose error is to approve it, and not to defend truth is to suppress it, and indeed to neglect to confound evil men, when we can do it, is no less
a sin than to encourage them."
Pope St. Felix III

"Behold, I give unto you power to tread on serpents and scorpions and over all the power of the enemy: and nothing shall by any means hurt you."
Luke 10:19

ADAM

Believe my friend
Upon the future,
For if we could see it
How our lives would change.
Not into the wind
But into the past,
We release our sorrows,
Never to be bothered by them again.
It is not death that brings sorrow,
But the sadness of death,
For if death had not existed
I would be alive . . . 36
In Christian Love,
"Dr. Joye"

Psalm 26 - A Psalm of David

"JUDGE me, O Lord; for I have walked in mine integrity: I have trusted also in the Lord; therefore I shall not slide. Examine me, O Lord, and prove me; try my reins and my heart. For thy loving kindness is before mine eyes: and I have walked in thy truth. I have not sat with vain persons; neither will I go in with dissemblers. I have hated the congregation of evil doers; and will not sit with the wicked. I will wash mine hands in innocency: so will I compass thine alter, O Lord. That I may publish with the voice of thanksgiving, and tell of all thy wondrous works. Lord, I have loved the habitation of thy house, and the place where thine honour dwelleth. Gather not my soul with sinners, nor my life with bloody men: In whose hands is mischief and their right hands is full of bribes. But as for me, I will walk in mine integrity: redeem me, and be merciful unto me. My foot standeth in an even place: in the congregations will I bless the Lord."

Preach the Word - II Timothy 4:1-8

"I charge thee therefore before God, and the Lord Jesus Christ, who shall judge the quick and the dead at his appearing and his kingdom; Preach the word; be instant in season, out of season; reprove, rebuke, exhort with all longsuffering and doctrine. For the time will come when they will not endure sound doctrine; but after their own lusts shall they heap to themselves teachers, having itching ears; And they shall turn away their ears from the truth, and shall be turned unto fables. But watch thou in all things, endure afflictions, do the work of an evangelist, make full proof of thy ministry. For I am now ready to be offered, and the time of my departure is at hand. I have fought a good fight, I have finished my course, I have kept the faith: Henceforth there is laid up for me a crown of righteousness, which the Lord, the righteous judge, shall give me at that day: and not to me only, but unto all them also that love his appearing."

Bibliography

Adams, Samuel. Cattle Mutilations—An Elusive Prey. Raleigh, North Carolina: Pentland Press, Inc., 2000.

Allnut, Frank. Antichrist—After the Omen. New Jersey: Spire Books, 1976.

Andrews, Colin. Crop Circles—Signs of Contact. Franklin Lakes, New Jersey: New Page Books, 2003.

Ankerberg, John and Weldon, John. The Secret Teachings of the Masonic Lodge. Chicago: Moody Press, 1989.

Baigent, Michael and Leigh, Richard. The Temple and the Lodge. New York: Aracade Publishing, 1989.

Bailey, Alice. Discipleship in the New Age, Vol 2. New York and London: Lucis Publishing Co., 1986.

Becker, Robert O. and Seldon, Gary. The Body Electric. New York: William Morrow, 1985.

Blake, Steve and Lloyd, Scott. Pendragon The Definitive Account of the Origins of Arthur. Guilford, Connecticut: The Lyons Press, 2003.

Blavatsky, The Secret Doctrine. Pasadena, California: Theosophical University Press, 1963.

Burrell, Paul. A Royal Duty. New York, New York: G.P. Putnam's Sons, 2003.

Carlyon, Richard. A Guide to the God's. London: Heineman/Quixote, 1981.

Chalker, Bill. Hair of the Alien—DNA and Other Forensic Evidence of Alien Abduction. New York: Paraview Pocket Books, 2005.

Churton, Tobias. The Gnostics. New York, New York: Barnes & Nobles, 1987.

Cohen, Tim. The AntiChrist and a Cup of Tea. Aurora, CO: Prophecy House, Inc., 1998.

Cotterell, Maurice. The Tutankhamun Prophecies–The Sacred Secret of the Maya, Egyptians, and Freemasons. Rochester, Vermont: Bear & Company, 2001.

Davies, Kevin. Cracking the Genome. New York, New York: The Free Press, 2001.

Drosnin, Michael. Bible Code II—The Countdown. New York, New York: Viking Penguin, 2002.

Druffel, Ann. How To Defend Yourself Against Alien Abduction. New York, New York: Three Rivers Press/Random House, 1998.

Dunn, Christopher P. The Giza Power Plant. New Mexico: Bear and Company, 1998.

Dupont-Sommer, Andre. The Essene Writings from Qumran, (trans. Geza Vermes). Oxford: Basil Blackwell, 1961.

Elkington, David. In the Name of the Gods. Sherbourne, UK: Greenman Press, 2001.

Filer, George. Filers Files—2003 Skywatch Investigations #24 - #27. "UFOFlap in Europe", "The Illusion of Knowledge", "Green Meteors and Cylinders", "Electrolyte Imbalances in Abductees". www.GeorgeFiler.com/

Finlay, Anthony. Demons—The Devil, Possession, and Exorcism. London: Vega/Chrysalis Books p/c, 2002.

Gardner, Laurence. Bloodline of the Holy Grail. Massachusetts: Element Book, Inc., 1996.

Gardner, Laurence. Genesis of the Grail Kings. Massachusetts: Fair Winds Press, 2002.

Gardner, Laurence. Realm of the Ring Lords. The Myth and Magic of the Grail Quest. Massachusetts: Fair Winds Press, 2002.

Garza–Valdes, Leoncio A. DNA of God? New York, New York: Double Day, 1999.

Geryl, Patrick and Ratinckx, Gino. The Orion Prophecy–Will the World be Destroyed in 2012? Prophecies from the Maya and the Old Egyptians. Kempton, Illinois: Adventures Unlimited Press, 2001.

Good, Timothy. Above Top Secret: The World Wide UFO Coverup. London: Sidgwick and Jackson, 1987.

Graham, O.J. The Six-Pointed Star. Don Mills, Ontario: The Free Press, 1948.

Graham, Tim and Archer, Peter. WILLIAM. New York, New York: ATRIA BOOKS, 2003.

Hall, Manly P. The Phoenix. Los Angeles, California: Philosophical Research Project, 1960.

Hall, Manly P. The Secret Destiny of America. Los Angeles, California: Philosophical Research Library, 1972.
Hancock, Graham and Faiia, Santha. Heaven's Mirror. New York, New York: Crown Publishers, Inc., 1998.

Hansen, George P. The Trickster and the Paranormal. Xlibris, www.xlibris.com, 2001.

Harris, Jack. Freemasonry—The Invisible Cult In Our Mist. Pennsylvania: Whitaker House, 1983.

Haselhoff, Eltjo H. The Deepening Complexity of Crop Circles–Scientific Research & Urban Legends. Berkeley, California: Frog, Ltd., 2001.

Haupt, Reginald C. The Gods of the Lodge. Savannah, Georgia: Victory Publishing Company, 1990.

Hitler, Adolf. Mein Kampf. New York, New York: Houghton-Mifflin Co., 1971.

Hesemann, Michael. The Fatima Secret. New York, New York: Dell Publishing, 2000.

Hoey, Brian. Prince William. Gloucestershire, England: Sutton Publishing Limited, 2003.

Hoffman, Michael A. Secret Societies and Psychological Warfare. Coeur d'Alene, Idaho: Independent History and Research, 2001.

Hurtak, J.J. The Book of Knowledge : The Keys of Enoch. Los Gratos, California: Academy for Future Science, 1977.

Ice, Thomas and Demy, Timothy. The Coming Cashless Society. Eugene, Oregon: Harvest House Publishers, 1996.

Icke, David. The Biggest Secret. Montana: Bridge of Love Publications USA, 1999.

Icke, David. Tales from the Time Loop. Wildwood, Montana: Bridge of Love Publications USA, 2003.

Jeffrey, Grant R. Armageddon. New York, New York: Bantam Books, 1990.

Jeffrey, Grant R. Jesus: The Great Debate. Tennessee: Word Publishing, 1999.

Jeffrey, Grant R. The Handwriting of God. Toronto, Ontario: Frontier Research Publications, Inc. 1997.

Jeffrey, Grant R. War on Terror—Unfolding Bible Prophecy. Ontario: Frontier Research Publications, Inc. 2002.

Jenkins, John Major. Galactic Alignment—The Transformation of Consciousness According to Mayan, Egyptian, and Vedic Traditions. Rochester, Vermont: Bear & Company, 2002.

Josephus, Flavius. The Jewish Wars (translated by G.A. Williams). Harmondsworth: Penquin, 1959.

Josephus, Flavius. The Works of Flavius Josephus: The Antiquities of the Jews I, Against Apion (translated by William Whiston). London: Milner And Sowerby, 1870.

Keith, Jim. Mind Control and UFO's: Casebook on Alternative 3. Lilburn, Georgia: IllumiNet Press, 1999.

Keith, Jim. Saucers of the Illuminati. Lilburn, Georgia: IllumiNet Press, 1999.

King James Version. Holy Bible. New Jersey: Thomas Nelson, Inc., 1972.

King, Jon and Beveridge, John. Princess Diana—The Hidden Evidence. New York, New York: S.P.I. Books, 2002.

Knight, Christopher and Lomas, Robert. The Hiram Key. Massachusetts: Element Books, Inc., 1998.

Knight, Christopher and Lomas, Robert. The Second Messiah. Massachusetts: Element Books, Inc., 1998.

Knight, Christopher and Lomas, Robert. Uriel's Machine. Massachusetts: Fair Winds Press, 1999.

Knight, Stephen. The Brotherhood—The Secret World of The Freemasons. USA: Dorset Press, 1986.

Kolata, Gina. Clone. New York, New York: William Morrow and Company, Inc., 1998.

Kramer, Paul. The Devil's Final Battle. Buffalo, NY: The Missionary Association, 2002.

Kramer, Samuel N. Sumerian Mythology. New York, New York: Harper Brothers, 1961.

Kramer, Samuel N. The Sumerians—Their History, Culture, and Character. Chicago: The University of Chicago Press, 1971.

Leonard, George. The Silent Pulse. New York, NY: E.P. Dutton, 1978.

Mackey, Albert. An Encyclopedia of Freemasonry. Chicago, Illinois: the Masonic History Company, 1927.

Manning, Jeane and Begich, Nick. Angels Don't Play This HAARP. Alaska: Earth Pulse Press, 1995.

Mannion, Michael. Project Mind Shift. London: M. Evans and Company, Inc., 1998.

Marrs, Texe. Circle of Intrigue. Austin, Texas: Living Truth Publishers, 1995.

Marrs, Texe. Codex Magica. Austin, Texas: River Crest Publishing, 2005. Marrs, Texe. Dark Majesty. Austin, Texas: Living Truth Publishers, 1992.

Marsden, Victor E. The Protocols of the Learned Elders of Zion. Boring, Oregon: CPA Book Publisher, 1934.

Martin, Malachi. Hostage to the Devil. New York: Harper San Francisco, ed., 1992.

Martin, Malachi. The Keys of This Blood. New York, New York: Touchstone, 1990.

Martin. Malachi. Windswept House. New York, New York: Broadway Books, 2001.

Marx, Karl. Das Kapital. London, England, 1867.

Mitcham, Larry. September 11 is in the Bible Code. Australia: New Litho Pty. Ltd., 2001.

Morton, Andrew. Diana in pursuit of love. Martinsburg, WV: Michael \ O'Mara, 2004.

MUFON Journal. "Filer's Files—Sitchin, the Bible, & genes." Morrison, CO: MUFON, May 2001, pg. 11.

MUFON Journal. Morrison, CO : MUFON, November 2002; May 2003; June, 2003.

Nave, Orville J. Nave's Topical Bible. Nashville, Tennessee: The Southwestern Company, 1962.

North, John. Stonehenge. New York, New York: The Free Press, 1996.

Ovason, David. The Secret Architecture of our Nation's Capital. New York, New York: Harper Collins, 1999.

Orwell, George. 1984. New York, New York: New American Library/Signet Paperback Edition, 1983.

Picknett, Lynn and Prince, Clive. The Templar Revelation. New York, New York: Touchstone Simon & Schuster, 1997.

Pike, Albert. Morals and Dogma of the Ancient and Accepted Scottish Rite of Freemasonry. Richmond, Virginia: L.H. Jenkins, 1924.

Pike, Theodore Winston. Israel Our Duty . . . Our Dilemma. Oregon City, Oregon: Big Sky Press, 1984.

Pringle, Lucy. Crop Circles—The Greatest Mystery of Modern Times. London: Thorsons, 1999.

"Project Grudge Report". See website at: http://www.majesticdocuments.

com/authentication/archives/national archives.html-grudge.
Prophet, Elizabeth Clare. Fallen Angels and the Origins of Evil. Montana: Summit University Press, 2000.

Pugh, Joye Jeffries. ANTICHRIST–The Cloned Image of Jesus Christ. Griffin, Georgia: Vision Publishing Group, 1999. www.drjoye.com.

Pugh, Joye Jeffries. Colours of Joye. Limited Edition Poetry (Joye Jeffries). Fitzgerald, Georgia: Gibbons House Publishers, 1975.

Queensboro, Lady. Occult Theocracy. California: Christian Book Club of America, 1931.

Rauschning, Hermann. Voice of Destruction. New York, New York: G.P. Putnam Sons, 1940.

Ravenscroft, Trevor and Wallace-Murphy, Tim. The Mark of the Beast– The Continuing Story of the Spear of Destiny. York Beach, Maine: Samuel Weiser, Inc., 1997.

Rice, John R. LODGES- Examined by the Bible. Murfreesboro, Tennessee: Sword of the Lord Publishers, 1971.

Riplinger, Gail A. New Age Versions of the Bible. Ohio: A.V. Publications, 1993.

Rorvik, David M. In His Image. New York, New York: J.B. Lippincott Co., 1978.

Rosio, Bob. Hitler and the New Age. Lafayette, Louisiana: Huntington House Publishers, 1993.

Roux, Georges. Ancient Iraq. London: George Allen & Unwin, 1964.

Russell, Bertrand. The Impact of Science on Society. 1953.
Schwartz, Gary E. The Afterlife Experiments. New York, New York: Pocket Books, 2002.

Shaw, Jim and McKenney, Tom. The Deadly Deception. Louisiana: Huntington House, 1988.

Silva, Freddy. Secrets In The Fields. Charlottesville, Virginia: Hampton Roads Publishing Company, Inc., 2002.

Simkin, J., Zelman, A. and Rice, A. M. Lethal Laws "Gun Control" is the Key to Genocide. Milwaukee, Wisconsin: Jews for the Preservation of Firearms Ownership, Inc., 1994.

Simmons, Simone. Diana The Last Word. New York, New York: St. Martin's Press, 2005.

Sinclair, Andrew. The Sword and The Grail. New York, New York: Crown Publishers, Inc., 1992.

Sitchin, Zecharia. The Lost Book of Enki. Vermont: Bear and Company, 2002.

Sitchin, Zecharia. The 12th Planet. New York, New York: Avon Books, 1976.

Sora, Steven. The Lost Treasure of the Knights Templar. Rochester, Vermont: Destiny Books, 1999.

Springmeier, Fritz. Bloodlines of the Illuminati. Texas: Ambassador House, 3rd edition, 2002.

Steiger, Brad and Francie. Gods of Aquarius. New York, New York: Berkeley Books, 1981.

Still, William T. The New World Order: The Ancient Plan of Secret Societies. Lafayette, Louisiana: Huntington House Publishers, 1990.

Strieber, Whitley. Transformation, The Break Through. New York, New York: Beech Tree Books, William Morrow, 1988.

Tesla, Nikola & Childress, David H. The Fantastic Inventions of Nikola Tesla. Stelle, Illinois: Adventures Unlimited, 1993.

The Way. The Living Bible, Illustrated. Tyndale, 1970.
Thiede, Carsten Peter and d'Ancona, Matthew. The Quest For The True Cross. New York, New York: PALGRAVE, 2000.

Tortora, Gerald J. and Anagnostakos, Nicholas P. Principles of Anatomy and Physiology. New York, New York: Harper & Row, 1978.

Vallee, Jacques. Dimensions. New York, New York: Contemporary Books, 1988.

Wallace-Murphy, Tim and Hopkins, Marilyn. Rosslyn. Massachusetts: Element Books, Inc., 1999.

Weidner, Jay and Bridges, Vincent. The Mysteries of the Great Cross of Hendaye—Alchemy and the End of Time. Rochester, Vermont: Destiny Books, 2003.

Westhues, Kenneth. The Pope Versus The Professor. Queenston, Ontario: The Edwin Mellen Press, 2005.

Wharfe, Ken. DIANA—The Closely Guarded Secret. London: Michael O'Mara Books Limited, 2002.

Williams, Paul L. The Vatican Exposed. Amherst, New York: Prometheus Books, 2003.

Wilson, Ian. The Blood and The Shroud. New York: The Free Press, 1998.

Notes

Chapter One
1   A. Cohen, The Soncino Chumash (London: The Soncino Press, 1962).
2   Flavius Josephus, Antiquities of the Jews I—The Works of Flavius Josephus (London: Milner & Sowerby, 1870), 3:1.
3   Damascus Document, Manuscript A, The Essene Writings from Qumran (Oxford, 1961), 2: 17-19.

Chapter Four
4   G. Roux, Ancient Iraq, p. 78.

Chapter Seventeen
5   Richard Carlyon, A Guide to the Gods (London: Heinemann/Quixote, 1981), p. 312.

Chapter Twenty
6   Tessa Ranford, cited by Knight and Lomas, The Second Messiah (Massachusetts: Element Books, 1998), p. 32.
7   Andrew Hennessey, pegasus@easynet.co.uk, Transformation Studies Group.

Chapter Twenty-One
8   Lady Queensboro, Occult Theocracy (The Christian Book Club of America).
9   Manley P. Hall, The Secret Destiny of America (Los Angeles: Philosophical Research Library, 1972), pp. 23-24.

Chapter Twenty-Four
0   Malachi Martin, Windswept House (New York: Broadway Books, 2001), p. 7.

Chapter Twenty-Five
11 Paul La Violette, "The Crop Circle phenomenon and field projection technology" (MUFON UFO Journal, April 2001), p. 6.

Chapter Twenty-Six
12   Jose M. R. Delgado, Congressional Record (No. 26, Vol. 118, February 24, 1974), Dr. Delgado served as Director of Neuropsychiatry, Yale University Medical School.
13   Brad and Francie Steiger, Gods of Aquarius (New York: Berkeley Books, 1981), p. 88.
14   Bertrand Russell, The Impact of Science on Society, 1953.

Chapter Twenty-Seven
15   Whitley Strieber, Transformation—The Break Through (New York: Beech Tree Books, 1988), pp. 240-241.
16   Barry H. Downing, Wormholes, Heaven, and the God Hypothesis (MUFON UFO Journal, November 2001), pp. 10-12.
17   Barry H. Downing, Wormholes, Heaven, and the God Hypothesis Part II (MUFON UFO Journal, December 2001), p. 12.
18   Chris Aubeck, Fairy Folk and Aliens: A Perspective (MUFON UFO Journal, June 2002), p. 11.
19   Barry H. Downing, Is UFO Midnight A Possibility? (MUFON UFO Journal, May 2000), p. 6.

Chapter Twenty-Nine
20   Michael Mannion, Project Mind Shift (New York: Evans, 1998), p. 229.
21   Nancy Talbott, Researcher Witnesses Crop Circle Formation (MUFON UFO Journal, January 2002), pp. 3-7.

22   Eltjo Haselhoff, Crop Circles—The Facts and the Fiction (MUFON UFO Journal, October 2001), pp. 3-7.
23   Eltjo Haselhoff, The Deepening Complexity of Crop Circles (Scientific Research and Urban Legends, 2001), pp. 25-26.
24   Dwight Connelly, Symposium speakers cover diverse topics—Dr. Linda Corley (MUFON UFO Journal, August 2000), p.3.

Chapter Thirty
25   Sir Iain Moncreiffe, Royal Highness Ancestry of the Royal Child (London: Hamish Hamilton, 1982), p. 62.
26   Jack Van Impe, Question of the Week (www.jvim.com, 4/25/02).
27   Grant R. Jeffrey, Jesus The Great Debate (Nashville: Word Publishing, 1999), "6th Century Painting of Jesus" p. 139.
28   Jack Van Impe, Update "Charles Gears Up to be the Prince of Faiths", (www.jvim.com, 4/24/02), Article taken from The Times of India, (April 16, 2002).
29   Frank Allnutt, Antichrist--After the Omen (New Jersey: Spire Books, 1976), p. 45.
30   Man, Myth and Magic Encyclopedia, Numerology (New York: BPC Publishing Ltd., 1970), p. 2023.
31   Man, Myth and Magic Encyclopedia, Alphabet (New York: BPC Publishing Ltd., 1970), p. 72.
32   Joye Jeffries Pugh, Antichrist – The Cloned Image of Jesus Christ (Georgia: Vision Publishing Group, 1999). www.drjoye.com

Chapter Thirty-One
33   http://www.humanunderground.com/anatomy.html
34   Holy Bible, Revelation 13: 7-8 (New Jersey: Thomas Nelson, Inc., 1972),

p. 304. King James Version.

35   Texe Marrs, Power of Prophecy, "Is Witnessing about Jesus Genocide?" (Vol. 99-4, April 1999), p. 3.

36   Joye Jeffries Pugh, Colours of Joye Limited Edition Poetry of Joye Jeffries (Georgia: Gibbons House Publishers, 1975), p. 9.

Made in the USA
Coppell, TX
25 November 2021